WITHDRAWN

Mobsters in our Midst

THE KANSAS CITY CRIME FAMILY

William Ouseley

KANSAS CITY STAR BOOKS
KANSAS CITY, MISSOURI

Published by Kansas City Star Books
1729 Grand Boulevard
Kansas City, MO 64108

First Edition, fourth printing

ISBN 978-1-61169-005-7

Library of Congress Control Number:
2011923635

Printed in the United States of America
by Walsworth Publishing Co., Inc.
Marceline, Mo.

To order copies call StarInfo at (816) 234-
4636 and say "operator," or order online at
www.TheKansasCityStore.com.

Cover photograph:
Nick Civella in a 1961 police
mugshot.

Back cover photographs
(clockwise from upper
left): River Quay explosion
aftermath, March 1977; "Big
Jim" Balestrere, 1951; Joe
Cammisano; Nick Civella after
a bond hearing, 1980; Villa
Capri Restaurant and Lounge;
Nick Spero; Fred Harvey
Bonadonna, 1977. Center
left: Willie Cammisano, 1950.
Center right: Carl "Cork"
Civella, 1961.

Introductory pages: 1,
Wreckage after explosion
that killed Gary T. Parker. 2,
Nick Civella in a 1946 police
mugshot.

All images are from the files
of *The Kansas City Star* or
William Ouseley except p. 189
(bottom), AP Images.

Contents

William Ouseley spent 25 years in the FBI, more than 20 of those investigating and prosecuting organized crime figures. As an expert witness on mob activities, he testified in federal courts and before the U.S. Senate Permanent Subcommittee on Investigations. He retired as supervisor of the Organized Crime Squad of the Kansas City FBI Field Division, and afterward worked as a security consultant and private investigator. He is also the author of *Open City: True Story of the KC Crime Family 1900-1950.*

Dedicated to my loving wife, Jo.

This monster — the monster they've engendered in me — will return to torment its maker from the grave, the pit, the profoundest pit. Hurl me into the next existence, the descent into hell won't burn me. I'll crawl back to dog his trail forever. They won't defeat my revenge, never, never.

— From a clipping of unknown origin saved by Nick Civ-ella. It was seized by the FBI at his home. The quotation is by George Jackson, who wrote it while serving time at Soledad Prison in California.

CHAPTER I

PRELUDE

We think of it as a sixth sense: an unexplainable internal radar that alerts an experienced law-enforcement officer. It tells us danger is imminent, or things are not as they seem, or something big is going down.

Most likely that sixth sense is what Sergeant Edgar Crosswell of the New York State Police experienced the afternoon of November 13, 1957. He and his partner, Trooper Vincent Vasisko, spotted 21-year-old Joseph Barbara Jr. about to enter a motel in the vicinity of the sleepy upstate New York hamlet of Apalachin. By pure happenstance, a routine bad-check complaint had brought the troopers to the same motel.

Ducking out of sight of the front desk, the officers overheard young Barbara make reservations for several guests, no names provided. The guests were coming to town, he said, to attend a "soft-drink convention" at the estate of his father.

Joseph Barbara Sr. held himself out as a legitimate businessman, owner of a local bottling company along with distributorships for beer and Canada Dry soft drinks. The elder Barbara's name commanded respect, and he had important connections. His gun permit was issued by the county's leading judge.

For years, however, Crosswell had come across Barbara's name in connection with gambling, other rackets and underworld associates.

In the late 1950s the existence of a national Mafia-like organization was generally disputed. Crosswell suspected that such a secret organization did exist, and that it reaped huge sums of money from rackets. As part of his assignment to the New York State Police Criminal Investigative Bureau at Binghamton, New York, Crosswell had made a point of tracking Barbara, and his inquiries confirmed suspicions about Barbara's sordid past. Crosswell learned that Barbara carried the gangland moniker, "Joe The Barber." As the "wise guys" say, the wealthy resident of Apalachin, New York, was "mobbed up."

Knowing what he did, Crosswell doubted the existence of any soft-drink convention. He would check it out.

A trip to the Barbara bottling works gave no hint of anything out of the ordinary. Not so at the Barbara estate. There, on a dead-end road, he spotted two cars with out-of-state license plates. It wasn't much to go on, but it was enough to fuel Crosswell's sense that something was in the wind.

There have been been various stories about what happened next. The most credible account has Crosswell, Vasisko and two U.S. Treasury agents driving to the estate at mid-day November 14, 1957, and finding an array of luxury cars parked there. As the officers busily copied down license numbers, they were spotted. Someone shouted a warning, setting in motion a wild exodus of well-dressed men, fleeing in all directions.

The officers, retreating to the bottom of the one road that led to the estate, sized up the situation, called for reinforcements and set up a roadblock. A stream of cars immediately jammed up. Sixty-three of Barbara's guests were rounded up and taken to the State Police Barracks in Vestal, New York. There they were identified and questioned.

Other guests, many in silk suits and patent-leather shoes, escaped on foot through nearby woods and fields. Four men riding in one cab and two in another were caught in the police net. Three more were identified through motel registrations and car rentals, and one by clothes left in a car stashed in a barn on the estate.

Exactly how many had attended would never be determined, but names recorded in law-enforcement reports that day represented a veritable "Hoods Who" of the American "Mafia." The organization was unrecognized at the time, but later became known around the world as La Cosa Nostra — "Our Thing." The list of luminaries included Joe Bonano, Carlo Gambino, Vito Genovese, Joe Profaci — bosses of four of the five New York City crime families. Other crime family bosses identified were John Scalish from Cleveland, Joe Civello from Dallas, James Colletti from Boulder, Colorado, Frank DiSimone from Los Angeles, Joseph Ida from Philadelphia and Frank Zito from Springfield, Illinois. Two attendees hailed from Cuba and one from Italy.

What were they doing at the Barbara estate that day? Reasons proffered ranged from the ridiculous to the bland: "visit a sick friend," "invited to a party," "personal business reasons," "car broke down nearby," "came for a good meal." For those plucked out of the woods, their luxury suits in tatters, came excuses such as "looking at real estate." Two claimed they were on their way to the railroad station, which was 70 miles away.

The men's excuses differed but their backgrounds clearly resembled one another. It would stretch the imagination to believe coincidence brought them together in that little village in upstate New York. One thing was clear: they weren't there for a soft-drink convention.

Scouting heavily traveled Route 17 near Vestal that fateful day, State Police Sergeant J.J. Benanti spotted a taxi cab with two men as passengers. About six miles west of Apalachin, Benanti pulled the cab over and asked for identification. The passengers gave their names as Joe Filardo and Nick "Civello" and produced identification showing their hometown was Kansas City, Missouri.

Oh, sure, they had been in Apalachin, they told Benanti at the Vestal State Police office, but they had not attended any meeting at the Barbara estate. Otherwise, they offered nothing in the way of a purpose for their visit. The two were released.

Benanti believed that Filardo and "Civello" — actually spelled "Civella" — could not have been in Apalachin for any reason other than to attend the meeting.

SERGEANT CROSSWELL AND HIS FELLOW OFFICERS had disrupted a meeting of Cosa Nostra's national leadership, a meeting forever to be known as the Apalachin Gangland Convention. The event, most agree, did more than anything before it to open Americans' eyes to organized crime.

For decades, Kansas City's organized crime society and its comrades-in-arms around the country had avoided sustained scrutiny and any effort to break them up. They took advantage of a formula that combined ignorance, forgetfulness and apathy on the part of the public along with political influence. The formula depended also on corrupted supporters, fellow travelers and others with a stake in the mob's success.

After Apalachin that same formula persisted, hindering law enforcement efforts far into the future.

Consider a statement from the managing director of the Kansas City Crime Commission, an influential organization sponsored by the business community, in the wake of the revelation about Filardo and Civella.

"There are no concrete reasons to believe that what remains of the old

Kansas City underworld is tied to activities of a national crime syndicate," Commission Director Harold L. Scott was quoted as saying in *The Kansas City Times*. Kansas City Police Major Jack Halvey agreed, claiming that organized crime no longer existed in Kansas City.

Both pointed to only a few small-time gamblers. Except for them, they said, "gangsterism is dormant."

Lost in such proclamations was the historical reality that the "old Kansas City underworld" had become part of the fabric of Kansas City life. No matter what appeared outwardly, the organization had never ceased to exist. After Prohibition ended in the early 1930s the city was thrown wide open to assorted forms of vice and rampant corruption, allowed to operate by means of an unholy alliance between the corrupt political machine of Thomas J. Pendergast and the crime family based in the North End or North Side, the area just south of the Missouri River that was then the northern limit of Kansas City, Missouri.

The 1930s were characterized by scores of gangland slayings, bloody, fraudulent, stolen elections, political chicanery, a full menu of racket activities and the criminal organization's ever-increasing influence and wealth. Things reached a boiling point in 1939, when banner headlines trumpeted the findings of federal and Jackson County grand juries leading to the indictments and convictions of boss Pendergast and of crime family leader Charles Carrollo.

With the fall of the Pendergast machine a reform movement swept the city, robbing the mob of much of its political clout. Then came a vote-fraud scandal in the middle 1940s and the heralded murders in 1950 of the "Two Charlies," Charles Binaggio and Charles Gargotta, both politically influential mob bigwigs. The Kansas City mob scene contributed to the formation of a U.S. Senate committee headed by Senator Estes Kefauver to investigate organized crime in America. Widely heralded hearings in Kansas City, some closed and some public, exposed the grip that syndicate criminals held on the city. Kefauver declared that Kansas City had come under the influence of as vicious a group of mobsters as existed anywhere in the country.

The mob was forced to ground, pulling in its horns, reducing the level of activity in what might be described as a strategy of submersion. Waiting for the pressure to ease, Kansas City's mobsters maneuvered behind the scenes, creating a false impression that rackets were a thing of the past. However, the mob was in it for the long run, and any belief in its demise was misguided.

The Kansas City criminal organization was part of the national alliance of crime families, La Cosa Nostra, a term familiar in the East. In cities west of the Mississippi, a crime family was also known as the Outfit or the Clique.

Cosa Nostra came to be as the result of a bloody struggle between Italian-Sicilian crime societies in New York City in 1931. With the cessation of hostilities, the groups consolidated and united similar crime groups in some 26 U.S. cities. These structured, disciplined "families," restricted to men of Italian descent, insinuated themselves into the political, economic and social fabric of their cities. They were dedicated to an everlasting lifespan and persevered intact through good times and bad, with succession to leadership as certain as that of the throne of Great Britain.

Although the makeup and culture of these groups stemmed in large part from the Mafia of Sicily, this was not the Mafia. No American crime family referred to itself by that name, even though it was a popular label among the public. The Mafia belonged to Sicily, and what developed in the United States was an American product that can be described as Mafia-like. Mystery inured to the mobsters' benefit, as demonstrated in a 1960 newspaper article profiling the Civellas of Kansas City. It reported the views of one law enforcement agency after another this way:

"Their world to this day is an enigma to us."

APALACHIN WAS A WATERSHED event leading to a general awakening and eventually a relentless effort to undermine and destroy organized crime. For Joe Filardo, Nick Civella, fellow members of Cosa Nostra, their associates, facilitators, political allies and those otherwise doing business with the mob, they were to be the focus of relentless scrutiny — daily, weekly, monthly and yearly.

CHAPTER II

THE RISE OF NICK CIVELLA

The road to Apalachin was a long and arduous one for Nick Civella. He became a member of the Kansas City Outfit probably in the late 1940s, an era when its power structure was difficult to sort out. There were those in the public eye who made headlines, but from the inception of the Kansas City Crime Family there had been others who remained in the shadows. It was they who held ultimate power. They were primarily Sicilian-born, the founding fathers of the organization, who settled in Kansas City's North End in the early 1900s.

Labeled "Mustache Petes" by younger mobsters, they adhered to the culture and protocols of the Old World Sicilian Mafia. Most notable were the DiGiovanni brothers — Joe "Scarface" DiGiovanni and "Sugarhouse" Pete DiGiovanni — along with "Big Jim" Balestrere and Joe Lusco. In what was known as the Black Hand era, they formed criminal factions that extorted fellow immigrant countrymen.

The competing North End factions came together in the late 1920s as the result of Prohibition, and a single Outfit was born. Its first out-front boss emerged in the person of American-born John Lazia, who was murdered in 1934. By the 1940s the "Big Five" were running things — Balestrere, Gaetano Lococo, Tony Gizzo, Charles Binaggio and Charles Gargotta. Some operated out front and others behind the scenes. The intricacies of their relationships and degrees of control in that era were secrets taken to the grave. With the sensational double murder of Binaggio and Gargotta in 1950, Tony Gizzo became the public face of the mob. When Gizzo died three years later, Nick Civella's name surfaced as the prime candidate to take over the reins. Still, Civella had old-line powerbrokers to contend with.

Balestrere, from the early 1900s to his death on October 19, 1959, was recognized as the most formidable of the powerbrokers. In the 1950s, when the Kefauver Committee was making the climate toxic for organized crime, Balestrere played the role of a simple man. He lived modestly and claimed to be nothing more than a retired senior citizen with an interest in an Italian restaurant.

In truth Balestrere represented Civella's main opposition to being named boss, and that was no surprise. It is fairly certain that Balestrere was behind failed attempts in the 1940s to have Civella murdered.

In Civella's corner were prominent figures including Joe Filardo, Joe Cusumano and Gaetano Lococo along with a number of mobsters whom Tony Gizzo had elevated as trusted aides, enforcers and enablers while he was boss. Among them were John Mangiaracina, Thomas "Hiway" Simone, Louis "Black Louie" Cangelose, Joe Guerra, Morris "Snag" Klein and Max Jaben, all of whom would loom large in crime-family affairs in the Civella years.

Cosa Nostra protocol required its ruling national body, the Commission, to approve the appointment of new bosses. Joe Filardo, considered well-connected "back East" where the national power lay, took on the task of securing the Commission's blessing for Civella's promotion. With that in hand, Balestrere was satisfied, and Civella took his place at the table as boss of the Kansas City Family.

Filardo, operating in the shadows, and Civella, operating out front, represented the old and new in Kansas City organized crime. Filardo was one of the "founders" from the Sugar House syndicate days, when the Outfit consolidated. He was a traditionalist who adhered to Sicilian Mafia concepts of honor, loyalty, strict rules and codes of conduct. Civella, a native of Kansas City, represented the Americanized generation of organized crime.

JOE FILARDO WAS BORN August 10, 1897, in Castelvetrano, Sicily. He entered the United States at New York City aboard the *S.S. Venezia* on December 18, 1913. He took up residence in Brooklyn, claiming employment as a buttonhole maker at a clothing firm.

The New York City police arrested Filardo on February 7, 1922, charging him with blackmail. Considering the era and the charge, and even without benefit of the police file, it's a good bet that this was a case of Black Hand extortion, the earliest manifestation of ethnic Italian-Sicilian crime. Black Hand criminals systematically extorted Italian-Sicilian immigrants, preying on their fear of the Mafia from their days in the old country and at the same time on their distrust of authorities. As a result Black Hand victims would not cooperate with police. That's likely to have occurred in Filardo's case; 15 days after his arrest the charges were dismissed. It's also likely that in his time in New York City Filardo established the Eastern connections that would serve him well with the men who rose to power in Cosa Nostra.

From there, Filardo moved to Springfield, Illinois, where he encountered countrymen from Castelvetrano who were associated with a developing crime family. Apparently, Filardo found the bootleg liquor racket attractive. In 1925 he was indicted by a federal grand jury in the Southern District of Illinois on Prohibition-related charges. Upon pleading guilty he was fined $300 and served three months in a county jail.

About 1926, it is believed, Filardo made his way to Kansas City and settled in. The next year an affair of the heart turned violent, leading to his arrest on March 19, 1927, on a charge of murder. The victim, one Tony Leone, had surprised his wife while she was "with" Filardo, and in the altercation that came afterward Leone was shot dead and Filardo wounded. When the complaining witness failed to appear, the charges were dropped — not an uncommon occurrence for men of Filardo's status. Subsequently Filardo and the victim's wife were reported living together.

Picking up where he left off, Filardo returned to the bootleg liquor business. About 1928, with other prominent members of the North End criminal element, he formed a cooperative venture known as the Sugar House Syndicate. The syndicate monopolized bootlegging activities from production to delivery. It also united the various factions of the North End into a singular criminal organization, the Outfit.

In 1931, in partnership with Castelvetrano countrymen Joe Cusumano and Jack Binaggia, Filardo established the Roma Bakery at 1303 Independence Ave. The bakery operated continuously for more than 50 years. Cusumano and Filardo were as close as two men could be without being blood brothers. They lived next door to each other and often were referred to as the "Two Joes" or simply, "the Bakery." In 1959, with the death of Big Jim Balestrere, the influence of the the Bakery became predominant.

Senator Estes Kefauver's committee identified Filardo as a Kansas City "Mafia" member and stated, "Men who were high up in the Mafia had milked the town." As the Outfit developed and prospered, Filardo took his place as one of the old-line Sicilian-born founders. He maintained a low profile as a behind-the-scenes power, and as such accompanied Nick Civella to the Apalachin meeting.

ALL THINGS CONSIDERED, NICK CIVELLA was a prohibitive underdog to make it to the top. He was born Guiseppe Nicoli Civello on March 19, 1912, in Kansas City's "Little Italy," the North End. He was the ninth child of Antonio Civello and Antonia Bovi Civello, and the fourth to survive childbirth. Theirs was a family of little means, and it was said that the father walked to his menial jobs to save the five-cent carfare. At the age of 10, Nick suffered his first arrest and was charged as an "incorrigible." In the Prohibition era he dabbled in bootlegging, earning a federal Prohibition rap and a three-month stint in a county jail. Unlike elder statesman Filardo, Civella accumulated an extensive arrest record for common street crimes, among them tire theft and robbery. The number of times he was picked up and held for "investigation" made it clear he was well-known to the police.

Unlike many youngsters in Little Italy, Civella did not look up to or seek the approval of the well-known racket figures who lived in the North End. Civella had disapproved of the heavy-handed Old World methods practiced by the Mustache Petes of the Black Hand, in which small merchants and others were victimized. Reportedly, they had mistreated Civella's father.

Lacking respect from the organization, he went his own way, joined by his older brother, Carl Civella, and some like-minded associates. The gang not only resisted the Crime Family's persistent efforts to recruit them, but did so boldly and foolishly, acting contrary to mob interests. The early and middle 1940s witnessed a rash of holdups of mob-protected gambling operations, holdups laid at the doorstep of Civella and his running mates.

Such disrespect and conduct was not to be tolerated, and the Family's efforts to recruit turned into efforts to murder. Were it not for tips secretly passed on by associates, who despite joining the Family remained loyal friends, Civella would not have survived. It is part of a Mafioso's DNA never to forget those who defy or disrespect the organization and never to be deterred from repaying defiance no matter how long it may take.

James Maroon, a member of Civella's band of thieves, was the first to fall. He was found in his car on December 2, 1940, shot to death and left in an alley behind the 500 block of Troost Avenue. Immediately, Civella fled the city for Chicago. On the day after Christmas 1940, Civella was observed leaving Chicago's Merry Gardens dance hall immediately after it had been held up, the cash box having been snatched. A Chicago policeman saw the robbery and commanded Civella to halt, then shot him twice when he failed to heed the order.

Civella's version was that he was simply an innocent bystander caught in crossfire. What appeared to be an open-and-shut case wasn't. Civella was found not guilty by a Chicago judge, and he returned to Kansas City.

While hiding out in Chicago, Civella befriended Sicilian-born Chicago racket figure "Cherry Nose" Gioe. Gioe had close ties to Kansas City and reportedly had come to Civella's aid in his time of need. Gioe was gunned down on Chicago's North Side on August 18, 1954.

Time ran out for another Civella crime partner on January 22, 1946, when the body of Joe "Buggy" Anch was found under the Lydia Avenue viaduct in Kansas City, shot five times and beaten about the face and head. The brutality of the murder made it abundantly clear that some people were angry with Anch, and the police investigation made it clear why: Anch was linked to numerous holdups of gambling games.

Eight days later Civella stopped in at Trucker's Liquor Store, 1901 E. 15th St., where by plan or happenstance he met up with a Jackson County sheriff's deputy, Louis Cuccia. Their conversation moved from the store to Civella's car parked out front. For some reason, Cuccia got in behind the wheel while Civella took the passenger seat. Sometime after 1 a.m. another car rolled up. Shotgun and pistol fire erupted, all aimed at Civella's vehicle. Cuccia was struck in the head and died several hours later at General Hospital, while Civella, ducking down, came away unharmed.

The police were well aware of ties between the murdered Joe Anch and Civella, as well as their links to the holdups of gambling games, which cost Anch his life. Civella was not about to provide them a motive for the shooting, but in their minds there was little doubt who the intended target was. Any doubts that remained were dispelled when Civella once again fled Kansas City for sanctuary in Chicago.

There once more, Nick was left to bide his time, riding out the storm. Meanwhile, he took the opportunity to further cement and expand his ties with the Windy City mob, ties he would capitalize on in the years to come. Finally the call came from Kansas City: the way was clear for him to return home. Exactly when he returned is unknown, but a gambling-related arrest in Kansas City on April 10, 1948, gives a clue that by then his exile had run its course.

Whether it was at the behest of Civella associates, or, as some believe, a request from Chicago Boss Tony Accardo, Tony Gizzo of Kansas City's Big Five gave his blessing for Civella's safe return. Because Gizzo and Accardo

Early powers in the Kansas City Outfit: Brothers "Sugarhouse" Pete and Joe "Scarface" DiGiovanni ...

... Joe Lusco ...

... and "Big Jim" Balestrere, who was among those hailed before the Kefauver Committee in 1950.

As the middle of the 20th century approached, the Kansas City mob's inner circle included, from left, Charles Binaggio, Charles Gargotta and Tony Gizzo. When Binaggio and Gargotta were slain in 1950, Gizzo became the public face of the Outfit.

Among other important figures were Gaetano Lococo, left, and the two men who ran the Roma Bakery, Joe Filardo, center, and Joe Cusumano.

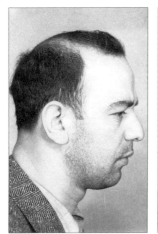  

Nick Civella in 1946, when his status in the Outfit was shaky.   Joe "Buggy" Anch

The car was Nick Civella's but Louis Cuccia occupied the driver's seat when gunmen drove by on a January night in 1946 and opened fire. Cuccia was killed.

Detectives poked around the Downtown Bridge Club during a raid in 1955, looking for false partitions. The gambling operation was at 1423 Baltimore Ave.

Carl Civella, nicknamed "Cork" for his explosive temper, was photographed by police in 1952 and by newspaper photographers in 1961 — the latter over his vigorous objections.

Nick Civella in 1960

had a long history together and were known to be close friends, it is plausible that Accardo interceded. Gizzo harbored a soft spot for the Civella boys, who in earlier times reportedly supplied stolen tires to a tire shop in which Gizzo had an interest.

Not only did Gizzo bring Civella back but he also took him under his wing. He made Civella his driver, an important post in Cosa Nostra's career development path. As the story goes, Civella proved himself an astute and competent racketeer, displaying organizational and planning skills even beyond those of Gizzo himself.

In many circles there was strong suspicion that Civella was responsible for orchestrating the nationally infamous murders of the "Two Charlies," Binaggio and Gargotta, in spring 1950 and thus greatly enhancing his stature. With their deaths, Gizzo took over as boss. Civella, his No. 1 lieutenant, was responsible for implementing and enforcing orders, and for running things on the street in behalf of the boss.

Befitting his rise in stature, Civella was cut in on gambling operations, assigned to oversee them and to employ muscle when called for. For instance, when Boss Gizzo became involved in a football parlay-card gambling enterprise, Civella visited other gambling operators and warned them they were not to be involved in any similar operation — or else.

A federal grand jury report issued in 1950 identified a "Nick Savella" as a partner in a gambling operation at 85th Street and Wornall Road. In 1953 the Downtown Bridge Club, 1423 Baltimore Ave., opened and ran for five years, raking in some $300,000, according to a grand jury report. Carried as "high-salaried" employees of the club were Nick and Carl Civella. Partners included Max Jaben, Louis Cangelose, Joe Lascuola and Thomas Cacioppo.

In 1960, Civella's Apalachin notoriety led a Jackson County Grand Jury to revisit the Downtown Bridge Club and indict Civella and his associates on gambling charges. After 2½ years of protracted court appearances, Civella beat the case on a technicality.

Gizzo died April 1, 1953, and Nick Civella was well placed to take over the reins. It was his good fortune that Gizzo had close ties with the Bakery. Joe Filardo's and Joe Cusumano's support was essential in overcoming Big Jim Balestrere's reluctance, and in obtaining the national Commission's approval of Civella's coronation.

APALACHIN WAS AT THE SAME TIME SINISTER and fascinating, spawning serious study and a great deal of speculation. It is impossible to know with certainty the internal workings, motivations and strategies leading to Filardo's and Civella's ending up at the conclave. It may be simply that their leadership status mandated they gather with bosses of other Cosa Nostra crime families to make policy — business as usual. It is known that similar meetings had taken place before, and Kansas City representatives probably attended them.

One of the most popular stories in Kansas City lore had Filardo, the man with the high-level connections, accompanying Civella to introduce him as the new boss in Kansas City. From what is known, however, the theory does not hold water. An intriguing backdrop to the affair came by way of a knowledgeable source developed years later. In that account, Civella approached Chicago's boss of the day, Sam "Momo" Giancana, asking Giancana to nominate him for an open seat on the national Commission. The Commission was heavily weighted with East Coast bosses, and Civella would give the West another voice. Civella's personality and driving ambition lent credence to that report, as did his close ties to Giancana and the Chicago mob. Whatever the reason, Apalachin forever marked Civella and Filardo for who they were, and what they represented.

As with those who came before him, Civella was at first bound to operate within the rules established by the invisible power brokers past and present. Once Big Jim Balestrere died and the Bakery's Filardo chose a less active role — encouraged by the fallout from Apalachin — Civella broke the mold. He became his own man, and would be the longest-serving crime-family boss in Kansas City history.

Apalachin changed the landscape dramatically. If Prohibition helped the growth of organized crime, Apalachin had the opposite effect. Unlike their predecessors, Civella and Filardo would not benefit from generalized apathy and sporadic scrutiny. Apalachin would haunt them and Cosa Nostra for years to come.

CHAPTER III

FALLOUT FROM APALACHIN

Apalachin spawned a series of grand jury investigations, all manner of other inquiries and extensive investigative reporting, ensuring the mob a place on the front pages in Kansas City and across the country. In June 1958, as Nick Civella completed a round of golf at an area country club, a U.S. marshal served him a subpoena. He was to appear with Joe Filardo before the U.S. Senate investigating committee chaired by Senator John McClellan, ably assisted by a young attorney named Robert F. Kennedy. The McClellan committee, probing the labor rackets and Teamsters boss Jimmy Hoffa, recognized the significance of the Apalachin meeting and refocused its attention on it.

Civella and Filardo next appeared before a Jackson County, Missouri, grand jury in mid-1958, and then were called before a federal grand jury in Chicago in February 1959. The Chicago inquiry was a part of an Apalachin-inspired U.S. Department of Justice push against rackets nationwide, in which the department established four special regional investigative units. In the glare of the spotlight in Chicago, Civella showcased character traits that marked him for years to come. He was provocative, abrasive, confrontational and wisecracking, relishing the chance to spar verbally with the authorities and the press.

According to a Chicago-datelined newspaper article, Civella labeled his 19-minute grand jury appearance "baloney," and characterized himself and Filardo as "nobodies" whom the government was attempting to turn into notorious characters. As for Apalachin, sure, they were stopped by the State Police nearby, but they weren't there to attend any convention.

"We were chasing girls," Civella said. They simply couldn't talk about it lest their wives find out.

Reporters asked how Civella made a living.

"I'm a legitimate businessman," he shot back, "and pay my income taxes."

Pressed as to what his business might be, he responded: "First I was a truck driver but I quit because it hurt my back. I am more legitimate than any witness that comes before the grand jury." As an afterthought he added, "I'm an investment broker, but don't print that."

Through it all Filardo, a man of quiet authority, remained subdued and aloof, offering a vivid contrast in conduct between the old-school Sicilian-born racketeer and the all-American Kansas City-born capo. The contrast would be replayed over and over in their appearances before a myriad of inquires that followed.

Focusing on the Apalachin conclave, a federal grand jury in New York City in May 1959 leveled charges of conspiracy against 26 men. Twenty were convicted but all were set free on appeal. Two were not tried because of poor health and four others never caught. Thirty-six others, among them Joe Filardo and Nick Civella, were named as unindicted co-conspirators.

For Civella, the die was cast. There seemed to be no way to escape the glare of publicity, much of which he brought on himself. Without fanfare, Filardo quietly responded to each and every call to testify, while Civella and his close associate, Max Jaben, only fueled the fires. They spent a month ducking local and federal grand jury subpoenas issued in July 1959 for them and a raft of Outfit figures now caught up in the furor over organized crime.

The best was yet to come. Summoned by a Jackson County grand jury Nick and Carl Civella appeared at the Jackson County Courthouse in downtown Kansas City on August 23, 1960. The media were well-represented. The hot-tempered Carl, nicknamed "Cork," took exception to photos being taken, and challenged a TV cameraman to take a picture of "this." He exposed his privates for the camera, earning himself an arrest on charges of indecent exposure.

Cosa Nostra members have a characteristic mindset about the criminal justice system. They view any legal action against them as unjust persecution by the state. They will go to any end to resist, no matter how minor the charge or how major the resulting publicity. If they beat the system, mobsters believe, their stature is enhanced, imbuing them with an aura of power and giving the impression that they are beyond the reach of authorities. In case after case, using a combination of political allies, legal machinations, claims of discrimination, leniency and too-frequent judicial errors, Outfit members have successfully escaped conviction, or come away with a slap on the wrist.

Consider what happened after Cork Civella exposed himself for the television cameraman.

He pleaded not guilty to the charge, which was a simple misdemeanor. When the case came before Municipal Court Judge Thomas Moran, the assistant city counselor argued that the best evidence of the event was the film itself. Moran did not bother viewing the film. Instead, he ruled that the cameraman had invaded Civella's privacy in a public building, and dismissed the charge. One might ask, what is the expectation of privacy in a public building?

Cork Civella was neither out of the woods nor about to give in, but in the end the system self-destructed. The indecent exposure charge was re-filed by means of an information on November 10, 1960, by the Jackson County prosecutor's office. Again, Civella pleaded not guilty. The case wound through a series of continuances granted by Judge Harry E. Whitney. The delays were so numerous that they violated criminal procedure rules, forcing the judge at trial time to declare a mistrial. Again, the charge was dismissed.

Next the prosecutor's office took the matter to a Jackson County grand jury, obtaining an indictment. The end came 14 months after Civella was first charged. Circuit Court Judge Tom J. Stubbs sustained a defense motion of double jeopardy, dismissing the charges for good.

When Nick Civella's turn to face Lady Justice came, his refusal to give in would have unintended consequences. The issue was state income taxes, Civella having failed to file returns for the years 1957, 1958 and 1959, leading to Jackson County grand jury charges in July 1960. The grand jury had also studied the Downtown Bridge Club gambling operation and, in a separate indictment, charged Nick and Cork Civella, Max Jaben, Louis Cangelose and Thomas Cacioppo with keeping a gambling table, a felony offense.

As trial time approached in the tax prosecution, Nick Civella, not enamored with the idea of testifying, signed a stipulation outlining his sources of income and exposing his 1957 federal tax return, providing a glimpse of his associates and purported business interests. His tax return listed income of $19,800, of which $12,480 was salary and $7,320 proceeds from real estate, rents and commissions, a modest figure for a crime family boss.

The salary was derived from the Downtown Bridge Club, where he claimed employment. Independently it was established that the partnership behind the operation included Jaben, Charles Bruno, Alex and Chester Presta, Tony Civella and Phil Maggio. According to a grand jury report the take for its five years of operation was $300,000.

Civella also derived income from interests in the Midwest Bonded Money Order Company, 1503 E. 76th Terr. in Gladstone, Missouri, and the Steve Plas Used Car Co. in Kansas City, Missouri. Ownership interests in the money-order firm were identified in a 1961 Federal Bureau of Narcotics report as including Nick Civella, Jaben, Cangelose and Tony and Louis Orlando. The firm was later described in a news article as having 60 to 100 outlets in liquor, drug and grocery stores on Kansas City's East and North sides.

Turning to real estate, rents and commissions income, Nick Civella reported a 12½ percent interest in the Holmes Hotel at 622 Truman Rd. in partnership with Jaben, Bruno, Alex and Chester Presta, and Tony Civella. A report issued by the May 1960 term of the Jackson County grand jury identified the hotel as used by about six prostitutes working out of the Santa Anita Bar next door. The jury labeled prostitution as another profitable activity for the organization.

Additional income came from a series of property acquisitions. Using six different company names and combinations of partners including Nick Civella, Anthony Civella, Alex, Chester and Louis Presta, Phil Maggio and Jaben, nine properties were acquired and then sold to the State Highway Commission.

A Bureau of Narcotics report titled "Organized Crime and Racketeering in Kansas City, Missouri," dated March 13, 1961, and prepared in contemplation of a federal grand jury inquiry, addressed the matter. In recent years, it said, a source of income for the Crime Family had been speculation in proposed right-of-way property for federally financed state and city trafficways, including a proposed Southeast Trafficway in Kansas City. Through political contacts the syndicate obtained advance information about the proposed routes and set up fly-by-night real estate companies in the names of various members and associates to buy properties along the proposed routes. The Holmes Hotel was named, along with the Main Street Hotel at 1426 Main St. The buyers were identified as Nick Civella, Philip Maggio, Alex and Chester Presta and Jaben.

THE ONSLAUGHT OF GRAND JURY SUBPOENAS continued well into the 1960s. Each was widely heralded by the media, keeping Nick Civella, Filardo and other Family members and associates in the spotlight.

The impact was not lost on Civella. Feeling pressure from stepped-up law enforcement scrutiny, he was forced to change his ways. By 1962 an FBI informant reported that Civella was spending the best part of his time north of the Missouri River at the Mirror Lake Country Club near Parkville in Platte County, and away from his usual haunts. The practice was in keeping with his own order instructing Outfit members to maintain a low profile and avoid adverse publicity — the strategy of submersion.

When he was forced into public view, however, Nick Civella persisted in a show of "attitude," fueling the fire. At a 1966 Clay County grand jury session to which Nick and Cork Civella, Filardo and other Outfit figures had been summoned, Nick directed a barrage of four-letter expletives at reporters on hand, branding them sex perverts. Brother Cork warned a reporter, all of 5 feet 6 inches tall and 135 pounds, "I'm going to get you, boy."

As befits an old-world Sicilian don, Filardo sat apart from the frenzy, detached from, if not scornful of the display.

FBI DIRECTOR J. EDGAR HOOVER had gone on record stating there was no national crime syndicate operating in the United States. On the criminal side of the ledger, the organization he built strictly enforced a host of federal crimes within its jurisdiction, none of which were directed specifically at organized crime-like activity. In fact, the concept of a crime cartel such as Cosa Nostra was foreign to most Americans — and even most law enforcement officers — with the exception of the old Federal Bureau of Narcotics.

As a result, Hoover was blindsided by reports of the Apalachin conclave. Because of his stature in law enforcement, more was expected of him and he received the brunt of criticism for not recognizing the syndicate's existence. Hoover did not take well to being embarrassed, and within 14 days of the Apalachin event he directed a strongly worded edict to all offices captioned, "Top Hoodlum Program." It ordered that manpower be dedicated full-time to organized crime. He would personally scrutinize the progress of this new program, meaning FBI managers' and agents' feet would be held to the fire. The FBI's organized crime program was born.

In Kansas City, retired agent William J. "Bill" Quinn recalled well Hoover's call to action. Summoned by his criminal squad supervisor, Quinn and two other agents learned that they would be working the new Top Hoodlum Program, and were expected to handle the chore in addition to their other investigative duties. Quinn, who retired as supervisor of the Kansas City FBI Organized Crime Squad, was to target gambling operations, an area in which he admittedly had little knowledge.

At FBI headquarters in Washington, Quinn remembers, there was concern over a lack of jurisdiction in this new area. At first, Kansas City was not viewed as a hotbed of mob activity, so no great pressure was placed on the local office. That would change as the intelligence base expanded, and with Robert F. Kennedy's appointment as U.S. attorney general. Word came to Kansas City to ramp up the effort, and the Kansas City office established an Organized Crime Squad. FBI headquarters sent a supervisor to manage the program, which was aimed at aggressively pursuing organized crime investigations.

Quinn told of a personal visit to the office by Attorney General Kennedy, at which Kennedy directed tough questions at squad personnel. He later learned that Kennedy had made it clear to administrators that he would rate the office by the number of electronic surveillance operations it conducted. The procedure had proven successful in developing vital intelligence, but was of no value as evidence in court because it lacked statutory authority. Kennedy would never acknowledge giving this instruction, but it was made clear to the squad it was what he wanted and therefore what the squad would do.

Early on, great strides were made by developing two productive sources. One provided a detailed outline of the structure of the Outfit, its leaders, members and activities, and the other source reported on the Outfit's influence in the Teamsters union.

Before taking over as squad supervisor Quinn distinguished himself in the labor racketeering field. One of his cases involved the murder of the cooperating witness he had developed, a Teamsters union official.

It was about the time of that murder that I and another agent, Vern Piccinotti, joined the squad. We were the "youngsters," who would work alongside 10 experienced senior agents. Among them was George F. Leuckenhoff, who would follow Quinn as squad supervisor. After 16 years work on the squad I would follow in their footsteps.

RESPONDING TO THE FINDINGS of the Kefauver Committee the Department of Justice established the Organized Crime and Racketeering Section in 1954, but it had little, if any, impact until the

Apalachin meeting. In April 1958, then-Attorney General William Rogers announced an all-out drive targeting the top 100 racket figures in the country. When it took office in 1961, the Kennedy Administration took a strong hand in furthering the drive, but after the assassination of President Kennedy in 1963 it faltered under the administration of Lyndon B. Johnson. Richard Nixon, having made crime in America a major campaign issue, infused new life into the drive against organized crime upon taking office in 1969. The Rackets Section thereafter was a constant, formidable influence in the battle.

Six years after Apalachin, 60-year-old Joe Valachi — a stocky, crewcut, raspy-voiced New York City mob soldier in the Vito Genovese crime family — appeared before the McClellan committee and a fascinated national television audience and spilled the beans. He described the birth, structure, membership, activities and more of the organization he referred to as Cosa Nostra. Valachi was the first insider to reveal such secrets publicly, and his testimony had a profound effect on the public and on the mob. It was on par with Apalachin in providing a boost to law enforcement efforts.

At Kansas City Police headquarters, Chief Clarence Kelley recognized the need and in late 1961 ordered the formation of an Intelligence Unit. It was to be overseen by the commanders of the Narcotics Unit, with primary responsibility in the hands of John Flavin, one of those commanders.

Initially seven detectives were assigned. Among them was Sergeant James Hitchcock, who later, as a captain, was named to handle day-to-day direction of the unit. The mandate of the Intelligence Unit was simple: Keep tabs on underworld figures and avoid becoming involved in criminal investigations. Lacking specialized training or orientation about the nature and makeup of the criminal organization, the detectives were left to their own devices to sort it all out and effectively did so.

To start with, they kept tabs on places known to be frequented by members of the Outfit such as the Northview Social Club at Fifth Street and Troost Avenue — informally known as "the Trap" — and the Original Toy & Jobbing Co. at 303 W. Ninth St., where Nick Civella used an office as his headquarters. As individuals were identified, their backgrounds were checked and their activities and associates scrutinized. The circle widened and the scope of the police Intelligence Unit broadened.

As the "youngsters" on the FBI's Organized Crime Squad, Piccinotti and I made it a habit to visit almost daily with the police Intelligence Unit. We talked with detectives who had been on the street day and night, learning more and more from them about organized crime. For me, as it was for many of the agents, those early talks began a close relationship maintained over my 20-plus years of work investigating organized crime. From its modest beginnings, the Kansas City Police Intelligence Unit grew in size and stature. The dedicated and talented commanders, supervisors and detectives who passed through the unit contributed significantly to the fight against organized crime in Kansas City.

Federal, state, county and local law enforcement joined in creating not only a formidable force against organized crime but also a fraternity of sorts. The Missouri Highway Patrol, the Kansas Bureau of Investigation and the sheriff's departments in Johnson County, Kansas, and Clay County, Missouri, all dedicated manpower to the effort. Intelligence units were formed in other police departments including Topeka, Lawrence, Wichita, Overland Park and Lenexa in Kansas, and in many Missouri-side police departments.

In addition to the FBI, other federal agencies were committed to the drive against organized crime, including the IRS, Bureau of Alcohol, Tobacco and Firearms, Secret Service, Department of Labor and Drug Enforcement Administration.

The combination of law-enforcement bodies represented a threat that the Family never before had faced.

CHAPTER IV

POLITICS

The methods and strategies employed by a Cosa Nostra crime family in its quest for money, power, influence and longevity have no boundaries. Traditionally the principal sources of a family's power and control have been gambling, politics, business infiltration, labor racketeering and murder.

For a crime family to indefinitely and freely pursue these and other endeavors, its members must avoid punishment and insulate themselves against law enforcement, prosecutors, judges and all others who would obstruct them. That goal is achieved through political influence — a factor that has been a part of Cosa Nostra from its inception, a critical element that sets it apart from other, less sophisticated criminal entities.

Political patronage allows a crime family to dole out jobs, increasing its can-do stature and that of its political factions. In 1966, then-U.S. Attorney Russell Millin described Kansas City's rackets leaders as continually seeking ways to "control and dominate public officials." He quoted Robert F. Kennedy as saying, "The racketeer is at his most dangerous, not with a machine gun in his hand, but with public officials in his pocket."

From 1928, when John Lazia seized by force the political machinery of the North End, the city was doomed to suffer under an alliance forged between him and political boss Thomas J. Pendergast. In that era the mob was above the law, brazenly displaying its political clout, dealing directly with politicians and public officials and openly running its rackets. Enforcers were put to work shaking down gamblers, pimps, bootleggers, drug dealers, fences and the like, generating millions of dollars in revenue that financed the corrupt Pendergast machine and filled the coffers of organized crime. The Outfit manufactured thousands of ghost voters and generated large blocs of votes through violence and intimidation at the polls, using every tactic imaginable to rig elections. In return it was protected, free to operate openly, with free access to public officials and the Police Department.

After Pendergast was imprisoned, a reform movement in 1940 swept many of his followers out of political office. That created hard times for the mob. It was no longer able to operate openly and notoriously, forcing it to invoke the strategy of submersion. The remnants of the battered Pendergast machine gave rise to various Democratic factions. Because the North End was dominated by the Crime Family, it was preordained that when Nick Civella became boss in 1953 he would also assume the mantle of political leader. Initially his visibility on the political stage was of no concern. However once he was thrust into the limelight by Apalachin and became the face of organized crime, that had to change. Outward displays of political involvement faded away in the face of continuous law enforcement and grand jury scrutiny, forcing him to discreetly maneuver behind the scenes and proffer denials of any interest in politics.

DURING THE CIVELLA REIGN the name most commonly associated with North End politics was that of Alex Presta. Presta began his political career in 1915, when he was 14 years old, by walking voters to the polls in the old First Ward.

Decades later, Presta claimed to have allied himself and his followers with the reformers who won the city in 1940 and elected John Gage mayor. When asked, Gage had no recollection of any part Presta played in that movement. At the time, Presta said, he headed a group of 75 to 100 young men called the Independent Democratic Club. Among them was 28-year-old Nick Civella, who served as an outside challenger at the polls. As it was, the First Ward voted decisively against Gage.

When Civella assumed out-front leadership of the Outfit in the early 1950s, the political clique running the First Ward was divided into two. On the western side, forces were headed by Tom Gavin and Jasper Brancato and on the eastern side by Joe Gallucci. When Gallucci stepped down in 1956, the two factions merged; Presta became the leader and Brancato his No. 1 man. By 1959 Presta was identified publicly as president of the First Ward Democratic Club. The club was affiliated with Henry McKissick, a former political faction partner in the 1940s with then-mob front man Charles Binaggio.

Interestingly, although Presta's influence stemmed from his ability to deliver thousands of votes, he was barred from voting because of liquor-related convictions in 1929, 1935 and 1939. His application for a presidential pardon was denied in 1961.

Presta's political ship hit rough seas in 1958 and 1959. Two Jackson County Grand Jury reports branded him as the political front man for the Kansas City criminal organization. Furthermore, in the 1958 report he was accused along with Max Jaben of having exerted political pressure on the district attorney's office; Presta and Jaben were said to have demanded the firing of an assistant district attorney, Austin Shute, who had been hard at work attempting to close the Downtown Bridge Club. The two had been identified as having an interest in the gambling operation. They also sought to end further investigation of the club and similar operations. The grand jury found that Shute had acted well within the province of an assistant prosecutor to investigate gambling and vice in Jackson County. The Downtown Bridge Club was closed, but Shute wound up out of a job anyway.

After the 1959 grand jury report, Presta spoke out, denying he had ever been a political front man for any underworld elements in or out of politics As for the "Mafia," he said:

"I've heard that name since I was a little boy. I have never been able to find out what it is or what the word means. Kansas city is clean as a whistle."

On the other hand, 1959 unexpectedly turned out to be a banner year for the Presta faction. In an upset, the Presta faction and four other factions wrested control of City Hall from the Citizens Association after its 18-year clean-government reign.

The highly regarded city manager, L.P. Cookingham, was quickly dumped. His replacement initiated a house-cleaning, dismissing department heads not protected by the merit system and simply changing the rules to rid City Hall of those who were merit-protected. Once again, patronage became the word of the day.

A little more than two years after being named as an Apalachin attendee, Nick Civella was the toast of the town. On December 13, 1959, a 25th wedding anniversary party was held for Nick and Katherine Civella at the Mirror Lake Country Club near Parkville in Platte County, Missouri. The club was owned by longtime mob facilitator Edward "Eddie Spitz" Osadchey. Five hundred to 1,000 guests were estimated to have attended. Crime Family figures were liberally sprinkled among a host of political and civic luminaries. Jackson County Sheriff Arvid Owsley reported that 162 cars were observed at the event. Among the political and civic figures said to have attended were City Council members Tom Gavin and Sal Capra, State Senator Jasper Brancato, faction leader Alex Presta, ward boss Henry McKissick, Jackson County administrative judge Hunter Phillips and Lyman Field, president of the Board of Police Commissioners.

ALTHOUGH CIVELLA AND PRESTA adamantly denied Civella's influence, other voices gave a different description of the North End political landscape. District Attorney William A. Collet, in a re-election campaign speech in July 1960, said Nick Civella operated behind the scenes and had the final say in all North End political decisions. Civella participated with faction bosses and at times with City Council members in conferences about city policies, Collet said.

Sheriff Owsley told a reporter, "As far as the connection between organized crime and politics, Civella is the No. 1 director," acting privately and meeting with political leaders when it was necessary.

The FBI was hearing things, too. In the early 1960s Civella hung his hat daily at the Original Toy & Jobbing Co. Following its mandate, FBI agents planted a bug in his office.

Politics was among the wide range of topics discussed by Civella and his cronies, confirming that he was politically active. Civella was overheard complaining that city jobs available to Presta through political connections were minor, and spoke of money he and Max Jaben had put into the last election. Civella talked of an unnamed candidate for Jackson County prosecutor whom he would back only after he met the man personally, and only if the candidate promised to give "consideration" to the North End. It was apparent Civella had the authority to decide who would get the backing of the North End faction.

Civella and Jaben were the two who most often talked politics. Before a primary election in 1962, Civella told of his satisfaction with all the Democratic Party nominees except for an unnamed candidate for prosecutor. In yet another conversation that month, discussing the coming political elections, he told Jaben how "Alex" kept him abreast of what transpired in the political arena. Civella took an active role in drumming up political contributions; in a phone call to Nick Evola at his Paramount Vending Co., Civella arranged for $3,000 to be donated to the First Ward Democratic Club.

With time, the wheels came off Presta's proud results in the 1959 city election. The council elected that year proved to be a chaotic nightmare, and the climate at City Hall became so that intolerable Mayor H. Roe Bartle turned to Civella. Why Civella? According to Bartle, he did so because of "rumors that would reach me with a great deal of regularity from many sources" — and "almost daily" from higher-ups in the Police Department — painting Civella as an important figure in the North End political faction.

In 1958, even before the election that upended the council, Bartle had turned to Civella, asking his support in a political race for Bartle's personal attorney and close friend. That year, Civella gave his regrets, but he had already committed to another candidate.

On two occasions in 1959, in hopes of restoring some order to the "erratic" City Council, Bartle sought out Civella. Agreeing to meet with him and Alex Presta, Civella claimed to have no political influence, referring to Presta as the political organization's head. That raised the question, Why had Civella agreed to the meeting?

In 1963, all the council members were swept out of office except one — Presta's nephew Sal Capra.

AFTER THE 1963 DEBACLE Presta retired from political activity and was replaced by Vic DiMaria, owner of a real-estate firm and a Jackson County assistant license inspector. Because DiMaria lacked Presta's experience in the rough-and-tumble world of faction politics, rumors abounded that Max Jaben was really the man to see.

Jaben, born Motel Grzebienacz in Poland, came to America in 1920 and to Kansas City in 1926. His star rose in the 1940s during the reign of Charles Binaggio. Gambling was Jaben's forte. He was involved in gambling operations in Colorado in league with notorious racket figures such as Eugene "Checkers" Smaldone, the future crime family boss in Denver. In 1949 Jaben was part of a cabal of Outfit thugs who muscled into all of Kansas City's policy gambling operations.

In the 1950s Jaben became part of Nick Civella's trusted inner circle, and was recognized as a person not to be fooled with. He had his hand in the Nevada gaming industry in behalf of the Kansas City Outfit, and along with Nick and Cork Civella was part of the initial group included in Nevada's "Black Book" of people banned from casinos.

Jaben's contacts and clout also extended to the east. On December 12,

1963, Kansas City Police received a tip about a high-level meeting at Uncle Tom's Barbeque at 3809 Broadway, operated by Outfit powerhouse Thomas "Hiway" Simone. The police found that Jaben had been meeting there for about two hours with the boss of the St. Louis crime family, Anthony Giordano, and with another St. Louis heavyweight, James Michaels, head of a Syrian criminal/political faction. When the meeting broke up, Jaben and the two St. Louis men were arrested in Jaben's car and charged with disorderly conduct. Michaels' and Jaben's involvement in politics gave rise to speculation that the meeting concerned the upcoming Missouri Democratic gubernatorial race in 1964.

Interviewed by a *Kansas City Star* reporter in 1966, Jaben denied being the hidden influence behind Vic DiMaria and denied that he was sought out for political advice. As for being connected with the mob, Jaben told the reporter, he was a "*Star*-manufactured underworld figure." He spoke of having been a political faction leader since the 1930s, claiming to have quit the North End faction because it made him no money, took a lot of time and brought him bad publicity.

Presta, too, denied Jaben's involvement. If Jaben had claimed to be part of the organization, Presta continued, then he had not paid his dues.

The issue of income taxes, which plagued so many of his ilk, caught up with Jaben in 1965. He was convicted of federal tax violations and on his way to serve a four-month sentence when the 63-year-old Presta came out of retirement and again took an active role in North End politics. To U.S. Attorney Russell Millin, the move was not sheer coincidence.

Despite Jaben's professed lack of political influence, it is interesting that former City Council member William R. Royster, then running for state representative, visited Jaben three times in jail. For this, Jaben had a simple explanation: Royster had dropped by solely out of friendship, and only because prison was on Royster's way when he went fishing. Royster, when asked, agreed with Jaben's version.

As a City Council member in 1961, Royster reprinted and distributed a flyer containing an article from *The Kansas City News-Press* boldly proclaiming "No Organized Crime Here, Police Commissioner Says." It quoted Police Board President Lyman Field, one of the attendees at Nick Civella's anniversary bash, as proclaiming to a Lions Club meeting in 1960 that there was no organized crime in Kansas City and that anyone who intimated there was should be viewed with suspicion.

Also in play at the time Jaben went to jail in 1965 was the newly elected governor of Missouri, Warren Hearnes. Although Presta was said to have personally favored Hearnes in the 1964 election, the North End faction failed to back him and thus Hearnes owed them nothing. On the other hand, it was not politically expedient to abandon the North End and that led to speculation that Presta had come out of retirement to foster a favorable relationship with Hearnes. Future actions of the Hearnes administration would tend to bear that out.

WHEN HE FIRST STEPPED ASIDE in 1963, Presta was quoted as saying, "Since I became a power, I elected a state senator (Jasper Brancato) a state representative (Frank Mazzuca) and put Sal (Capra) in the City Council," describing these as particularly important accomplishments. The importance of Capra's and Brancato's elections, however, would be sorely tested when their character and reputations were called into question.

In 1973 the federal government charged Capra and Brancato with a criminal conspiracy to evade millions of dollars in state sales taxes, estimated by the Missouri state revenue director at $45 million to more than $100 million. The *St. Louis Globe-Democrat* described the matter as "one of the biggest state government scandals in recent years."

The accusation was that Capra and Brancato had fudged badly on state sales tax returns, which could be deemed mail fraud because they were submitted through the U.S. Post Office. That made it a federal matter.

The prosecution brought howls of anti-Italian discrimination, selective prosecution and misapplication of federal law. A special federal prosecutor, Michael DeFeo, said the government's mandate was to step in when local law enforcement was blocked by political influence and the tentacles of organized crime were involved.

The act of tax cheating was exacerbated, the government said, by a brazen exercise of political influence. From 1965 to 1972, Brancato and Alex Presta frequently had met with and called employees of the Kansas City Office of the Sales Tax Division in the Missouri Department of Revenue. They had influenced employment, tenure, assignment of duties, collection activities and the conduct of audits. Brancato had issued directions to initiate or forgo enforcement of sales-tax laws. Also, he was accused of counseling employees of the local Sales Tax Division to send the Missouri Department of Revenue only one-third of the sales taxes it was owed, to keep one-third for themselves and to remit one-third to Brancato for his protection against potential difficulties that might arise.

"This Sales Tax Division," Brancato had said, "is my baby."

Capra was accused of submitting fraudulent sales tax returns from 1969 to 1972 from two taverns in which he had an interest. For that, he was indicted in August 1973 on two counts of mail fraud. Compounding the fraud, it was alleged that Capra told the operators of another establishment in which he had an interest that they did not need to report the full amount of their gross receipts; a "friend" in the Missouri Department of Revenue could take care of any problems if they arose. Furthermore, certain Department of Revenue auditors referred individuals with tax problems to Capra for assistance.

When Capra learned of the federal probe he filed amended sales-tax returns to the state.

Capra was tried on the federal charges of sales-tax evasion and in September 1975 he was acquitted by a jury. There was no question that the state had been defrauded, the jury foreman said, but the jury found the use of the mail was only incidental to the act. Capra's own attorney stated he was wrong in not paying the proper taxes.

The ax fell on Brancato in late 1973, two months after Capra was charged. Brancato was indicted on 10 counts of mail fraud charging that from 1968 through 1971 he had understated by about $800,000 income subject to sales tax from his Ramada Inn at 5100 Linwood Blvd. Following in Capra's footsteps, he filed amended tax returns upon learning he was under investigation. Later, the indictment against Brancato was dismissed.

STATE REPRESENTATIVE Frank Mazzuca, the third officeholder Presta had bragged about, died in January 1969. He was replaced in a special election by Alex Fazzino, who had grown up in the North End. Fazzino's political base was the Northeast Democratic Club and his business base was the Passantino-Fazzino Bonding Company.

Immediately after winning the seat he was embroiled in controversy. The issue: where did Fazzino live? He had a residence at 1809 Pendleton Ave., outside the district to which he had been elected, but he claimed 574 Harrison St. as his place of abode. That was the home of Dr. Sam Scardino. Seeking answers, reporters met conflicting and unanswered questions at every turn. The Jackson County Democratic chairman, Thomas R. Slaughter, called

Fazzino's residence claim a fraud.

Nevertheless, Fazzino weathered the storm and took his seat in the Missouri General Assembly. His career in office would be rocky. Throughout his tenure Fazzino would come to the aide of notorious figures, claiming he was only supporting his constituents and often stretching the limits of that claim.

Consider three of many examples:

First was the case of a longtime crime family member and one of Nick Civella's closest allies, Thomas Cacioppo. In December 1972, in one of the last acts of the Hearnes Administration, Lt. Governor William Morris, acting in Hearnes' absence, signed a pardon for Cacioppo after he was approached by an unnamed elected official who Morris explained was "a very close friend" of Cacioppo. The reason given by Morris was that Cacioppo's conviction had occurred many years in the past and, if the man had lived an honest life ever since, then he deserved a pardon. No, Morris was not aware that Cacioppo had been publicly named a top echelon member of the Family by the Kansas City Crime Commission.

State records showed that the unnamed elected official who made the request was State Representative Alex Fazzino. He had assured Legal Counsel Paul Williams that Cacioppo had no connection with organized crime. Williams, whose name repeatedly surfaced in such affairs, ignored negative reports from law enforcement and recommended the pardon, which sat on Hearnes' desk until Morris took action.

A second instance was the case of Anthony "Tony Ripe" Civella, Cork Civella's son and Nick Civella's nephew. He was seeking relief from an order by the Kansas City Liquor Control director revoking his license for Sunday liquor sales. Hearnes signed a "pardon," even though the liquor control director said that, in fact, the state had no jurisdiction in a city administrative ruling. At the top of the so-called pardon was a typed note: "12/15/72 Mailed to Representative Alex Fazzino, 1809 Pendleton, KCMO." That was the very address Fazzino disclaimed as his home. At the time, Tony Civella was under indictment, along with his uncle, in an extensive Outfit bookmaking operation, and the Civella name was not exactly unheard-of in and out of Kansas City.

The governor, however, said he had never heard of Tony Civella.

I just sign what Paul Williams sends over, Hearnes said. Also, Hearnes had no idea why the pardon was sent to Fazzino. Williams himself had little recollection of the affair, apparently having done nothing to check Civella's background.

A year later, former Governor Hearnes revealed that Fazzino had admitted to him that he had interceded in behalf of Tony Civella in the pardon matter.

There was little doubt that Fazzino and Tony Civella were close. On October 16, 1973, Fazzino was present in the early morning hours at a mob-frequented establishment operated by Tony Civella, Georgie Porgies at 2510 N.E. Vivion Rd. in Gladstone. Two patrons claimed they were ganged up on and beaten, and they identified Civella as one of their assailants. When the case was heard in municipal court Fazzino appeared as a defense alibi witness for Civella, who was found guilty. Fazzino appeared again on Civella's behalf at an appeal hearing.

A third instance occurred in April 1980, when Fazzino accompanied 32-year-old Rita Armillio to the Jackson County sheriff's headquarters at Lake Jacomo. He was there to lend weight to her request for a license to purchase a .38-caliber revolver. Armillio was an employee of the Villa Capri Restaurant, a favorite meeting place for the Family. According to Jackson County Sheriff Robert Rennau, Fazzino represented Armillo to be his niece.

In fact, Rennau found, she was not Fazzino's niece. She was, however, the girlfriend of Cork Civella. Fazzino denied that Civella had any part in the affair and acknowledged that he had misrepresented the facts, but said:

"I wasn't trying to deceive anybody. There was nothing devious about what I did."

Alcohol, Tobacco and Firearms agents suspected Armillio was obtaining a weapon for Cork Civella, who as a convicted felon could not possess one. When Fazzino was called to appear before a federal grand jury looking into the case, he took the Fifth Amendment. It would not be the last time he did so.

Eventually, Fazzino was caught up in a career-ending FBI bribery investigation involving two wholesale fireworks dealers. At his trial, they testified that Fazzino had solicited bribes in exchange for his influence in defeating proposed fireworks legislation detrimental to the dealers. The jury found Fazzino guilty and sentenced him to four years in prison and a $10,000 fine. During the 10 months between his sentencing and his appeal, which was denied, Fazzino remained free on bond, and won re-election as state representative. Upon reporting to prison in August 1985, Fazzino was removed from office. He served eight months of the sentence and was released to a half-way house, where he was allowed to leave during the day and go free on weekends.

If there was a moral to the story, others failed to learn it. Fazzino was one of five Missouri legislators prosecuted, beginning in 1977 when House Speaker Richard J. Rabbitt was convicted of mail fraud and extortion and sentenced to seven years. In 1983 State Representative Gary Smith and State Senator Lee Vertis Swinton were convicted of misappropriating funds from estates they were handling. In 1990 Fazzino's successor, Henry Rizzo, ran afoul of the law.

In Fazzino's times of trouble, Rizzo, then a Jackson County legislator and president of the Northeast Democratic Club, was vocal in his support of the embattled state representative. In return, before going to prison Fazzino endorsed Rizzo as the man to replace him.

Through four months in 1989 Rizzo, his brother John Rizzo, and an employee of theirs at their Chevrolet dealership wrote more than 100 fraudulent checks totaling some $3.5 million dollars. The check-kiting scheme was aimed at keeping their ailing dealership at 1615 Independence Ave. from collapse. They were charged in a 17-count federal indictment in November 1990 with defrauding two Kansas City banks. Rizzo's seat in the Missouri House was saved when a deal was struck for his plea to a misdemeanor: accessory after the fact. He received a three-month sentence.

And of all of these troubles, what seemed to bother Rizzo the most? Politicians, he complained, had become the targets of excessive scrutiny by the authorities.

CHAPTER V

VIOLENCE — A WAY OF LIFE

THE AURA SURROUNDING the Outfit is one of violence. Murder and the threat of it are intrinsic to its success, and Kansas City's history is dotted with gangland murders. At one time they were described as "spot killings," but in today's vernacular they are called the "hit" or the "contract killing." Outfit rules dictate that the boss authorizes these acts of violence.

As boss, Nick Civella took a reasoned, thoughtful and restrained approach to the matter. As a rule murder was committed for tactical, defensive, or disciplinary purposes and at times for personal reasons. In killings attributable to the Outfit, all of those factors have come into play.

The 1959 murder of 34-year-old Melvin L. Meinsen was notable for this: It appears to have been the first gangland slaying in Kansas City after the Apalachin meeting in November 1957. The tentacles of the case also extended to other mob-related events.

Meinsen had the assets of the con man. He was described as a fun-loving sort with a glib tongue and an easy smile. He racked up an impressive string of arrests in Los Angeles, Des Moines, Las Vegas, Fort Worth, Oklahoma City and Stamford, Connecticut, along with about 20 arrests in the Kansas City area.

In July 1958, he and two associates were caught passing hundreds of bad checks estimated to total $200,000 to $500,000. The scam extended across several states and preyed on small-town businesses, sadly victimizing those least capable of standing the loss. Meinsen was arrested. He pleaded not guilty and went free on bond. Working the justice system, he delayed his day in court in Missouri until January 11, 1960, while other states waited in the wings for their chance at him.

However, more potent forces moved to the head of the line.

On December 15, 1959, Meinsen pulled into the driveway of his residence at 5219 E. 41st Terr. As he approached the front steps his wife opened the door for him. To her horror, behind her husband appeared a man with a white handkerchief covering the lower part of his face. He carried a 12-gauge shotgun, and blasted Meinsen. The couple's 13-year-old daughter screamed at her mother to shut the door. It was riddled with 11 pellet holes.

Meinsen staggered toward the back of the house, followed by the gunman. A second round from the shotgun killed him. The weapon was found lying along the edge of the street in front of 5211 E. 40th St., broken in two pieces. Apparently it had been thrown from a getaway vehicle. Considered a "spot murder," the question was, What had Meinsen done to incur the wrath of the Family?

The answer lay in another of Meinsen's scams, this one involving extorting abortion doctors. A close associate of Meinsen provided details of the scheme to a Kansas City police detective:

Meinsen recruited young girls to visit abortion doctors and claim to be pregnant. While the girl was with the doctor, Meinsen or an associate would barge in, acting the part of an outraged father, threatening to expose the doctor and demanding money in return for the "father's" silence.

Joseph Getelson, a Kansas City physician appearing before a state grand jury, testified about paying $75,000 to $80,000 in extortion money to Meinsen. On one occasion, he said, after paying Meinsen $15,000, Felix Ferina and another Outfit member assaulted Meinsen and took back the money. Getelson, whose name later surfaced in another murder case, identified Nick and Cork Civella along with Ferina as patients of his. Meinsen had stepped on important toes.

He was summoned to a meeting with Outfit figures, who warned him that he was messing with the wrong doctors and ordered him to stop. Failing to heed the warning proved fatal. Felix Ferina, a known Outfit enforcer, was considered the prime suspect in Meinsen's murder, which was never solved.

Six months after the Meinsen murder gangland violence erupted in a far more sensational way, and Felix Ferina once again was a central figure.

KENNETH BRUCE SHEETZ PROUDLY said of his profession, "I am a well-recognized, reputable burglar." He denied being a habitual dope peddler, but it was narcotics that brought him a world of trouble.

The trouble started about 9 p.m. July 16, 1959, when an attractive, 32-year-old blonde "working girl," by previous arrangement, met Sheetz at

11th and Washington streets. In Sheetz's powder-blue 1956 Cadillac they motored to Union Station, discreetly shadowed by officers of the Federal Narcotics Bureau and the Kansas City Police. At the station, they ordered drinks at the Westport Room. Sheetz stepped away briefly to meet a man loitering in the station. As the officers looked on, the man handed Sheetz a package. Sheetz returned to his drink and then left with his companion.

Several months passed before the two met again. After a brief drive with Sheetz, the woman proceeded by cab to near Fifth Street and Troost Avenue. While the taxi driver waited, she walked to some bushes at Fourth and Troost, grabbed a package that she was looking for and had the cab take her to the vicinity of 31st and Troost. Waiting for her there were federal narcotics agents and Kansas City policemen, who took possession of the package she retrieved from the bushes. Their next stop was the residence of Kenneth Bruce Sheetz, where he was placed under arrest.

Sheetz had been set up. The woman, described as a once-respectable housewife whose drug addiction led her to prostitution, had agreed to work for the authorities after she was arrested for narcotics violations. The packages she had received from Sheetz, paying him a total of $75, contained narcotics.

In turn, Sheetz agreed to work with the Federal Narcotics Bureau. He joined an undercover narcotics agent and the two traveled through 20 Midwestern states, establishing themselves as buyers of narcotics. In Omaha, Sheetz introduced the agent to Anthony Biase, a well-known criminal figure suspected of being a major drug supplier. Streetwise and wary, Biase made contact with "people" in Kansas City to insure it was safe to deal with Sheetz. Getting the green light, he transacted three narcotics deals.

With Sheetz' later grand jury testimony, Biase was indicted in Omaha in March 1960. Biase then demanded that his Kansas City contact who had vouched for Sheetz put Sheetz down. The stage was set and Sheetz, certainly not unaware of his predicament, still chose to return home to Kansas City from Omaha.

About 10:20 a.m. the morning of June 20, 1960, after taking care of some personal business, Sheetz went to his one-story frame house at 4501 Michigan Ave. As he opened the front door he sensed a presence, causing him to withdraw. He tried to pull the door shut, but before he could he was shot in the stomach. Sheetz turned and was shot in the back. The shot spun him around so that again he faced the front door. Shot once more, this time in the head, he dropped to the floor, and then took one more round in the back. Just before being shot the fourth time one of the assassins said something like, "This is for Tony" or "Tony sent me."

Somehow, Sheetz lived. At first, abiding by the code, he told the authorities, "I know who shot me, but I won't tell."

Later he fingered Felix Ferina and Anthony "Tiger" Cardarella as the shooters. To the consternation of the Family, the gangland shooting garnered front-page banner headlines, and state and federal indictments issued less than a month later kept the "hit" a hot item. Ferina and Cardarella were charged in Jackson County with the attempted murder of a federal witness. Federal charges of conspiracy to prevent Sheetz from testifying against Biase in the Omaha narcotics prosecution were leveled against the two, along with Anthony Biase and a man named Carlton Young. Biase was charged in a separate indictment with narcotics trafficking.

Cardarella was alleged to be the shooter in the failed attempt on Sheetz' life. Young, a Teamsters Union Central Conference business representative working in Kansas City, was implicated in the conspiracy. He was said to have acted as an intermediary for friends in Omaha, relaying a message to Mrs. Sheetz before the shooting that her husband had better keep his mouth shut.

The intrigue and manipulation characterizing the Sheetz saga seemingly had no bounds. It began at General Hospital, where Sheetz was recovering, when prosecutors, defense attorneys and police gathered to take his deposition. Representing Cardarella, attorney James Mullin attempted to pull a fast one. Looking to elicit a false identification, Mullin entered the scene with his "client" at his side, someone similar in height and build to Cardarella. The scheme quickly fell apart when Sheetz and a policeman recognized the impostor, Cardarella's brother George. Questioned by the police, George Cardarella readily admitted his role in the scheme to fool Sheetz.

In fact, the substitution was not a novel idea, but one borrowed from co-defendant Felix Ferina. In 1946 Ferina was in magistrate court in Kansas City, facing a burglary charge. His attorney had noted the uncanny resemblance between Ferina and his brother, just out of the Navy, so he had Ferina put on his brother's uniform and sit behind the defense table. Meanwhile, Ferina's brother, in civilian clothes, took his place as the defendant. Each witness asked to identify Felix Ferina pointed to the brother. Case dismissed.

In the Sheetz case, Ferina was the first to stand trial, which began in November 1960 in Jackson County Circuit Court. Sheetz was the prosecution's star witness. For the defense, Clyde C. North Jr. took the stand as an alibi witness. North, a Johnson County, Kansas, resident who was in the real estate and loan business, testified that on the morning of the Sheetz assault he met with Ferina. After a cup of coffee, he said, he took Ferina to inspect a house North had on the market at 10001 State Line Rd. They left there about 10:45 a.m. and looked at two other houses before returning to North's office at 11:30 a.m.

It just so happened that North's uncle, as North admitted in his testimony, was Joseph Getelson, whose relationship with Ferina came to light in the Meinsen murder investigation. A question not fully explored at trial was whether Ferina's look-alike brother had accompanied North that morning — if, in fact, any houses ever were inspected.

After five hours of deliberation the trial jury was hung and a mistrial was declared. The two holdout jurors pointed to North's testimony as key to their decision.

A month later the case was retried. Once again Sheetz identified Ferina as one of his assailants, and once again Clyde North repeated his alibi testimony.

Between trials, the defense had reached into its bag of tricks and come up with two additional — and most interesting — alibi witnesses. One was Paul Silvio, an Outfit associate and partner with Nick and Tony Civella in Antonio's Pizzerias at 43rd and Main streets and at 2512 E. Vivion Rd. in the Northland. Silvio testified that on the morning of June 20, 1960, he had breakfast at the Vivion Road Antonio's and that Anthony Cardarella was there along with Albert Brandmeyer.

The other additional witness was Brandmeyer, who was a partner of Carl Civella in B&C Meat Company. He testified in support of Silvio's story. If these three alibi witnesses could be believed, then Sheetz had misidentified Ferina and Cardarella as his assailants.

The prosecutors counter-punched with their own new witness, the owner of the residence that Ferina and North allegedly visited on June 20. He was Ted C. McMurrough, a regional sales manager. McMurrough testified that he, his wife, and two salesman were at his home at 10001 State Line Rd. that morning and that neither North or Ferina had come by to inspect the house. In fact, the first time he had ever seen Ferina was when he took the stand to testify.

Alex Presta, North End
political operator

Max Jaben, part of the Civella
inner circle.

Sal Capra, a Presta protege

Jasper Brancato

Alex Fazzino, left, with his successor, Henry Rizzo

From *The Kansas City Star*, January 11, 1966

Missouri Governor Warren Hearnes

Melvin Meinsen

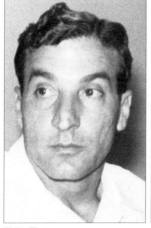

Felix Ferina

Anthony "Tiger" Cardarella

Kenneth Sheetz, burglar and informant, was shot as he approached the front door of his home.

Anthony Biase

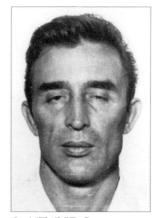

Carl "Tuffy" DeLuna

Stanton Gladden, firefighters union leader who survived a car bombing in early 1961.

The wrecked Gladden vehicle, parked outside the family home.

Edgar Grass,
Gladden rival and
Teamsters backer

In the end, the trial jury acquitted Ferina, which forced the prosecution to drop the charges pending against Cardarella. The two had dodged one bullet.

They did not fare as well in federal court, where in April 1961 a jury delivered verdicts of guilty for Ferina, Cardarella and Biase, while the judge directed a verdict of not guilty for Carlton Young. Alibi witnesses Paul Silvio and Albert Brandmeyer went back on stage but this time their story apparently didn't hold sway. Cardarella and Ferina were sentenced to 10 years, while Biase received five.

Still, the Sheetz saga was far from over. The same month the case went to trial in federal court Clyde North was indicted by a Jackson County grand jury for furnishing perjured testimony in the two state trials. Eighteen months went by while the case was continued time and again. Ted McMorrough, the key witness to North's perjured testimony, moved to Texas.

Meanwhile, in December 1962 a source told the Kansas City Crime Commission that Cork Civella had excused a $5,600 gambling debt owed by Clyde North in exchange for his testimony at the Ferina trial.

The North case was called on January 14, 1963, two weeks after Lawrence Gepford became Jackson County prosecutor. Gepford dismissed the case, telling the court the chief witness was outside the jurisdiction and would not return to testify. Gepford's chief assistant, J. Arnot Hill, ran against Gepford in 1964 and in the campaign labeled Gepford's excuse as flimsy. Hill claimed that he had tried to get the case set for trial in November 1962 and that there would have been no trouble in getting the key witness back to testify then, so there should have been no trouble in calling him two months later.

There was yet one more chapter to be written in this sordid story. Caught up in the web was Sicilian-born Frank LaRocca. He had immigrated to the United States in 1906 and for years had operated LaRocca Grocery at 815 E. Fifth St.. The Kefauver Committee had identified LaRocca as a member of the Kansas City "Mafia" in its 1950 hearings in Kansas City.

Now, more than a decade later, the 74-year-old LaRocca was called to testify before the federal grand jury investigating the Sheetz assault. In March 1963, he was arrested and charged with lying when he told the grand jury that he was not the purchaser of the pistol found a block from the Sheetz crime scene.

At LaRocca's trial, government witnesses testified he purchased the

.38-caliber revolver in August 1957 at Elmer's Sporting Goods in Gunnison, Colorado. For the purchase he used the name John Sutomano. Furthermore, LaRocca had returned to Gunnison in October 1957 to buy 12 similar revolvers for "Christmas presents." The weapons had to be ordered and were then delivered to the home of Frank Costanzo of Gunnison, who at Elmer's Sporting Goods had vouched for LaRocca as being John Sutomano. They were paid for in cash by LaRocca.

He was found guilty of lying to the grand jury and sentenced to a five-year maximum prison term, which was reduced on March 26, 1965, to probation and a $1,000 fine. It had taken the better part of five years to close the book on the Sheetz shooting.

THERE IS A SAYING that one man's misfortune is another man's riches. It could well apply to Felix Ferina and Carl "Tuffy" DeLuna. The Outfit's powers, it seems, were not pleased with the flap created by the botched hit on Sheetz, and Ferina ended up in the doghouse as well as the Big House.

As a result, DeLuna, whose sister was married to Tony Civella, became Nick Civella's prime enforcer. When the Outfit's No. 2 man, Thomas "Hiway" Simone, died in 1968, DeLuna moved up another rung in the Outfit hierarchy. He became a favorite of Nick Civella, and was tabbed as potentially Civella's successor.

A postscript: The woman who set up Sheetz was hospitalized twice for her drug addiction and died in 1962 of a drug overdose. Cardarella, after years of involvement in Outfit affairs, was found stuffed in the trunk of his car on February 27, 1984, apparently strangled. A little more than six months later, Felix Ferina's body was found in his car, shot three times in the head.

Many more would fall victim to the revolver, shotgun, bomb and to strangulation at the hands of Outfit enforcers.

CHAPTER VI

LABOR RACKETEERING

AS EARLY AS THE 1920s John Lazia, who was then the out-front boss of the Kansas City Crime Family, recognized and seized upon the potential that lay in Kansas City's unions. As years went by and the labor movement grew, labor racketeering became a Cosa Nostra staple.

For Nick Civella, labor — and particularly the Teamsters union — would be the source of power and influence that would vault him into national prominence within Cosa Nostra.

The story traces back to 1937, when a rough-edged Teamsters business agent named Floyd R. Hayes, representing Local 41 in Kansas City, embarked on an organizing campaign. One of Hayes' first targets was his own uncle, the head of Reardon Truck Lines. Reardon looked on the Teamsters as a bunch of punks and wanted nothing to do with the union. Within three months, every piece of equipment owned by Reardon Truck Lines was damaged or inoperable. Reardon did not bend, but under similar duress most other truck lines and related businesses fell in line. Truckers who resisted and hired strikebreakers faced pitched battles with union goons.

Hayes' union organizing involved cash kickbacks in return for labor peace, "sweetheart contracts," padded billings and other schemes. At the outset Hayes was mob-free, but the union's potential for money, jobs, power and influence was far too enticing to keep the Outfit at bay. By the 1940s elements of organized crime around the country were escalating efforts to infiltrate the Teamsters, and they had the perfect man to pave the way in James Riddle "Jimmy" Hoffa, a Detroit Teamsters official. As for the Kansas City mob's push for the Teamsters, the best evidence is that it bubbled to the surface about 1952. That year, the attempted murder of Local 955's president, Lee Quisenberry, was attributed to the Family. To protect himself and pacify the Family, Quisenberry hired Outfit-affiliated Sam Ancona as an assistant business agent.

About the same time, Orville Ring, an ambitious and savvy man, won the presidency of the largest Kansas City Teamsters local, 541. He brought on board a group of street-wise toughs: Ernie Anderson, Carl "Curly" Rogers, Del Nabors, Bobby Williams and Tripoli "Trip" Milone.

Some of the toughs soon turned on Ring. Both Anderson and Rogers were aligned with the Outfit, and in 1952 Anderson arranged a meeting with the boss, Tony Gizzo. If he knew what was good for him, Ring was told, he would do what Gizzo ordered. What Gizzo wanted was for all Teamsters to vote for Gene Purdome as Jackson County sheriff. That put Ring in a bind; he supported a different candidate. A year after Gizzo's approach, Nick Civella made an approach recommending Ring go along with Civella and his people, who Civella proclaimed were "running the town." If Ring would swing the labor vote for "their candidates," Civella said, Ring would be made the "biggest S.O.B." in the city. A second item appeared on Civella's agenda: he would handle all union shakedowns and payoffs. Civella warned Ring that if he resisted and wanted to continue living he should resign.

Under these pressures from the mob, Ring wisely resigned on March 1, 1954. When FBI agents appeared at his door he freely recounted his tale of woe.

The election to replace him was carried out in April 1954 in the Teamsters style of the day: The general membership of the local was not notified. With only 136 of the 5,000 members present, Ernie Anderson was elected president of Local 541.

ALSO NOTEWORTHY IN 1954 was an election personally presided over by Jimmy Hoffa, who had risen to president of the International Brotherhood. In it, the trustee of Kansas City's troubled Teamsters Local 41 — assigned to the task two years before by Hoffa's assistant Frank Fitzsimmons — was elevated to president of the local.

He was Roy Lee Williams, who was destined to play an enormous role in Teamsters-mob affairs, particularly in Nick Civella's reign as Family boss.

Williams was born March 22, 1915, in Ottumwa, Iowa, one of 12 children. He was reared in southeast Missouri. In 1935 he entered the freight industry as a driver for the C.W. Pascal Co. and three years later he joined Kansas City Teamsters Local 41. In World War II, Williams served a distinguished stint in the Army. Four years after the war ended, Hoffa appointed Williams trustee of Wichita, Kansas, Local 795, which was facing internal difficulties.

By the time Williams arrived in Kansas City in 1952 he was already a trustee of Joint Council 56, which oversaw all Teamsters locals in western Missouri and in Kansas. Subsequently he would be elected president of the joint council in addition to his presidency of Local 41.

Not surprisingly, politics was the setting for Williams' first encounter with Nick Civella. In late 1953 or early 1954, he sat on a political committee that included Civella as a representative of a North End political club. The two served as referees for the political clubs operating in Jackson County; their aim was to build a unified front by sorting out candidates based on their chances of winning. The relationship between Williams and Civella developed into a strong friendship. Eventually, however, Williams would experience elements of the relationship that were not so friendly.

Over time the Outfit successfully stacked the deck at the Teamsters halls with Roy Lee Williams as majordomo. Owing their positions to the North End were Ernie Anderson, winner of the unannounced election for president of Local 541; John Balestrere, brother of the powerful Big Jim Balestrere, as assistant business agent of Local 955, and Sam Ancona, secretary-treasurer of Joint Council 56 and president of Local 955. Ancona also held an unofficial post as direct liaison with Nick Civella, reporting to him and passing on his orders to Teamsters officials.

ILLUSTRATIVE OF THE EXPLOSIVE MIX of politics, labor and organized crime was the case of the firefighters union and its combative president.

The Kansas City Fire Department had been a wellspring for patronage jobs in the 1920s and 1930s. As night follows day, patronage flowed again once the old-line Democratic factions — including the Alex Presta-led North End — took over the City Council in 1959. Using the mob-infiltrated Teamsters as the wedge, the restored old-liners set out to retake control of the Fire Department.

In July 1959, Teamsters Local 774 mounted a drive to organize the firefighters, most of whom belonged to Local 42 of the International Association of Fire Fighters. Blocking the Teamsters and their North Side allies was a feisty battalion chief who was the Fire Fighters union president, Stanton Gladden.

Gladden had built a strong union local, and he had also professionalized what had become a shoddy Fire Department. Publicly, he decried how "North Side elements" were seeking to politicize the department as a source of patronage. In several heated disputes, he crossed swords with the new City Council majority. He was also a longtime rival of Fire Chief Edgar M. Grass, a Teamsters supporter. At one point, Fire Department Director Harry A. Eibe stepped in, issuing an ultimatum to Gladden and Grass: If either persisted in critical public statements it would result in immediate dismissal.

Joining the fray, Jackson County Prosecutor William A. Collet addressed the conflict in a re-election campaign speech: "There is talk Civella takes instructions from James Hoffa. The Teamsters and the North Side organization work together.... There is an alliance in an attempt to organize the Fire Department. That is going on today — there is no question about it."

In his quest to gather evidence of North Side involvement, Gladden came across an affidavit executed by then-Fire Captain Robert E. Anderson. It charged that Chief Grass had offered Anderson the answers to a promotion examination if he would switch his allegiance to the Teamsters. Anderson left the department after the affidavit was found, becoming an organizer for the Teamsters Union. The affidavit became public, aired by City Councilman Joseph Welsh on June 3, 1960, and Gladden was fired for violating the Fire Director's ultimatum about making critical public statements.

Nine days later, Gladden publicly revealed the events transpiring on the morning before the affidavit was aired. Gladden got word from an "acquaintance" that Cork Civella wanted to talk with him. Believing that it would be worth meeting with anyone who might offer a solution to the conflict, Gladden agreed. Room 100 at the Pickwick building on McGee Street between 10th and 11th streets, where Civella had an office, was the site selected.

Right off the bat, Civella made it known that his only interest was in protecting Anderson. To do so he was prepared to use his influence to get Gladden appointed fire chief and Grass appointed director of the Fire Department. In return, Gladden was to insure that Welsh would not make public Anderson's affidavit. As Civella saw it, publicizing the affidavit would cause embarrassment to the Teamsters in the Fire Department and to the city administration. Civella told Gladden that his offer could not be guaranteed, "but there are certain councilmen that we can rely on and we feel confident we can get this done."

Gladden declined the offer, saying he had previously turned down a similar proposal. He saw no reason to do differently this time.

That previous offer had been made at a meeting at the office of Charles Hipsh, a Democratic leader, and attended by council members William Royster, Sal Capra, Charles Fisher and Charles Shaefer, by Fire Chief Grass and by Alex Presta. The offer of promotion purportedly was made to better the relationship between Gladden and Grass. Gladden described Grass as having proven himself impossible for his organization, the Fire Fighters union, to work with and the plan would do nothing to improve the situation. Gladden rejected the offer, adding he didn't want the fire chief's job in any case.

In a statement to *The Kansas City Star* the day after the affidavit was read, Cork Civella said his "friend" Anderson planned to repudiate the affidavit because it was made under duress. Following the script, Anderson appeared at the office of Councilman Fisher, chairman of the Fire and Water Committee, to renounce his affidavit. He claimed Gladden had poured drinks down him at the Fire Fighter's union hall before he completed the document.

About 6:15 a.m. February 9, 1961, at his home at 8000 E. 83rd St., Gladden went to move one of the family cars, a red 1958 Plymouth. It was parked in his driveway, blocking the car he planned on driving to work. As he turned the ignition an explosion ripped the car apart, blowing the hood over the roof of the house into the back yard, 200 feet away.

Gladden was thrown to the driveway, miraculously still alive but with multiple fractures of both ankles. The force of the explosion blew both his 17-year-old and 13-year-old sons out of their beds. Gladden was severely shaken and fearful, feeling an overwhelming dread for his family. The mangled auto normally was driven by his wife. It could have been her and the boys who were injured or killed by the bomb.

A Fire Fighters union official later shed light on what may have triggered the attempted murder. Earlier in the week of the explosion, Gladden had been approached with yet another peace offering. It had come from an individual identified only as a Democratic politician who worked with North End and other political factions; he claimed to be a spokesman for some members of the City Council. A promotion to deputy fire chief, the politician told Gladden, was his to take. Gladden took the question to the executive committee of Fire Fighters Local 42, which voted to reject the offer. Less than 24 hours later, the bomb went off.

Word of the attempt on Gladden's life reached Attorney General Robert Kennedy and he dispatched Special Attorney James Featherstone to Kansas City to investigate. For Agent Bill Quinn and the FBI's Organized Crime Squad, the inquiry that followed broadened the scope of their knowledge and understanding of the alliance between the Outfit and the Teamsters.

THE KEY FOR NICK CIVELLA was to dominate Roy Lee Williams, whose star was rising within the union. Williams was willing to do business in limited areas such as putting Civella-sponsored people to work, but reluctant to honor every Civella request. To Civella, that was unacceptable.

The turning point came when Williams opposed a plan under which Local 41 would pay an area doctor $1 per Teamsters member, in return for which each member and dependent would get an outpatient visit. The unwritten part of the deal was that Civella would get cash kickbacks. Local 541 had adopted such a plan and the Boss wanted Williams' Local 41 to adopt it, too.

After a union meeting at a downtown Kansas City hotel, Williams was accosted by two men — Thomas "Hiway" Simone, Nick Civella's partner in oversight of their Teamsters interests, and another gangster type. Their message was clear and to the point:

Go along with the plan or Williams' two children, his wife and then Williams himself would be killed. If he cooperated he would be taken care of, which Williams took to mean allowed to retain his union position.

Williams appealed to Jimmy Hoffa, saying that the plan would cost the local $4,000 a month and strain its coffers. Hoffa simply instructed him to raise the membership dues.

Reluctantly, Williams agreed to the plan.

Confirmation of the cash kickbacks came when the doctor complained to Williams that Civella was demanding too big a cut of the fees, making the plan unaffordable. The doctor wanted out. Nevertheless, the plan remained in place, so evidently the doctor simply was not allowed to walk away.

Now it was abundantly clear to Williams where he stood. Whenever he and Civella disagreed, his union superiors asked him to comply with Civella's wishes. It was only a matter of time before any resistance to Civella's ambitions would end the civility of their relationship.

The defining issue involved the Teamsters' Central States Pension and Welfare Fund, headquartered in Chicago.

FOLLOWING THE LEAD of other unions, Jimmy Hoffa in 1955 negotiated the first pension plan for 100,000 Teamsters in the South and Midwest. Employers were required to pay $2 per member per week. The money was placed with banks, which controlled investment strategies, and in the first year the plan produced $10 million for the Central States Pension and Welfare Fund. Ten years later, the number of members had doubled, employer contributions had risen to $7 per member per week, and the Fund took in $6 million a month. By 1977 assets of the Fund would total $1.4 billion.

From the beginning the potential size of the Fund was irresistible to Hoffa, who coveted personal control over the money. He soon manipulated the makeup of the Fund's board of trustees, allowing him — rather than banks — to dictate how assets of the Fund would be handled. One of those he ordained a trustee in 1955 was Roy Lee Williams. In Hoffa's view the Fund should be the union's own bank, lending money to people who in return would do something for Hoffa, his friends and the Teamsters. A year later the first loan was made directly by the Hoffa-controlled Fund. The door was wide open.

From that point on, the lion's share of Fund loans involved a cash kickback, a mob connection, friendship, or all three.

Coinciding with these events, Las Vegas was poised to assume the title of gambling mecca of the world. Ever since the notorious "Bugsy" Siegel constructed the Flamingo Hotel, the first plush Vegas hotel and casino, in the 1940s the mob looked to expand its interests in Nevada gaming. The problem was the enormous amount of money required to build a gambling emporium. Normal financing channels were not inclined toward such ventures.

The solution lay with the mob's friend and ally, Jimmy Hoffa, and his Fund. It would be described as the mob's "money store."

Hoffa and his mob allies dictated who would be the beneficiaries of a Fund loan, and what strings would be attached. Almost always the beneficiaries acted as fronts for the mob. The selected parties were required not only to kick back cash, but also to relinquish control of casino management, allowing the mob to steal millions in gambling proceeds in an act known as "skimming." Also benefiting was Hoffa's handpicked Fund administrator, Allen Dorfman, who had played various roles for the mob, among them idea man, strategist, manipulator, go-between and scam artist. Dorfman's insurance companies wrote more than 90 percent of the insurance carried by businesses borrowing from the Fund. Often the insurance purchase was mandated by a clause in the loan agreement.

Nick Civella counted as friends people who pulled weight in the Fund. Among them were Hoffa; his attorney, Morris Shenker of St. Louis; Dorfman, and his father, Paul Dorfman, who acted as go-between for Hoffa, the mob and the Fund trustees. This put Civella on the inside, fully aware of all that was transpiring. Not to be excluded from the gold rush, Civella started pushing Williams as a Fund trustee to follow his lead and to support Civella's candidates for Fund loans. Williams stiffened, refusing to go along with Civella's wishes, and in dramatic court testimony years later he described what happened next.

A union meeting at the Teamsters hall, then at 116 W. Linwood Blvd., had just ended and Williams headed for his car. There he encountered two formidable-looking men, one on each side of his vehicle.

"Get in and park your car over in the other lot" one of the men instructed. Complying, Williams was then shoved into another car, blindfolded and sandwiched between the two men in the back seat. After a 20-minute drive he was pulled out of the car and taken into a building and seated on a stool, a bright overhead light temporarily blinding him. His eyes adjusted, but he was surrounded by blackness and could see nothing.

Out of the darkness came a voice.

Williams would be expected to cooperate closely with Nick Civella or else. Next came a threat he had heard once before. Referring to his two daughters by name and age, the speaker made it clear that if Williams failed to cooperate his daughters would be killed, as would his wife. He would be the last to go. Did he understand fully? His reply was in the affirmative. He was marched out of the building and taken back to his car.

Desperate for some relief, he paid Jimmy Hoffa a visit. A sympathetic Hoffa heard Williams out, and then explained the facts of life:

"You can run but you can't hide. My advice to you is to cooperate or get your family killed. Roy, these are bad people, and they were here a long time before you and me came. And they will be here a long time after we're gone. They've infiltrated into every big union, every conference and pension fund, even the AFL-CIO. I'm tied tight as I can be."

A similar plea was made to Hoffa's righthand man, Frank Fitzsimmons, who mirrored Hoffa's sentiments, telling Williams, "I know the same people Jimmy knows, and I can't help you."

There was nowhere else to turn, so Williams capitulated. Later, he admitted: "I made no bones about it. I was controlled by Nick, and I think everybody knew it. And when he threatened me, why, that's when I became his boy."

WITH WILLIAMS IN THE BAG, Civella had cemented his position with the Fund, insuring he would be a player in ripping off the Nevada gaming industry. For him, things were looking good — calm seas and smooth sailing ahead.

Then Bill Quinn and fellow FBI agents, supported by Special Prosecutor James Featherstone, entered the picture. In an effort stemming from the Gladden investigation, the agents uncovered a well-designed scheme to embezzle about $200,000 in union funds through systematic kickbacks, bill-padding and other assorted payoffs.

Williams, Floyd Hayes and five other Teamsters were indicted in 1962 and they were tried the next year. Government witnesses laid it all out in their testimony. Although they tied Williams to the kickbacks, the trial jury nonetheless found him not guilty. The 66-year-old Hayes and the five other Teamsters were not so fortunate. Hayes received a four-year prison term.

Considered hard-core and tough, a pioneer in Teamsters labor racketeering, Hayes had done nothing in this life that indicated he would ever cooperate with law enforcement. His criminal history dated to 1917, when he served one year in the Oklahoma State Penitentiary for car theft. Later he spent 60 days in a San Diego jail on a bootleg liquor charge, and then added an income-tax conviction to his resume. Joining the Teamsters, Hayes became a Local 41 business agent in 1935. In the years to come he held various positions in that local and in Joint Council 56.

On the heels of his conviction and sentencing, however, Hayes was left feeling that Williams and the union had betrayed and abandoned him. Finally, he succumbed to Agent Quinn's prodding to cooperate and help himself. Hayes' value lay in the fact that he had been a friend of and mentor to Williams, someone Williams confided in. With Hayes, Williams talked freely about how all major decisions and union problems were run by Civella before a final decision was made, and how no one was fired or hired if Civella voiced an objection. For Agent Quinn, Hayes was a fountain of knowledge about Teamsters affairs. He confirmed that, within a year of Williams' election as president of Local 41, Civella's influence in the union had become substantial.

Among the investigators, expectations soared that this time around Williams would be convicted. Yet a conviction of Williams would have dire consequences for Civella, and Civella could not allow that to stand.

Hayes was nobody's fool, fully cognizant of the perilous position he was in. At the time, there was no such thing as a witness protection program, so Hayes would have to fend for himself. Thinking it most likely that the mob would resort to a car bomb, he installed a remote-control starting device on his car.

He miscalculated, however, when he failed to alter his pattern of activities, particularly his weekly Thursday evening bowling league at King Louie East. On June 11, 1964, their bowling session concluded, Hayes and his wife left King Louie with a group of friends. Following his routine, Hayes alone headed for their car, which was parked by itself away from other vehicles.

His wife waited about 75 yards away, while Hayes went through what had become an everyday drill of retrieving the remote device, backing away and then activating the starter. Just as he reached his vehicle, a car sped into the lot and screeched to a stop by Hayes, a shotgun protruding from the passenger-side window.

He was felled by the first blast. The gunman hopped out, leaned over Hayes and finished him off. Screaming as she started toward her husband, Mrs. Hayes was shot by the driver of the murder car, miraculously suffering only a superficial wound to her midsection. In the end, cautious as he may have tried to be, Hayes' passion for bowling proved fatal.

The threat to Civella's Teamsters puppet had passed. By the 1970s, Roy Lee Williams was elected 13th vice president of the International Brotherhood of Teamsters, and then director of the Central Conference. Civella was ready to ride him to a place of prominence in Cosa Nostra.

CHAPTER VII

GAMBLING AND THE SUPER BOWL BLUES

CALL IT THE LIFEBLOOD, the mainstay, or the money pot: gambling has long been a staple for crime syndicates.

In Kansas City, gambling has historically been an integral part of life. Its impact occasionally has been exposed but too often downplayed. The Kansas City Crime Family's domination of gambling resulted largely from the political influence it wielded for decades.

In the wake of the Apalachin meeting, it stood to reason that organized gambling would be a priority for investigators in Kansas City and nationwide in their push against organized crime syndicates.

The effort was severely hampered, however, by an absence of laws specifically addressing the sophisticated way crime syndicates went about their business. The problem was addressed in a report issued in 1967 by a presidential crime commission, which stated: "(Organized crime) transcends the crime known yesterday, for which our criminal laws and procedures were primarily designed. The American system was not designed with organized crime in mind."

Among investigators' few tools was an outdated 1948 statute prohibiting the importation of lottery tickets, primarily for the once-popular Irish Sweepstakes. A 1952 law imposed a 10 percent excise tax on all wagers accepted by gambling operators and coupled it with a $50 yearly occupational tax. The law generally was ignored by mobsters, but it did afford the IRS another tool to pursue racket figures, which their agents did with vigor.

Two 1961 laws made it illegal for bookmakers and gambling operators to use interstate facilities to ply their trade and a 1962 law prohibited transportation of gambling devices from one state to another. The 1961 laws appeared to address illegal gambling effectively, but in reality the interstate requirement presented an almost insurmountable hurdle. Bookmakers worked from their home or rented store fronts, apartments and the like, where they could conduct business over the telephone free of the fear of legal wiretaps and bugs. Mobsters may have been grade-school dropouts, but they knew the law as well as the investigators did.

The only avenue left for investigators trying to establishing the interstate nature of an operation was to try to secure cooperation from bettors. Usually that attempt was futile. Bookmakers offered the public a service, the same as the neighborhood dry cleaner, and placing bets was a voluntary act. When push came to shove, a bettor sided with his friendly bookmaker. An avid better did not want to see his bookie put out of business, and the fear of speaking against a criminal organization was more than enough to keep a bettor's lips sealed.

Nonetheless, in the formative years of the organized crime program in Kansas City, substantial time and effort were spent chasing down Family and other assorted gambling figures operating on both sides of the state line. The effort proved valuable in improving surveillance skills and interview techniques, developing informants, preparing search warrants, conducting raids, interpreting gambling records and testifying in court.

Nevertheless, results were hard to come by. It was hard enough producing evidence, but even when the work led to a prosecution the impact was negligible. In early federal gambling prosecutions related to the bookmaking network of the Kansas City Outfit, four of the five lower-echelon subjects indicted were convicted. All refused to cooperate, so the investigations came to a dead end. Unless lower-echelon workers could be persuaded to open up, there was no way to move to the next level or to expose the full scope of the network and the mob's gambling monopoly.

IN THE EARLY 1960s NICK CIVELLA conducted business daily in an office at the Original Toy & Jobbing Co. on West Ninth Street, meeting with trusted Outfit members and associates. It was an ideal place to put a secret microphone, which is exactly what a team of FBI agents did in 1961. The agents quickly established that Civella's bookmaking business was run out of the building and was managed by Morris "Snag" Klein, whose reputation as a gambling whiz was well established. Klein came to prominence in late 1939 as an ally of Tony Gizzo, and then his criminal career blossomed during the reign of Charles Binaggio. In Civella's behalf,

Klein successfully increased the gambling business, overseeing policy gambling, bookmaking on sporting events and horse racing, and football parlay-card betting. It was Klein's job to obtain the critical point spreads on sporting contests and then to disseminate them to other Outfit-connected bookmakers, including Civella's nephew Tony Civella.

The hidden microphone, supplemented by informant reports, provided an overview of the Civella-controlled gambling enterprise and more. Conversations involving Max Jaben, Thomas and Charles Cacioppo, Louis Cangelose and other Outfit figures ran the gamut from interests in Las Vegas to out-of-state mob contacts to federal investigations to political matters to security precautions to various merchandise transactions. At the time the information was not admissible in court, but it did provide critical intelligence and confirmed information developed by other means.

Civella's notoriety and constant law-enforcement scrutiny forced him to change his ways, no longer able to remain physically close to the action. He had established himself north of the Missouri River, spending most of his time at his home, at the Mirror Lake Country Club or at various other Northland locations. He appointed his protege, Carl DeLuna, as his go-between with Frank Tousa, who had taken over management of the bookmaking operation. The business was thriving.

Thirty-eight individuals were identified as active bookmakers through whom bets eventually were funneled to Tousa. Card and dice games controlled by the Outfit were held at the Trap at Fifth Street and Troost Avenue, at another social club at 525 Gillis St. and at a building at 1109 E. 12th Street. All policy operations — also called "numbers" gambling — in the greater Kansas City area were managed by Max Jaben. Sam Palma was responsible for the football parlay card business on the Kansas side, once Jaben's domain, signifying his rising prominence in the outfit.

In the 11 years since Apalachin, an enormous intelligence base had been established by investigators at all levels, and an army of investigators and prosecutors savvy in the ways of organized crime were on the job. Convictions in organized crime cases increased each year, and new laws directed at syndicated crime were passed.

Nevertheless, the Kansas City Outfit remained intact, its leadership beyond the reach of the law. It was clear that if real strides were to be made far more effective tools were mandatory, and with the exception of people in high places, there was general agreement on exactly what was needed most.

THE SOLUTION LAY in authorizing federal law enforcement to use electronic surveillance legally. Such a law was formally proposed as early as the 1950s, but in the face of an odious political climate it was a long time coming. The delay was yet another windfall for the mob.

Considering why organized crime flourished nationally, the political resistance to electronic surveillance was telling.

Historically, organized crime was allied predominantly with big-city Democratic political machines similar to the Pendergast machine in Kansas City. As a result, few powerful big-city Democrats were willing to take action against that political-criminal nexus. In 1950, it was proposed that a special Senate committee be formed to probe organized crime in America. To a large degree, the idea stemmed from the sensational 1950 Binaggio-Gargotta murders in Kansas City and a vote-fraud scandal there in 1946. President Harry S. Truman along with some senior Democratic senators and the then-junior senator from Texas, Lyndon Johnson, opposed it. Nonetheless the Kefauver Committee, led by Senator Estes Kefauver of Tennessee, himself a Democrat, was established in 1950 and aggressively went to work.

The successes of the Kefauver Committee only worsened the distaste in the mouths of some Democrats. It was particularly galling to Truman because Kefauver brought national attention to Missouri, exposing mob influence and muscle employed in getting Democratic candidates elected — including Truman himself. In that climate, it was understandable that the White House and Congress had no stomach for the Kefauver Committee's recommendation that electronic surveillance be legalized and a witness immunity law passed.

Ten years later, Robert F. Kennedy was appointed attorney general, bringing to the office knowledge gained from serving on Democratic Senator John McClellan's Committee probing mob-related labor racketeering. Kennedy, also a Democrat, established a "get Hoffa" unit and infused new life into the Justice Department's organized crime and racketeering section. Convinced that legalizing electronic surveillance was a must in any organized crime legislation, Kennedy promoted just such a package. He sent it to Congress in 1962 and it was rebuffed. With the assassination of President John Kennedy and the ascent of Lyndon Johnson, all of the life and intensity that Robert Kennedy had pumped into the drive against organized crime sputtered and died.

Kennedy left the attorney general's post, but he had trumpeted organized crime as a fact of American life that had to be confronted. In that vein a sweeping piece of legislation was launched that included authority for electronic surveillance. It stemmed in large part from Johnson's own National Crime Commission, despite Attorney General Ramsey Clark's attempt to have the commission avoid the subject altogether. In 1966 the commission split with the Johnson Administration, holding that electronic surveillance was necessary in the fight against organized crime.

Over the strenuous objections of President Johnson and Clark, Congress enacted the Omnibus Crime Control and Safe Streets Act of 1968. It was the mobster's worst nightmare. The law authorized the use of electronic surveillance when approved by the attorney general or a designated assistant, and also approved by a federal judge.

However, the joy felt by investigators was short-lived. Although President Johnson reluctantly signed the bill on June 19, 1968, he labeled the electronic-surveillance provision "unwise" and petitioned Congress to repeal it. When that failed, he announced that a 1967 Justice Department edict barring eavesdropping and wiretaps except in national security cases would remain in effect despite the new law. The edict had been brought about in part by the embattled Jimmy Hoffa, who seized on the exposure of a hidden FBI microphone in a Las Vegas establishment and prodded political allies such as Senator Edward Long of Missouri to make hay of it. The result of all this: court-authorized electronic surveillance was on the books but off limits.

Richard Nixon, a Republican, seized on the issue in his successful presidential campaign in 1968. One month after he took office as President in January 1969, his attorney general, John Mitchell, authorized the first use of electronic surveillance under the 1968 statute. The course of history for the mob was forever altered.

BACK IN KANSAS CITY, what first appeared a routine bit of intelligence would morph into the Organized Crime Squad's first venture in the world of electronic surveillance. On an ordinary day in mid-1969 I tagged along with fellow agent Michael Jeweler to contact one of the productive informants he had recruited. The source was involved in gambling and one of the tidbits he threw out concerned an individual operating as a bookmaker out of a dress store on 11th Street. The store stood directly across from the north entrance to City Hall.

Jeweler had a full plate so it was agreed that I would take a look at the situation. I identified the owner of the shop, a nondescript storefront, as Louie Rice. Rice's family was in the dress business, yet this store seemingly had little to offer clientele. The matter was intriguing.

The shop's location, however, simply was not conducive to conducting surveillance for long stretches or from an automobile. The only avenue left was the tedious process of hanging out in the area on foot — sometimes inside City Hall and other times outside on the front steps or the street itself. I did so day after day, and was amazed at how little attention I drew. I saw little activity at Rice's shop, but noted the license plates of those who did visit.

From them surfaced the name of Paul Sere, and that proved to be the first piece of the puzzle. The second piece came to light when I watched Rice take a noonday break from his shop. I slipped across the street for a bite to eat at a little cafe next door to Rice's operation. While I was seated at the counter a man walked in, inquiring of the cafe's owner the whereabouts of "the guy next door," meaning Rice. The man was none other than Pat Sellaro, a main cog in Civella's bookmaking operation. It was a thin thread, but Sellaro's query suggested a direct connection between Rice and the Outfit.

Sere was a partner in a bookmaking venture run by Robert Thompson. I knew Thompson all too well, having in years past spent considerable time probing his gambling activities but having been unable to establish the elusive interstate requirement. It was time to re-visit Mr. Thompson. Unlike hardcore Outfit bookmakers, I believed, Thompson and Sere would not be overly cautious. Their operation probably would be easier to exploit with this new tool, court-authorized electronic surveillance.

Fortunately for investigators, the first assistant U.S. attorney, Calvin K. Hamilton, was an experienced, capable and savvy prosecutor who understood the menace of organized crime. After reviewing the case built against Thompson and Sere, Hamilton agreed that an application for authority to employ electronic surveillance was justified. With the help of a special attorney designated by the Department of Justice, all the necessary hoops were jumped through. On December 5, 1969, a U.S. district judge signed an order authorizing the first legal wiretap in the Western District of Missouri.

With the tap on Thompson's home telephone came proof of the effectiveness of electronic surveillance. Previously, only one or two individuals in a large network might have been charged, but now an entire bookmaking ring was broken up. Ten individuals were indicted and convicted, including Thompson, Sere, Sellaro and Rice.

In the past investigators would have developed only limited evidence of the scope of an operation; now the structure and interdependency of such operations became clear. The evidence established that part of the wagers funneled to Thompson and Sere were re-bet or "laid off" to another bookmaking operation. It was run by a Kansas City, Kansas, vice king and convicted bookmaker named Joe Kostelac, who operated from his Cougar Club. Another portion was laid off to Pat Sellaro, representing the Outfit's main book. In a 13-day period Thompson and Sere accepted wagers totalling at least $70,000 in 1969 dollars.

BEFORE ANY INDICTMENT COULD BE RETURNED and the investigation made public, there was work to be done. The Thompson-Sere connection to Sellaro was the road leading directly to the "Office," the gambling fraternity's name for the nerve center of the Crime Family bookmaking operation. It was run by Frank Tousa out of the Northview Social Club — the Trap. Building on the wiretap intercepts, the investigation established probable cause that the phone at the Trap was being used by Outfit figures in an interstate gambling enterprise. However, a conflict arose with officials in Washington responsible for reviewing and approving the application for electronic surveillance. Because the targeted telephone in the social club was a public pay phone, they were concerned that the wiretap might infringe on someone's rights of privacy.

No amount of arguing and reasoning could convince them that, in this case, the word "public" was a misnomer. Besides serving as bookmaking central, high-stakes card and dice games went on at the Trap. Situated as it was in a building owned by Boss Nick Civella, the club was a mob congregating point where Outfit business often was hashed out. The possibility of some John or Jane Doe off the street walking into the club to use the pay phone was nonexistent.

None of it made any difference to the officials in Washington. Either we agreed to limit our monitoring only to those occasions when Frank Tousa was on the phone, or the wiretap would not be approved: Take it or leave it. From our standpoint, it was a lousy deal that we had to swallow, and a golden opportunity lost.

By later standards the authorized time limit for the first two wiretap cases — 13 days and 10 days — would be considered extremely modest. We had to play the hand that was dealt to us.

On January 7, 1970, FBI technical agents disguised as telephone company personnel shinnied up the telephone pole to install the tap, a process that in later years would be considered Stone Age technology. They succeeded in doing this within sight of the social club, where little out of the ordinary is missed, and the next day the wiretap was operational and producing results.

Frank Tousa was hard at work in the Office overseeing a string of subagents. With them Tousa kept current on the amounts of bets taken in, discussed the betting line, which could change daily, and issued instructions. Often he scolded his minions for misdeeds. This was a relatively slow time for sports wagering because the wildly popular football season was almost over, and there were only college and pro basketball games to bet on.

Nevertheless, Super Bowl IV was coming on January 11. The game had not reached the betting frenzy it has today, but with the Kansas City Chiefs pitted against the Minnesota Vikings, interest was at a peak in the city.

A bookmaking enterprise is in business to make a profit. To reduce risk and ensure a profit, the bookmaker aims to balance the books. In its simplest form, this means ensuring that substantially the same amount is bet on each team in a contest. Profit is derived from a fee or "lug," normally 10 percent, which losing bettors fork over. With Super Bowl IV, the Office was faced with a dilemma. The lion's share of wagers was going to the hometown Chiefs, skewing the book out of balance. The situation proved so unacceptable that the Boss himself called Tousa, expressing his concern. Tousa informed Nick Civella that the Office had been unable to lay off $47,360 in bets. Laying off is a method of balancing the books by re-betting the overage with another bookmaker, sometimes a bigger one and often one in another part of the country.

"Well, that's ridiculous," Civella commented.

Where, he asked had all these bets come from?

"Right here," Tousa replied, meaning Kansas City.

Civella wanted to know who was doing something about it, but having rarely faced such a situation, the Outfit's sources for laying off bets were limited.

As other Outfit figures got on the telephone line, attempting to find sources for laying off the bets, investigators' worst fears were realized. Obligated to comply with the restrictions on our monitoring, we had to turn off the recorder, allowing several prime subjects to skate. However, thanks to

Super Bowl IV and Kansas City bettors, the Boss was caught in the net.

Nine months later, on October 2, 1970, a federal grand jury returned an indictment charging violation of interstate gambling laws by Nick Civella, then 58; his nephew Tony Civella, 42; Frank A. Tousa, who was 46, and Martin Chess of Las Vegas, Kansas City's source of the betting line.

The time had come to arrest the Boss, and the privilege fell to Agent Lee Flosi and myself, having run the case, and Agent Shea Airey. We motored to the Mirror Lake Country Club. At the ninth hole we interrupted a round of golf Civella was playing with his wife and placed him under arrest. It had been 11 years since Civella, also in the midst of a round of golf, received a subpoena to testify before the McClellan Committee looking into the Apalachin gangland convention.

When U.S. Magistrate J. Whitfield Moody set Civella's bond at $5,000, Civella's normal sense of outrage at the government flashed. He protested, labeling the bond a double standard and emphasized that he was a responsible person.

"People with means usually get personal recognizance," he complained. "I haven't been in any trouble for 35 years. We are entitled to the same rights as others."

In the truth it is Civella and his ilk who practiced a double standard, intentionally subverting the law and invoking it only when it suited their needs.

IN THE SCHEME OF THINGS, the run-of-the-mill bettor was never allowed to call the Office directly. If caught, the average bettor was considered more likely to cooperate with the government, so his knowledge of the operation was restricted. For some high-dollar bettors, however, the story was different.

Sol Landie was a big-time bettor. A fixture in Kansas City, Kansas, for 25 years and co-owner with his brother of the Square Deal Scrap Metal Company at 218 Kansas Ave., the 49-year-old Landie wagered thousands of dollars daily. He did so directly with Frank Tousa. His calls from across the state line to the tapped phone at the Office vaulted him to the status of critical witness for the government — and threat to the Outfit. Taken before a grand jury and granted immunity from prosecution, Landie freely admitted to his interstate betting activities.

At 3:50 a.m. on the morning of November 22, 1970, a ringing doorbell interrupted the sleeping morning hours at the home of Sol and Ann Landie's neighbor. At their door, dressed in her sleepwear, a distraught Ann Landie blurted out:

"They have robbed me, and they killed Mr. Landie. I know he is dead. They shot him twice."

She had been raped. Four black men had broken in to the Landie residence, accosting them in their bed in a brutal invasion of their home.

Upon arriving at the Landie residence at 7914 Washington St., detectives Clarence Luther and Gary McCready were directed to a bedroom where Sol Landie lay in his bed, shot to death. At his shoulder, a white pillow bore the marking of what appeared to be a bullet hole. The pillow probably was held over his head when he was shot. The bedroom and the rest of the house had been ransacked, yet pieces of expensive jewelry and valuables had been left intact — a clue that this had been something more than a robbery.

Quickly and efficiently homicide detectives arrested four assailants, one of them only 16 years old. In confessing to the atrocity, the assailants implicated John Frankoviglia as the man who had hired them and orchestrated the fatal assault.

At the murder trial of Frankoviglia, 17-year-old Gary Johnson, one of the assailants, testified that Landie was killed because he was "supposed to have been a witness for the federal people who indicted somebody."

They had been instructed to make the crime appear to have been a robbery. Having admitted shooting Landie to death, 20-year-old Marquise Williams also testified that Landie was killed because of "the indictments."

However, the murder had none of the earmarks of an Outfit execution. Although the killing was put by prosecutors and the press at the doorstep of Civella, the fact that black teenagers were involved and the manner in which the crime was carried out dictated otherwise. The Outfit was not in the habit of using non-members in these matters. In fact, for Civella the result was a publicity nightmare.

Informants reported that the murder was an off-the-reservation affair orchestrated by an Outfit member who probably was trying to enhance his stature in the organization.

In the end, six people were convicted.

ABOUT THAT TIME, the Department of Justice designated Kansas City as the base for what turned out to be an extraordinarily vital element in the push against organized crime in the Midwest. The new unit was formally designated as the Kansas City Field Office of the Department of Justice Organized Crime and Racketeering section, but it was more commonly known as Federal Strike Force 17.

The concept was simple but brilliant. A team of federal prosecutors dedicated exclusively to organized crime matters would coordinate the investigative efforts of various federal law enforcement agencies, which would assign an investigator to act as a liaison.

February 8, 1971, was the date set for the Strike Force to begin operation. Its leader would be Kansas City native Michael DeFeo, an exceptionally astute and talented federal prosecutor who had been in charge of the Los Angeles Strike Force. He was assisted by a staff of three other exceptionally able prosecutors. Although separate, the Strike Force forged a solid working relationship with the U. S. attorney's offices on both sides of the state line. Once established, DeFeo and his Strike Force assumed the lead in the Civella gambling prosecution.

Murder or intimidation of government witnesses was envisioned in the second major organized crime legislation, the 1970 Organized Crime Control Act. One provision of the law allowed the government to secure depositions for use in a trial if a witness died or could not, for other reasons, testify.

With Landie already gone, the government moved to depose two other critical witnesses who were big-time bettors, jewelry store owner Alvin Hurst and automobile dealer Lester Moore. The idea was to afford a degree of safety and to preserve their testimony. The two had been intercepted placing large wagers from Kansas directly with Frank Tousa at the Office.

The prosecution was destined to be a torturous legal battle with more twists and turns than a fictional courtroom drama. Initially the Landie murder and other factors caused delays and required returning to the grand jury for a superceding indictment in March 1971. As the inquiry progressed and expanded, yet another superceding indictment was returned on October 7, 1971. It added as defendants Thomas "Dude" Fontanello, 60, who helped manage the book, and bookmaking subagents Philip "Bing" Saladino, 59, and Joseph "King" Barletta, 63. Along with Nick Civella, Tony Civella, Frank Tousa and Martin Chess, the indictments now totaled seven defendants.

A combative Nick Civella would fight tooth and nail. He used every legal maneuver that he and his attorneys could muster. While these legal battles ground on, Outfit business went on unabated — as did day-in-and-day-out scrutiny by law enforcement.

That the Boss himself had been charged in a gambling case and the FBI could legally wiretap did nothing to deter the Crime Family's gambling enterprise. For one, the business was too lucrative. For another, it led to so much more.

The bettor who can't pay borrows from a loan shark; the businessman who can't pay puts himself and his business at the mercy of gangsters; the thief who can't pay has to steal more and sells to mob fences; a company purchasing agent who can't pay places orders with mob-connected outlets, and on and on. When gambling cases are brought to court, the cumulative impact of the crimes is often lost. Light sentences and fines are meted out, and neither the gambler nor the Family sees fit to alter course.

As long as the Family controlled gambling it would remain in the headlights, and for the next 10 years every opportunity was seized upon to disrupt it and prosecute those involved.

CHAPTER VIII

RIVER QUAY 1

THE DISTRICT KNOWN AS THE RIVER QUAY is a
landmark, the place where Kansas City first took form. In the early
1800s steamboats plying the Missouri River took advantage of a natural rock
ledge that formed an ideal landing place to unload cargo destined for the
town of Westport about four miles south of the river. Along the riverfront,
stores and shops opened, providing groceries, equipment and other staples of
life.

By 1847 the area consisted mainly of rough wooden structures with
a few brick buildings. Broad sidewalks provided access to the saloons and
eating establishments that cropped up. Some days, as many as a hundred
wagons laden with provisions set out for the Southwest and West. It was
a frontier community, inhabited in part by riverboat gamblers, prostitutes,
cutthroats, con men and assorted other riffraff.

Organized as the Town of Kansas, the riverfront village was
incorporated by formal charter on February 22, 1853, as the City of Kansas.
Boom followed in 1854 when the town became the gateway to the new
Territory of Kansas, and bust came in 1861 when the Civil War disrupted
growth. Before the war, a city market was established in the heart of town
and it remained the heart of business activity and city life through most of
the 1860s.

The city's future as a commercial hub was insured with the coming of
a railroad bridge across the Missouri River in 1869, opening the West to
the rail lines of the East. An economic upswing continued in the 1880s as
the population grew and residential areas developed south of the bluffs that
overlooked the City Market. In 1889 the city officially became Kansas City.

By then, the financial and retail districts had moved south to Ninth,
10th, 11th and 12th streets. In 1914 a new Union Station opened well to the

south, near 24th Street and Grand Avenue. As business departed the City Market area in the late 19th century, disrepair and deterioration followed. Sleazy hotels, drinking joints and flophouses infiltrated and eventually the City Market area became populated by the homeless, drug addicts, drunks, winos and bums. Except for Saturday morning activity from farmers selling produce, by the 1960s the area around the City Market was a dead zone.

In the early 1970s a visionary Kansas City businessman, Marion Trozzolo, moved his LPF Plastics firm to the old Exchange Building, once the hub of the city's grain trade, at 502 Delaware St. Trozzolo dreamed of transforming the rundown area. Taking a cue from the landing place once favored by riverboats, he grabbed another term for a landing place, "quay," and devised the name "River Quay" for the area. A publication promoting his idea described the goal as "…a creative restoration of the Quay into a shopping and entertainment center with a delightful maze of boutiques and shops, quaint restaurants and galleries, antique shops and gourmet grocery shops."

Attracting like-minded individuals was Trozzolo's starting point, and a business group called the River Quay Association was formed. Properties were acquired and buildings were renovated with an old-time look. To attract business, rents were kept low — usually $2 to $3 a square foot. Ideally, the Quay's entrepreneurs would work together like a family, maintaining a clean, wholesome and safe atmosphere.

The area encompassing the River Quay extended from the Missouri River on the north to Interstate 70 on the south and from the Broadway Bridge on the west to Locust Street and the ASB Bridge on the east. The River Quay development formally opened in April 1971 and made steady progress into fall 1972.

AS THE RIVER QUAY CAME ALIVE, other businessmen noticed. One of them was Fred Harvey Bonadonna, an outgoing, personable sort in his early 30s whom everyone called Freddy. For five or six years he had operated a neighborhood bar and restaurant called Mr. B's at 207 Southwest Blvd.

Reared in the North End, Freddy Bonadonna as a youngster walked somewhat on the wild side. Frequently he got in fights and acted up. In his formative years, Bonadonna claimed, young Italian-Americans were arrested on sight if they strayed out of the North End. Many lost the desire to find jobs. Coveting the high life, they looked up to the gangsters, who drove new cars and carried big money in their pockets. Their admiration of the hoodlums led youngsters into a life of crime.

Ironically it was Bonadonna's father, himself a mob associate, who changed the direction of Freddy's life by guiding him into the military. Upon leaving the service the younger Bonadonna worked in a factory and got married. He drifted away from his old associates, losing touch with who had or hadn't joined the criminal organization.

One evening, a close friend stopped by Mr. B's to visit with his pal Freddy. The conversation turned to the new development down by the City Market. Freddy had heard talk about the River Quay, but he hadn't given it much thought. Convinced it was worth a look, he and his pal took a spin to see what was going on. As they walked the Quay's tree-lined streets, Bonadonna was taken by the quaint antique shops and the Old World atmosphere.

The two stopped in at Ebenezer's at 309 Delaware St. The business, which opened in April 1972, was the first drinking establishment in the district. On this night, Ebenezer's was packed with customers enjoying themselves to the hilt. The atmosphere was electric and the place was doing a land-office business. Bonadonna, a fun-loving guy in his own right, was caught up in the scene and taken with the concept behind the developing area. His business instincts kicked in. He recognized the Quay as a golden opportunity not only for himself, but also for his brother, Tony Mike Bonadonna. Tony Mike was earning less than $150 a week with little hope of improving his lot in life.

With his mind made up and not one to procrastinate, the very next morning Freddy Bonadonna headed to the Quay to scope out a business location and to speak with the person identified as the main man, Marion Trozzolo. Several potential sites were pointed out to him but Bonadonna already knew the one he wanted — a building at the corner of Delaware and Third streets. The reason was simple.

Early on, it had been drilled into his head that the success of a business depended on parking. What had caught Bonadonna's attention was a huge, city-owned parking lot directly behind the location. It was exactly what he was looking for.

There was a fly in the ointment, however: the site he coveted had been promised to someone else. Because no other place satisfied him, Bonadonna would have to put his name on a list to be notified if something came up.

Not to be discouraged, he made several forays to the Quay to check on developments. His effort paid off.

On one such visit he discovered that the potential lessee of the Third and Delaware location had given Trozzolo a bad check. Quickly, Bonadonna made his pitch and a disgusted Trozzolo gave Freddy and his brother Tony Mike the lease then and there.

The building was a disaster. The walls had holes, some penetrating all the way through. Windows were missing, lath hung off walls, the plumbing was rudimentary and there was no electricity. Freddy threw himself into rehabbing the place and while renovation was in progress he joined the River Quay Merchants Association, made up of a small group of businessmen, artists and craftsmen. Bonadonna was not one to sit in the back row, so he involved himself in everything going on in the Quay. He wholeheartedly supported the vision of a district dotted with a variety of shop owners, devoid of loud music and also of liquor joints that did not serve food or that featured adult entertainment.

The first name he chose for his new business was The Oar House — appropriate, he thought, because of the nearby Missouri River. Other association members pointed out that when the phone at his place was answered, "The Oar House," it could sound like "The Whore House." Freddy Bonadonna settled on the name Poor Freddie's, the spelling changed slightly from that of his own nickname.

Poor Freddie's grand opening came September 15, 1972, and the place was an instant success.

"My business exploded within the first three days," he recalled. "It was so much business I couldn't handle it."

Not long afterward, Joe Cammisano sauntered in. Bonadonna was familiar with the Cammisano family, particularly Joe, who had run girlie joints on Kansas City's West 12th Street Strip for years. The Strip encompassed wall-to-wall bars featuring go-go and exotic dancers, adult entertainment and businesses fronts emblazoned with garish signs advertising GIRLS-GIRLS-GIRLS. It was a favorite place for prostitutes to peddle their wares.

Without fanfare, Cammisano let Bonadonna know he thought his decision to invest in the River Quay was a waste of money. Unfortunately, Cammisano later would change his mind.

Meanwhile, by late 1972 all was not well in the Trozzolo camp. He owned about 20 properties, mainly along Delaware Street, and had become overextended financially. A young New Orleans businessman and developer got wind of Trozzolo's predicament, and flew in for a three-day inspection.

The developer's name was Joe Canizaro. He was known as a man who got things done in a hurry, and he was sufficiently impressed to negotiate a $500,000 loan from the Columbia Union Bank of Kansas City. With it, he bought out 90 percent of Trozzolo's interest and formed the River Quay Corp. Canizaro said he was committed to investing in the future of the district, wanted to maintain its original concept and opposed any infestation of drinking establishments.

IN HIS OWN EYES, FREDDY BONADONNA saw the Quay as an opportunity for Italian-Americans like himself to better their lot in life. Growing up in Kansas City's Italian community, he had experienced discrimination that limited the hopes of many of his neighbors. Now, he wanted to share his success story. He trumpeted the enormous potential he saw in the River Quay, bragging about the area and about his own success. As it turned out, there would be unintended consequences.

Since his days running Mr. B's on Southwest Boulevard, Bonadonna had patronized the B&C Meat Co., which was owned by Cork Civella and Albert Brandmeyer. Freddy may not have known the identity of many Outfit members, but the Civella name and its relationship to organized crime was another story. Over time, Bonadonna gradually got to know Cork Civella, and the two would chat when he went in to pick up a meat order.

After moving to the River Quay, Bonadonna continued to do business with B&C, and on one of his visits Civella asked how Freddy was doing with his new operation. Bonadonna made a fatal mistake. He boasted that he was taking in $10,000 a week, a bit of an exaggeration. Civella was impressed, and Freddy soon would feel the consequences of his braggadocio.

Not long after their chat one of Civella's associates, Paul "Paulie Pig" Scola, made it known that he was going to open a place in the Quay. Like Joe Cammisano, Scola had been one of those who belittled Bonadonna's decision to open in the Quay. Now Bonadonna had a chance for payback. Unknown to Scola, the location he was interested in at 317 Delaware — the only desirable rental left in the Quay — had been promised to Freddy and his brother.

Freddy was of a mind to close on the lease, leaving Scola out in the cold. He was worried about the type of place Scola would open and about his

Teamsters local leaders: (from left) Floyd R. Hayes, Lee Quisenberry and Orville Ring

Thomas "Hiway" Simone

Roy Lee Williams

Morris "Snag" Klein, gambling whiz.

Nick Civella, mid-1960s

Anthony "Tony Ripe" Civella

By the late 1960s, Frank Tousa was the Outfit's gambling manager.

Carl DeLuna, Civella's go-between with Tousa

Sol Landie, a high-stakes bettor, and his wife

John Frankoviglia

The Landies' home in Kansas City, scene of his murder

Marquise Williams

His head covered with a jacket, Nick Civella was escorted into the Kansas City federal courthouse in October 1970 by FBI agents (from left) Lee Flosi, Shea Airey and William Ouseley, the author. The agents arrested Civella on a golf course in Platte County after he was indicted in the Super Bowl gambling case.

Fred Bonadonna's venture in the River Quay, Poor Freddie's.

Marion Trozzolo, founder of the River Quay.

Joe Canizaro

Fred Harvey Bonadonna

Delaware Daddy's, opened by an associate of the Civellas.

Long before he grew interested in the River Quay, Joe Cammisano had made appearances before police cameras in 1950, left, and in 1961, above.

associates, and he was confident that Cork Civella was behind Scola's move.

Freddy's brother Tony Mike thought differently and urged him to allow Scola in. After arguing the point, Freddy relented to avoid what was sure to become an ugly dispute. He even went his brother one better, offering to help Scola get his place established. That proved to be another bad decision.

Scola's business was to be called Delaware Daddy's and on August 3, 1973, he applied for a liquor license. True to his word, Freddy pitched in, assisting Scola with advice and recommendations as the business was made ready to open.

Each morning Scola and several of his associates stopped in at Poor Freddie's to drink coffee and chat with the manager, a woman known by the name of Sherry. Delaware Daddy's liquor license was approved on October 17, 1973.

In no time, Bonadonna realized he had made a mistake. Before he knew it Delaware Daddy's lured away Sherry and several of Bonadonna's waitresses and copied Poor Freddie's menu. The die was cast. It was abundantly clear that Scola's plan was to compete directly with the Bonadonnas and run them out of business.

More than ever Freddy was convinced that the heavy hand of Cork Civella was pulling the strings. For one, where did the money come from to open Delaware Daddy's? Scola had cried on Freddy's shoulder about how bad off he was financially and how much money he owed. A later review of Liquor Control records revealed there was no loan or other source of funding listed on Scola's liquor application.

Cork Civella soon began visiting Scola's place regularly, looking over the operation and taking it all in. Delaware Daddy's became a hangout for many known Civella associates. Especially noticeable was John Amaro, a relative of Scola's. Anytime Scola, Joe Cammisano or any of their running mates was around, Amaro was there, too.

OF THE MANY CHARACTERS who were becoming attracted to the Quay, John "Johnny Green" Amaro was destined to play a particularly important role. Amaro's connection to the Outfit was well-known to law enforcement; among other endeavors he had been an Outfit bookmaker. Amaro maintained his residence in the Kansas City, North, development known as Filumena Acres, where the Civellas and other Outfit figures lived. For many years Amaro had owned Bena's Drive-In in Claycomo, Missouri.

In August 1974 the Scola family expanded its Quay interests by opening Three Little Pigs. It was licensed in the name of Linda Scola, Paul Scola's sister-in-law. Amaro became a regular visitor and even said he had worked there for two months.

In November 1974 John and Angelo Vitale, also related to the Scolas, opened the Village Gate at 419 Delaware. Amaro began hanging out there, and in 1975 became the owner of record of the place under the name Big John's.

Like other Outfit members, Amaro benefitted from the political largesse of the Hearnes administration and of State Representative Alex Fazzino. In 1972 the Missouri Board of Parole and Probation recommended denial of Amaro's request to be pardoned for a prior felony conviction, which was believed to have been for bookmaking. As grounds for the rejection, the Parole Board pointed to evidence that Amaro was a member of organized crime. Despite the board's objections and objections by law enforcement, on June 27, 1972, Hearnes signed Amaro's pardon.

Once again, Hearnes' legal assistant, Paul Williams, eased the way. He simply dismissed as hearsay the Parole Board's allegation of Amaro's ties to organized crime. In a memo, Williams described Amaro as a childhood friend of Fazzino's. Fazzino declared the allegations against his friend were untrue and vouched for Amaro as "a fine man with a good war record, good family, etc."

As for Amaro's organized crime ties, Williams pointed to his long friendship with Fazzino, saying, "Sometimes that is persuasive, you know."

What about the Kansas City Crime Commission's having publicly listed Amaro as a mob associate?

Not familiar it with it, Williams said.

WITH POOR FREDDIE'S PROSPERING, the Bonadonna brothers were in a position to expand their business interests in the Quay. With a partner they purchased a building at 401 Wyandotte St. Subsequently, it was leased to Louis Ribaste, of whose association with the Outfit Freddy Bonadonna claimed to know nothing.

In turn, Ribaste divided the space, making room for multiple bars. The next thing Freddy Bonadonna knew, Pat O'Brien, an Outfit bookmaker, had subleased a section of the building. His New Orleans-themed bar, Pat O'Brien's, and Ribaste's western-motif bar, Judge Roy Bean's, both had hidden owners, according to intelligence sources. Ribaste's and O'Brien's known close ties to the Family tended to support that.

The River Quay was developing a split personality. In its happy public persona, increasing numbers of visitors enjoyed shopping, dining and entertainment there; on the dark side, ominous undercurrents piqued the interest of law enforcement.

Experiencing both sides was FBI Special Agent Lee Flosi, a member of the Organized Crime Squad. Flosi was raised in Chicago and spoke Italian fluently. From the time he arrived in Kansas City Flosi and I hit it off, and we would work closely as partners for the next 10 years.

As a bachelor in those days, Flosi combined work and pleasure by checking out the Quay's dining and entertainment scene. In 1972 it was dominated by Poor Freddie's.

Bonadonna and Flosi immediately clicked, and a friendship developed that grew in strength and complexity as time passed. Once Bonadonna learned that Flosi was an FBI agent and well versed in matters concerning the Outfit, it was only natural that he began to spill out his worries about the Outfit's increasing involvement in the area. For Flosi, this was troubling: on the one hand Bonadonna was talking to him as a friend, but on the other hand the information was relevant to law enforcement.

Bonadonna was not an ordinary businessman, free to take his fears to the authorities. It was in his nature to openly and aggressively resist the mob efforts to infiltrate the Quay, but because of his ethnicity and his father's being mob connected, he could not. Freddy truly liked and respected Flosi, yet the predicament he was in caused him also to view Flosi as a lifeline. As conflict in the Quay escalated, the two had to exercise extreme care. To protect Bonadonna, a decision was made to treat his information as coming from a confidential informant. In FBI files, Bonadonna was referred to only by a code number, meaning his name would be kept secret even from other agents of the bureau.

THE EARLY SUCCESS OF EBENEZER'S and of Poor Freddie's spurred public interest in the River Quay. With the arrival of more establishments came support from city officials. A shuttle bus was instituted, running from Crown Center to the Quay. The Chamber of Commerce featured the Quay in a film production promoting the city. The years 1973 and 1974 saw an upswing in the number of businesses opening their doors.

Besides Delaware Daddy's, Judge Roy Bean's and Pat O'Brien's, the list included Papa Nick's, Bobby D's Warehouse, Yesterday's Girl, Three Little Pigs, Village Gate and the Victoria Station Restaurant. Most were liquor establishments, an issue that would develop into a festering sore.

Now that the Quay was firmly established as a popular entertainment and shopping district and a city attraction, it was a far different-minded Joe Cammisano who paid a return visit to Poor Freddie's.

Admitting he might have been wrong belittling Bonadonna's wisdom in moving to the Quay, Cammisano — to Freddy's chagrin — let him know that he was now considering a business venture in the area. Cammisano proceeded to recount the area's history as a red-light district with seedy bars and prostitutes; if he came to the Quay he would make it the way it once was. In turn, Freddy made it clear to Cammisano that his plan would not hold water with the River Quay Merchants Association nor with Freddy himself.

On the heels of Cammisano's early visit came news that Jack Taylor, the owner of Jack's Furniture in the Quay, had leased out the building on the west side of Wyandotte Street between Fourth and Fifth streets. The lessee was Mike Heller, owner of Bobby D's directly across the street. Heller had solicited potential renters and had lined up Joe Cammisano and Lonnie Roccaforte, another bar operator on the 12th Street Strip, along with Steve Como and Ross Abbate's wife, Donna Abbate.

For Bonadonna, this was a devastating turn of events. The lease on the same building had once been offered to Freddy, but the timing had not been not right for him.

Upon learning the names of the renters that Heller was courting, Freddy contacted the owner, Taylor. He discovered that the lease with Heller was unsigned; Heller had been sitting on it for about two months. Bonadonna implored Taylor to let him know if Heller didn't follow through, saying he and his brother might be interested in leasing the building. Instead, Taylor used Freddy's overture to warn Heller that if he didn't act the Bonadonnas would take the property. That prompted Heller to immediately sign and return the lease. In the process the impression was left with Joe Cammisano that Freddy had made the play to keep him and the others out of the Quay. In Cammisano's eyes, that was a mark against Freddy Bonadonna.

With hope of taking control of the building lost, Bonadonna encouraged Heller to add a clause in the subleases prohibiting pornography, go-go and exotic dancers, strippers and the like. Heller complied and again

Cammisano saw it as a move directed at him and yet another mark against Bonadonna.

Then came a stream of applications for liquor licenses along the block: Cammisano for the Fabulous Forties at 406 Wyandotte, Lonnie Roccaforte for Huck Finn's at 404 Wyandotte, Steve Como for The Godfather Lounge at 408 Wyandotte and Donna Abbate for Mama Angelina's at 400 Wyandotte. The 12th Street Strip was rapidly morphing into the Wyandotte Street Strip, and any hopes for maintaining a family atmosphere in the Quay were slipping away. Prospects for real conflict gained momentum when Bonadonna, unwilling to concede the Quay to the mob, geared up to secretly do battle by blocking the issuance of those liquor licenses.

With so many new establishments arriving, and the character of so many owners at issue, questions arose about financing and hidden ownership. For a business owner, it's a good thing to have a friendly bank and the Central Bank at 2301 Independence Ave. fit the bill. The bank had a quarter-million dollars tied up in the Quay.

In June 1979 *The Kansas City Star* documented a history of loans dating to the early 1950s made by Central Bank to people connected with organized crime. Bank officials replied by saying the background of a customer was of no concern to them. They would not withhold loans to convicted felons or mob figures — even if they knew who they were, which they didn't — as long as it was likely the loan would be repaid. A skeptic might ask, Is a person under a deportation order, or under indictment, or convicted and facing jail, or whose property securing the bank's loan is torched, all of which are easily verifiable, considered a good risk?

Former Outfit leader Charles Carrollo received a $25,000 mortgage in 1953 when he was under a deportation order and subsequently deported. Anthony Simone received $111,000 in a number of transactions at a time he was under federal indictment for his part in a large-scale bookmaking ring. Sal Manzo received $22,400 secured by property at 3427 Independence Ave. that was damaged in an arson fire in September 1977. That did not dissuade the bank from extending him a $97,000 loan in February 1978. Tony Civella received $35,000 in June 1976, when he had been convicted and faced a 3½-year prison sentence.

Other mob figures and associates receiving loans included Big Jim Balestrere, Willie Cammisano, Alex Presta, Max Ducov, Vince Abbott, Joe Ragusa, Ross Strada and Tudie Gulotta.

In the River Quay, these establishments and operators received funding from Central Bank:

- Ebenezer's Inc. — Mike Egan, $15,000 mortgage.
- Faces — Doris (Mrs. Joe) Cammisano and Anthony Simone, $20,000.
- The Godfather Lounge — Frank Pisciotta, $45,000. The business was damaged by fire of suspicious origin in September 1977.
- Huck Finn's — Lonnie Roccaforte, $6,139.
- Il-Pagliacci House of Pasta — Joe Cammisano, John Amaro, Lonnie Roccaforte, $40,000 loan commitment based on approval of liquor license.
- Mama Angelina's — Donna Abbate, $72,000 loan.
- Judge Roy Bean's — Louis Ribaste, $16,000 in addition to a $35,000 outstanding loan as of November 13, 1974.
- Village Gate — John Vitale, $46,478.
- Big John's — John Amaro. Purchased Village Gate (Fandango Inc.) for $77,092, assuming $54,571 owed to Central Bank
- Market Liquors — Frank Pisciotta.
- Delaware Daddy's — Dante Spini, $25,000.

Ignoring questions of character when dealing with clients, as was the Central Bank's wont, had consequences. That was illustrated by the web that trapped the bank's executive vice president, Edward Kratty Jr.

In summer 1976 Anthony J. Begulia, a bank customer, called Kratty and asked him to provide a credit reference for him under the name Tony Bruno. On two occasions Kratty did so when he was contacted by the Frontier Hotel casino in Las Vegas. Thereafter the bank received from the casino $5,000 in unpaid markers, or IOUs, in the Bruno name. The bank simply returned them to the casino, unpaid.

An FBI investigation revealed that Begulia, using the name Tony Bruno, also had applied for credit at Caesar's Palace and there, too, had given Kratty as a reference. So had Pat J. Fazzino, who later was convicted in a 1983 bookmaking case. John J. Sciortino, a convicted Outfit bookmaker, did the same at the Aladdin casino. Nothing, however, indicated that Kratty had personally verified their standing with the bank as he had done with the Frontier casino.

In indicting Kratty and Begulia in April 1979, the government alleged that Kratty had agreed beforehand to vouch for the Bruno name. Kratty, in his trial in June 1979, denied that and testified that he was only trying to accommodate a good customer of the bank who was also demanding and pushy. The trial jury found Kratty credible and acquitted him. Nonetheless, he had been dragged through the mud and the bank's reputation had been sullied.

For years, defrauding Las Vegas casinos by obtaining credit — often by falsifying credit applications — with no intention of repaying the debt was a favored scam. Apparently the Aladdin Hotel was on alert, as indicated by this note on Sciortino's credit application uncovered in the investigation:

"We've had a rumble he (Sciortino) may be part of a group that intended on setting us up and then at some point forcing their credit limits up refusing to pay."

Across that, in red ink, was written:

"No credit. All from K.C."

Besides Sciortino 11 names were identified in that group, among them River Quay figure Louis Ribaste and "Tony Bruno," Begulia.

CHAPTER IX

CARL SPERO

AS THE RIVER QUAY DEVELOPMENT continued to prosper, the number of individuals with ties to organized crime and with a direct or indirect interest in the Quay was growing. Among them was Carl Spero.

The Spero name would become synonymous with gangland violence that plagued the city in the 1970s and 1980s. The Spero family included six brothers, Joe, Nick, Carl, Michael, Sam and Vincent, and one sister. In criminal endeavors, Nick and Carl were the ones who gained notoriety Early on, however, they proved themselves to be anything but criminal masterminds.

Carl was born in Kansas City on November 9, 1939. As an adult, he stood 5-feet 11-inches tall and weighed about 190 pounds with a rugged build. He had dark hair and dark brown eyes and was referred to by the Civellas and their inner circle as "Curly." Carl Spero and brother Nick Spero were tough as nails, but at the same time outgoing, likable and charismatic. As a brash 16-year-old, Carl confessed to committing 37 burglaries, most of them to finance flashy sports cars for himself and his friends. For that, he spent four years at the federal reformatory in El Reno, Oklahoma.

On October 1, 1961, after pleading guilty to a charge of attempted burglary in Jackson County, Carl was sentenced to two years but received a five-year bench parole. In July 1963 he was charged with robbing *The Kansas City Star* credit union. Free on bond from those charges, which later were dismissed, and still on bench parole, he was arrested in September 1963 in St. Louis after a foot chase as he fled the scene of an attempted burglary of a jewelry store. A month later he was arrested again, this time in connection with the $33,000 burglary of the Ash Men's Store in Mission, Kansas. Caught in the act of breaking into a shoe store in Columbia, Missouri, on

November 17, 1963, he was arrested, and confessed to looting Flowers Shoe Store in Sedalia, Missouri, five days earlier. Topping if off, in November 1963 a federal grand jury indicted him in a burglary committed in Independence, Missouri.

The spree was enough finally to prompt Jackson County authorities to declare Carl Spero in violation of his bench parole and send him to jail for two years. Adding sentences received for his other misdeeds, he did not leave prison until September 1967.

The string of failures and the time in prison evidently had no effect on Spero — except to turn him from burglary to armed robbery.

From 1969 into the 1970s a string of robberies targeting jewelry salesmen was orchestrated by a loosely knit band including Carl and Nick Spero, Harold "Sonny" Bowen, Johnny Joe Calia, Frank Robertson and Jimmy Joe Sollome, names that would turn up time and again as events surrounding the Spero brothers unfolded.

By various means, visiting jewelry salesmen were identified and their routines established. When the time was right and conditions optimal, they were robbed of their sample cases.

Carl Spero was no more successful in this new endeavor. He was quickly identified and arrested after a jewelry salesman was robbed on May 16, 1969, as he pulled into a Holiday Inn in Mission, Kansas. Authorities in Johnson County, Kansas, charged Spero with armed robbery. Less than a year later, after pleading guilty, he was transported to the Kansas State Penitentiary at Lansing to begin serving a five- to 10-year sentence.

Perhaps Carl Spero's misfortune prompted the band of robbers to look to greener pastures. For whatever reason, the team took its show on the road, traveling to Portland, Oregon. There, on October 21, 1970, a jewel salesman was held up at his home and robbed of about $44,000 worth of merchandise. Immediately afterward a second salesman was robbed of his sample case containing $12,000 worth of jewelry. Witnesses put Nick Spero, Calia and Bowen together both shortly before and after the second robbery. Of the victims, only the second salesman could make an identification, picking out Calia. Calia was charged in Portland with the $12,000 heist and made bond. The team went home.

Returning to the West Coast, the crew on February 20, 1971, robbed a jewelry salesman in Palo Alto, California, and the very next day robbed another salesman in Sunnyvale, California. However, the team's batting average continued to fall. This time, Bowen, Sollome and Robertson were arrested in Santa Clara, California, and charged with both robberies. Bowen appeared in court in California in July 1971. He was convicted and sentenced to a prison term.

IN KANSAS CITY ABOUT THE SAME TIME, FBI agents arrested Johnny Joe Calia on a warrant for unlawful flight to avoid prosecution. He had failed to appear in Portland, Oregon, to face the charge of armed robbery. The arrest put in motion a series of events attesting once again to the power of political influence, and to the largesse of Governor Warren Hearnes' administration when it came to mob figures.

To set the scene: Years before, in January 1966, Hearnes visited Kansas City to meet with the Board of Police Commissioners. His visit occurred four days after the apparent gangland murder of Outfit member Sam Palma, which focused attention on mob activity. Asked about it at a press conference, Hearnes said that he had instructed the Police Board to look into the "possibility" of organized crime's existence in Kansas City and its political links. As for himself, Hearnes said he had been unable to learn of any protected organized crime element.

Where had the governor of Missouri been all that time? It had been a little more than eight years since the Apalachin summit. After that had come a local and national media blitz, grand jury pronouncements and stepped-up law enforcement activity — all of which made the name Civella as recognizable as that of the governor himself.

When reporter Charles Gray of KMBC-TV conducted a live interview with Hearnes that January, the governor skirted the question generated by the Palma murder about the Kansas City criminal organization. According to Hearnes, he had not made inquiries of his appointed Kansas City Police Board concerning political protection or organized crime. However, after the murder the board had reported to him that it had no evidence the mob was protected by politicians. Furthermore, Hearnes had asked the director of the Missouri Highway Patrol, E.O. Hockaday, to get in touch with U.S. Attorney Russell Millin to evaluate the status of organized crime. Hockaday explained that he had missed connections with Millin and the matter had slipped his mind.

Five years later, when Hearnes still was governor, the Kansas City Crime Commission added to the bulk of readily available information about organized crime by issuing a publication, "Hoods Who." It documented names, places, businesses and activities connected to the crime syndicate.

In that context came the tortured tale of Johnny Joe Calia. His story began when he was convicted in Johnson County, Kansas, of fourth-degree arson. Calia had torched a residence in Overland Park in December 1969. Sentenced to a year in the Johnson County Jail, he had served 28 days when he was freed on parole. After violating the parole, he was returned to county jail in March 1971. On July 16 of that year, he was released again.

Three days later, Oregon issued a fugitive warrant for Calia, who had missed his court date there in the robbery of the jewel salesman because he was jailed in Johnson County. Had the Oregon authorities been aware of Calia's incarceration and issued the warrant while he was still jailed in Kansas, they would not have had to deal with the Missouri administration of Governor Warren Hearnes and his legal assistant, Paul Williams.

On August 5, 1971, Oregon issued an extradition warrant for Calia, and four days later it made a formal request of Missouri to extradite him. Paul Williams handled the matter. Calia received a hearing and a month afterward the Oregon governor's extradition secretary was told in writing that Missouri would not act because of a charge pending against Calia in Jackson County, Missouri.

Indeed, Calia had been under indictment in Jackson County for receiving stolen property; his co-defendant had been none other than Carl Spero. However, extradition records indicated that three days before Williams wrote his letter of refusal to Oregon he was advised that the Jackson County charges against Calia had been dropped. Williams would claim he did not recall getting that information.

The next move by Calia's lawyer and Williams, made about six months later, stretched the imagination. Rather than inconvenience Calia, they suggested, the Oregon jewelry salesman should travel to Kansas City to view a police lineup and ensure that his identification was correct. Oregon authorities not only rejected the request but also labeled it an "unheard-of procedure." They expressed concern for the witness' safety.

Pressed to explain the bizarre maneuver, Williams came up with the story that someone in the district attorney's office in Multnomah County, Oregon, where Portland is situated, had agreed to the idea because the victim already planned to be traveling to the Midwest. The district attorney's office emphatically denied the story, which was unsupported in Williams' own extradition file.

When that didn't fly, Williams claimed there was "persuasive evidence" that Calia had been in Kansas City at the time of the Portland robbery. Calia's own lawyer denied that, saying he had no recollection of having provided such "persuasive evidence" to Williams. The lawyer's only concern was the accuracy of the witness' identification.

Nothing, it seemed, would deter Williams. Returning to the issue of witness identification, he wrote Oregon authorities that "an earnest plea" had been made that Calia had not been properly identified. Requiring a witness to view a lineup in Kansas City might be an unusual procedure, Williams said, but it would be a rather severe penalty for Calia to have to return to Oregon if in fact the identification was faulty.

The veracity of witness identification, it would seem, is a matter for a trial jury and not someone like Paul Williams.

The Hearnes administration never did extradite Calia. That was left to the new governor, Kit Bond. After Bond took office in 1973, a surprised assistant district attorney in Portland received an inquiry from Missouri asking whether he still wanted Calia. When it was explained that a new administration had taken over, the Oregon official indicated he now understood it all. Eventually, Calia was sent back to Portland — 18 months after the extradition warrant had been issued.

He stood trial in the robbery of the jewelry salesman, was found guilty and on July 26, 1973, he reported to begin a 10-year sentence. Inexplicably, Calia was granted a parole after serving only 1½ years. He was released February 6, 1975, and returned to Kansas City, where he joined the Speros and others in the intrigue, perfidy and violence that characterized the era.

STRANGE CARS PARKED on the secluded streets of the Village of Oakwood in Clay County, Missouri, were an uncommon occurrence in that toney neighborhood, and quickly noted. So it was that some time between 11 and 11:30 p.m. on April 11, 1973, a beige-colored Cadillac convertible parked in the 5800 block of Northeast Clements Ave. was reported to police. Within an hour a Gladstone policeman was on the scene to check it out. He found a partly opened trunk, its lid secured by a piece of wire. Looking inside, he caught a glimpse of a body in the beam of his flashlight.

It was the remains of Nick Louis Spero, 37 years old, married and the father of four daughters. Clad in loud red, yellow and blue slacks and a blue sweatshirt, Spero had been shot at close range, once in the head and once in the chest, with what was believed to have been a .38-caliber revolver. The coroner estimated that Spero had been killed between 9 and 11 p.m. that night. The Clay County sheriff labeled the murder a first; to the best of his knowledge, Nick Spero's was the first gangland-style slaying ever in the county.

Like his brother Carl, Nick Spero started at an early age as a burglar. Several of his criminal exploits were downright laughable. When he was 17, he received a 60-day sentence for burglary, and four days after being released he was caught in the act in another burglary. He pleaded guilty and received a one-year sentence. Several years later came what might be called the Pink Hat Caper. Arrested after the discovery of a smashed display window at Adler's, 1208 Main St., Nick Spero was found with five pink women's hats stuffed under his coat, all bearing Adler's labels. In December 1959, Spero and Glenn "Curly" Mitts, while being chased by the police, threw a package of burglary tools out of their car. A broken screwdriver in the canvas bag matched pieces from an attempted burglary of the Grand Avenue Temple Methodist church at 205 E. Ninth St., leading to their arrest.

In 1962 a poodle named Jolie owned by a couple from Mission, Kansas, was taken from their car at a Mission shopping center. A $200 reward was offered, and three days later a woman named Nancy Lee Dalton called to say she had the dog. She and the couple arranged a meeting at a Kansas City bar and after paying the reward the owners were reunited with Jolie. Witnesses identified the car used by Dalton as belonging to her friend Nick Spero.

For 18 months before his murder Nick Spero had been employed by Hyman Freightways in Kansas City's East Bottoms. Before that he drove a truck for Yellow Freight. He was a member in good standing of Teamsters Union Local 41, where his brother Michael Spero was business agent. In the wake of Nick Spero's murder, stories circulated that he had been shooting his mouth off about Teamsters affairs, and about his ambition to gain influence in the union. Allegedly this did not sit well with the Outfit; Local 41 was recognized as Nick Civella's domain. When it came to Teamsters affairs anyone with a mind of his own was treading on thin ice.

The motives behind gangland slayings are as complex as the people who inhabit the shadowy world of organized crime. As is often the case, it was not until years later that information surfaced shedding new light on why Nick Spero was murdered.

At the time of the murder, Nick Civella, his nephew Tony Civella and other mob functionaries were under federal indictment for interstate gambling as a result of the wiretap that the FBI had placed at the Northview Social Club. A key witness in the case was frequent bettor Lester Moore, a car dealer in Ottawa, Kansas.

The high-living Moore, after a casual social contact at a nightspot on the 12th Street Strip, developed a close friendship with Nick and Carl Spero. Moore had been placing sports wagers with a local bookmaker, Harry Huntman, but Moore found that Huntman did not pay off reliably. The Spero brothers offered to hook Moore up directly with the Outfit's main bookmaking operation. Moore, no penny-ante gambler, got direct access to Frank Tousa, the manager of the bookmaking ring. As a result of the FBI wiretap the car dealer found himself in a precarious position.

The Outfit feared that Moore potentially could put Boss Nick Civella in jail. In an effort to neutralize that threat, the Speros were called on to take care of the matter. Because the Speros had introduced Moore, the Outfit felt it was only right that the Speros do whatever it took to ensure Moore never made it to the witness stand.

Carl Spero, who was closest to Moore, refused, living up to his reputation as a strong-willed maverick. Brother Nick was pressured to see that Carl did what he was told. Nick, too, refused, reasoning that Moore was not part of the Outfit and not subject to Outfit rules. In his view, the Office had been happy to take Moore's money and now it simply would have to suck it up and accept the risk that went with dealing with a "peckerwood" — an outsider.

Nick, as it turned out, had ended up in the trunk of his car as payback for defying the Outfit. Carl Spero, however, was out of the Outfit's reach.

ON THE NIGHT HIS BROTHER'S body was found, Carl Spero was at the Kansas State Penitentiary, serving a sentence for a 1970 armed robbery. On May 7, 1973, less than a month after the slaying, Carl Spero walked out of the prison. Soon, word circulated that he was not about to let his brother's murder go unavenged.

In later years, Carl Spero would speak of making inquiries into his brother's killing but finding only a cloud of smoke meant to keep him off balance. Curly Mitts, the accomplice of Nick Spero in their 1959 burglary at the Grand Avenue Temple, was mentioned as the party responsible for the murder. When Mitts was murdered in June 1975, stories circulated that he was killed to placate Carl Spero. A more likely scenario was that the Outfit simply let Carl believe that it had had Mitts killed to keep him in check.

Carl Spero, back on the street, was looking around for something to get into. In his circles, the buzz was about the River Quay. As a convicted felon Spero was barred from obtaining a liquor license, so any involvement by him would have to be hidden. His opportunity came when Steve Como negotiated a sublease with Mike Heller for space in the building in the 400 block of Wyandotte Street. Como planned to open a bar to be called The Godfather Lounge.

A loan was made to Como by an investment company owned by a Clay County automobile dealership. The dealership was owned by Lester Moore, who had moved his operation from Ottawa to Liberty. Moore's pal Carl Spero worked there part time.

The involvement of Moore's business in the loan gave support to rumors that Spero was a silent backer in The Godfather lounge, as did Spero's regular visits to the place. However, Spero's opportunity was lost when the liquor application for The Godfather was denied. The place was sold to Frank Pisciotta, another Outfit associate. Spero moved on, destined for a historic confrontation with the Civella Crime Family.

CHAPTER X
RIVER QUAY 2

CARL SPERO AND HIS ILK were far from what Freddy Bonadonna had in mind for infusing new blood into the River Quay. Bonadonna's overriding concern, however, was that Joe Cammisano was gaining a foothold. That development occurred in part because of outside influences.

At the time that Cammisano made a point of letting Bonadonna know he was interested in the Quay, a cloud of doubt hovered over the 12th Street Strip, the raucous area where Cammisano had operated bars for years. The Strip was home to bars with names such as Pal Joey, Peyton Place, Can Can Lounge, Pink Door, It Club and Pink Pussy Cat, featuring bikini-clad go-go and exotic dancers. It catered to the clientele of nearby hotels and conventions. A favorite trolling ground for prostitutes, the Strip often accounted for one-third to one-half of Kansas City's monthly prostitution arrests. It was dotted with $7 hotel rooms — $9 with bath.

It was no secret that the Strip's days were numbered. In the early 1970s a new convention hall was in the works catercorner south and west of the 12th Street Strip, and in December 1973 came the formal announcement of plans to construct a $50 million luxury hotel where the Strip stood on 12th Street between Wyandotte and Central streets. In the proposal was an application under the Missouri redevelopment law authorizing the City Council to declare the block blighted and to condemn the buildings there.

With the future of the 12th Street Strip in doubt, business owners hesitated to invest in their deteriorating establishments. Some sought greener pastures such as the River Quay, only seven or eight blocks north. That altered the Quay's destiny forever.

Joe Cammisano's boast of bringing his style of adult entertainment to the Quay was only part of the worry felt by Freddy Bonadonna. The

Cammisanos were at the top of the list of crime figures most familiar to him, and Bonadonna was confident that Joe's brother, the fearsome mobster Willie "The Rat" Cammisano, was the force behind everything Joe was doing. Freddy Bonadonna knew about the Cammisanos because his father, David Bonadonna, was associated closely with Willie. That was a formula for intense conflict in Freddy's life, and one more reason his resistance to them had to be kept close to the vest.

FROM YEARS OF FATHER-SON TALKS and conversations overheard as a curious teenager, Freddy Bonadonna knew about Willie Cammisano's reputation and deeds. He was reputed to have killed or ordered killed any number of people. Willie was violently protective of his family, a noble calling except for the methods he used to resolve conflicts. Freddy could list the names of Anthony Nigro and Stino Circo — and others — as individuals who had crossed the Cammisanos and fallen victim to Willie's wrath.

Even though he was Willie Cammisano's son-in-law, Anthony Nigro had to pay the price for stepping on the wrong toes. The story from sources on the street was that Nigro and a tavern owner named Joe Porrello had formed a team that broke into homes; they had burglarized at least one home of a person closely connected to the Outfit. Nigro disappeared on February 25, 1967. His body was found in a North End sewer just short of six years later. A month after Nigro's disappearance, the 35-year-old Porrello was ambushed and shotgunned to death in front of his home at 105 Benton Blvd.

The story of Stino Circo provided insight into the way things were done within Cosa Nostra. Circo was considered a small-time, knock-around guy. In February 1961 he was arrested in possession of 40 fur pieces, but released when police were unable to show that the furs were stolen. Furs seemed to be Circo's thing; he was arrested again in 1965, again in possession of furs. This time the furs were established as stolen property, but because they were valued at less than $50 Circo received only a 30-day sentence in the Clay County jail. After that he evidently abandoned criminal endeavors — at least there were no further arrests — and in 1973 Circo was working as a salesman for a home improvement company.

In an ill-advised move, Circo took up with a married relative of the Cammisanos. By doing so, he ran afoul of the protective shield that surrounded the Cammisano blood family. The affair would not be tolerated.

Circo's misstep No. 1 was followed by misstep No. 2, when he failed to heed the Cammisanos' warning to stay away from the woman. Then came misstep No. 3, when Circo and the woman ran off together. Three strikes and he was out.

I learned of the affair from an informant who told me that Circo would have to pay the price for disrespecting the Cammisanos; he was a dead man walking. I paid Circo a visit, told him what I had learned, and warned him of the grave danger he faced. Circo responded in cavalier fashion: if I knew that much about him, it meant he was being watched by law enforcement. He thought that was all the protection he needed. In effect, he blew off my warning.

Time passed and the expected news of Circo's murder did not materialize. Had my informant been misled? I tried to get in touch with Circo but he failed to respond. Finally, I learned the answer. My informant found that a Circo family member or family connection had the ear of Joe Cusumano and pleaded with him to intercede in behalf of the wayward Stino Circo. Cusumano, partner with Joe Filardo in the Roma Bakery, was a respected elder statesmen in the Family. In true Old World fashion, Cusumano resolved the matter by ordering Circo's life spared as long as Cusumano was alive.

Joe Cusumano died November 15, 1973. Two days later, on a Saturday night, Stino Circo was found in his car parked at Fifth and Gillis streets in front of a North End gambling spot, shot five times at close range, three times in the head. To the homicide detectives on the scene it appeared that the killer or killers had been sitting in the car with Circo.

As was often the case, I was at the office working late when one of the detectives called. It looked like a mob execution, I was told, and the victim's car was registered to a Stino Circo. By any chance did I know him? I told the detective I would be right down. I spent the rest of the night working with the homicide detectives.

ALTHOUGH THE SPECTER OF THE CAMMISANOS hung over his head and his worst fears about the direction of the River Quay were coming to pass, Freddy Bonadonna was not about to give in.

The man who had taken over most of Marion Trozzolo's interests in the Quay, Joe Canizaro, was an experienced developer. He knew that complete control was critical to success. Why risk renovating only those properties he had acquired from Marion Trozzolo while properties outside his control deteriorated or were used in a way that harmed his development? To gain the control he wanted, Canizaro announced at a press conference on June 4, 1974, that within 90 days he would ask the city for approval to begin condemnation proceedings. He was ready, he said, to invest $39 million in the River Quay development.

Canizaro's plan was met with howls of resistance from Quay businessmen, who feared that the New Orleans developer was about to raise their rents. They closed ranks, forming the Market Area Businessmen's Association to fight the proposal and retained as legal counsel Denver Vold, who also held a seat on the three-member city liquor appeal board, a situation that would come into play later.

Canizaro took the opportunity to address his own concerns, making it clear there were too many bars in the area:

> "If Kansas City is interested in seeing the Quay be successful you have to keep out the bad element that tends to go to an area where there are a large number of bars. I'm concerned about the character of some of the people who are getting licenses. If that kind of thing continues, if any more (licenses) are issued to those kind of people I'm going to lose any more interest in developing the Quay."

Supporting Canizaro, Liquor Control Director W. Yates Webb documented 22 liquor establishments in the 40-block area and four applications that were pending. Webb believed that number was excessive, and he denied two pending liquor applications. His rulings, however, were reversed on appeal. The River Quay was caught in a bureaucratic snafu in which one arm of the city acted in direct opposition to the aims of other arms.

Public concern over the issue and resistance by Freddy Bonadonna were causing headaches for Joe Cammisano. He wanted to capitalize on the boom times the Quay experienced in 1974, but his efforts to obtain a liquor license faced several hurdles. For one, Joe Canizaro was in a position to exert influence. For another, before a bar could open the support and acquiescence of adjoining landowners was required.

Freddy Bonadonna had no intention of lifting a finger on Joe Cammisano's behalf. Then Freddy's father, David Bonadonna, talked to him.

Freddy had to help Cammisano get his liquor license, his father said, adding that those marching orders came directly from Willie Cammisano. At first Freddy declined, recounting his fear that Cammisano and others would bring their 12th Street Strip joints to the Quay.

That opposition earned Freddy a summons to Willie's garage hangout at 536 Monroe Ave. The building could be more accurately described as his fortress. It was brown cement-block and stucco with cement floors and a double-layered steel overhead door with multiple locks. A metal pedestrian door also had multiple locks and a sheet of plexiglass bolted to its interior side. Windows were barred. The building was as intimidating as Willie the Rat himself. Now Willie told Freddy how he wanted to proceed.

If Freddy cooperated, Willie said, he would see to it that a troublesome liquor control agent, Nelson Martin — who had a running conflict with Freddy — was prevented from bothering him. Furthermore, Willie also would guarantee that no adult-type bar — except for his brother's — would be allowed in the Quay.

Freddy was torn. On the one hand, he feared Willie Cammisano and knew his own father was in precarious position. On the other, he was worried about the future of the River Quay. He had to appear agreeable, but he still secretly wanted to keep the Cammisanos out. He was committing himself to a perilous course of action.

Freddy went to Joe Canizaro. In a private meeting, he described the type of bars that Joe Cammisano ran and made known his opposition. For the good of the Quay, he told Canizaro, do whatever it takes to keep the man out.

He also described his predicament. He had to bring Cammisano to see Canizaro, and outwardly he had to support him. Canizaro must appear receptive to them; otherwise Freddy feared for his life.

As he had been instructed to do, Freddy brought Cammisano and Lonnie Roccaforte to see Canizaro, who effectively played his part. With that out of the way, Freddy felt better about his next step, which was to circulate a petition to River Quay businesses approving Cammisano's and Roccaforte's new business ventures. Naturally, he faced questions about his unexpected change of attitude toward those ventures.

Canizaro, as promised, waded in. He made known to city officials that he opposed issuance of any more liquor licenses for the Quay. It wasn't necessary to prod Liquor Control Director Webb, who was already on board. Webb let Cammisano and Roccaforte know he would deny their license applications based on density. They let him know they were proceeding with their applications anyway.

Freddy's efforts with the petition gained him nothing from Joe Cammisano. Instead Cammisano angrily chastised Freddy, accusing him of blocking him every step of the way. Illustrating his disdain and displeasure, he made a show of tearing up the petition in front of him.

Alas, all Freddy's efforts went for naught. His petition and his pretense of support did nothing to change Cammisano's opinion. Furthermore, despite the initial denial of all four liquor license applications for the Wyandotte Street building, all were approved on appeal.

By September 1974, Canizaro had to abandon his attempt at condemnation proceedings in the face of the opposition mounted against him. A formal announcement was made by his spokesman at a meeting of City Council officials and members of the Market Area Businessmen's Association.

Joe Cammisano had made it into the Quay, and the district entered a death spiral.

ORDINARILY, SOMETHING AS INNOCENT as leasing parking spaces to further your business would not create turmoil, but this was the River Quay. Freddy Bonadonna was astute enough to recognize the importance of parking. Others in the Quay were not.

The story of the parking spaces began on an ordinary day in October 1974, when Bonadonna noticed a blacktopping job in progress in the parking lot just east of Poor Freddie's. From Day One the location for his business had been based on the availability of parking, if it ever became scarce. Now, Bonadonna knew, an opportunity was at hand. He visited with the manager of the City Market, Willis Castle, and learned that the city was leasing parking spaces in the newly blacktopped lot. The monthly rate was $10 per space, and 32 spaces were available. Immediately Bonadonna agreed to lease them.

He also learned that the remaining 28 spaces were leased to a River Quay business, William Volker & Co. He paid the business a visit and offered a plan: In the daytime, when the business was open, it could use Bonadonna's 32 spaces and in the night hours, Bonadonna could use Volker's 28. The business was agreeable to the arrangement. Now, Bonadonna had access to 60 spaces.

To offer free parking while increasing his business, Bonadonna came up with the idea of charging $1 to park in the lot. The parking ticket would be redeemable at Poor Freddie's as if it were a dollar bill. It would be a win-win deal — for all except his rivals.

No sooner had the signs gone up announcing Poor Freddie's parking than the pack came sniffing around. Paul Scola, his brother-in-law Angelo Vitale, John Amaro, Lonnie Roccaforte and, of course, Joe Cammisano eyed the situation with interest and suspicion. Freddy explained how he came by the parking spaces. Encouraged, they indicated an interest in following suit with another parking lot to the south.

Curious as to whether they had followed through, Bonadonna again went to see the City Market manager. Indeed, Castle told him, inquiries had been made, and he had agreed to make improvements including a stairwell from the south lot to Delaware Street, the main street of the Quay development. Bonadonna assured Castle that, if the other parties didn't come through, he would take the south lot, too. He walked away believing the matter had been resolved.

Months passed and parking lots became the farthest thing from Bonadonna's mind. Then Castle rang him up. In December 1974, Castle said, he had informed the interested parties that the lots were ready to go, but no one had appeared to execute the lease. Subsequent calls went unanswered.

Feeling a sense of responsibility in the matter, Bonadonna tried to find out what Scola, Vitale and the rest planned to do about the lots, and was assured it would all be taken care of in a week's time.

Instead, Castle soon was back on the phone reporting that still no one had come to see him. For a second time Bonadonna made inquiries, and now a different tune was sung: Why should we have to pay for lots belonging to the city? Besides, the rental fee was too high.

By April 1, 1975, Castle, who had spent city funds on improvements, was fed up and angry. Bonadonna couldn't blame him. Having committed himself to lease the lot if others didn't, Freddy offered Castle a compromise deal. He would pay $250 a month in rent, the most he could afford, to lease the spaces for weekend use only. To recoup some of the added expense and try to further increase business, he increased the parking fee to $2, again redeemable at Poor Freddie's. The other bar owners, who simply did not want Bonadonna to control the spaces, went ballistic, cussing him out, bad-mouthing him to others and generally making his life miserable. It was the opening shot in the parking lot wars.

THE POLITICAL LANDSCAPE ALTERED DRAMATICALLY
on February 25, 1975, and it would have a profound impact on the River
Quay. After 16 years in office, City Councilman Sal Capra, in whose district
the Quay lay, was upset in the city elections by a young man named Robert
Hernandez.

Capra had been elected in a similar upset in 1959, one in which his
uncle Alex Presta, the once-powerful North Side political faction leader,
was instrumental. Capra's indictment in August 1973 in a scheme to evade
state sales taxes may have dimmed his chances in the 1975 election. He was
acquitted but he lost his seat on the City Council.

THE 1975 ELECTION LOSS WOULD NOT BE THE END of
Capra's grief. Five years afterward, Capra would face even more, resulting
from some of the people he knew. The occasion was the 1980 World Series
between the Kansas City Royals and the Philadelphia Phillies. Capra had
upper-deck tickets to the October 19 game at Royals Stadium.

Beforehand, Missouri State Senator Harry Wiggins was enjoying his
meal at Leonard's Restaurant at 321 Gregory Blvd. when he received a call
from Capra. By 1980, ex-councilman Capra was a paid consultant to the
Board of Police Commissioners, and intergovernmental affairs consultant to
the Area Transportation Authority. Capra told Wiggins he wanted to see him
at the restaurant.

Playing the role of Good Samaritan, Capra told Wiggins he was trying
to help 70-year-old James E. Burke, who once was Thomas Pendergast's
lawyer, with tickets to the game. Burke, Capra told Wiggins, was in poor
health and would have difficulty reaching Capra's upper-deck seats. Capra
proposed a swap with Wiggins for his seats in the lower level and Wiggins,
who knew Burke well, agreed.

The game had reached the second inning when Wiggins decided to go
downstairs to say hello to Burke. To Wiggins' shock and dismay, it was not
Burke he found in his seats but rather Nick Civella and Pete Tamburello,
both free on appeal from a federal conviction. Futilely demanding to know
where Burke was, he was told they knew nothing about him.

"We're not telling you anything," Tamburello added.

Calling Capra, Wiggins demanded to know who was sitting in his seats.

Capra responded that he would try to explain to him sometime. For Wiggins, the show was far from over. The senator ran into reporters and photographers covering the crowd at the game and let them in on his discovery. He led them to a wild scene.

It was now the sixth inning. With cameras on and questions flying, the media blitzed Civella and Tamburello. Civella got up and walked back about four rows, where he encountered a KMBC-TV reporter who asked, "You're Nick Civella, aren't you?"

"You know who I am," Civella said and asked the newsman what he was doing there. Tamburello pushed, shoving the television camera while Civella slapped at a camera held by a *Kansas City Times* photographer. Then Civella's minions appeared, threatening to knock the *Times* photographer down if he kept taking photos. Meanwhile, fans shouted for all of them to sit down.

The final score was Philadelphia 4, Kansas City 3.

The ever-devious Civella laid the blame for the incident on Wiggins, claiming it was Wiggins who had delivered the tickets to his home that morning. Wiggins vigorously denied it, saying he would never have gone to Civella's home even if he knew where it was, which he didn't. It can be said of Capra that he did the right thing, backing Wiggins and contradicting Civella's fairy tale.

The next day the Board of Police Commissioners asked Capra to resign from his $800-a-month consulting position, which he had held since 1977. Capra admitted to *The Kansas City Times* that he knew there was a chance the tickets would go to Civella when he asked Wiggins for the swap, and learned it for sure the morning of the game. He would not identify who picked the tickets up from his home.

Capra also resigned his $15,000-a-year position with the Area Transportation Authority, which he had held since 1975, remaining until June 1981 when his contract expired. Less than a month later, he was rehired by the ATA. When a Jefferson City newspaper asked about Capra's rehiring, it was told that he was paid to "smooth the way" at City Hall. However, the ATA Chairman could not say with whom Capra consulted. ATA officials described Capra as effective, but one state senator labeled the position a wasteful patronage job.

LET'S RETURN NOW TO THE MAN who beat Sal Capra in the City Council election of 1975, Robert Hernandez. Freddy Bonadonna met

Hernandez in 1966 when Freddy opened Mr. B's on Southwest Boulevard. At the time, Hernandez was a college student and member of a group seeking to form a West Side political club that would hold its meetings at Mr. B's.

In 1975, Freddy had no idea that the Hernandez who had unseated Capra was the same person he knew from Mr. B's — until Hernandez appeared one day at Poor Freddie's. The two became fast friends. Freddy could never have counted on a relationship with Sal Capra, but now he had the ear of a City Council member, one who represented the district that included the Quay. This did not sit well with the North End, nor did the fact that Poor Freddie's was a meeting place for politicians, city councilmen, the mayor and other local luminaries.

BY 1975 THE ONCE-BRIGHT FUTURE of the Quay was severely tarnished. Attention now centered on the myriad of difficulties facing the area, and on a prevailing climate that had become unwholesome.

Joe Canizaro announced that he had taken a $300,000 financial beating. Without complete control over the development, he said, he was unable to win sorely needed investors — even for a scaled-down plan in which he would sell off many of his holdings and concentrate on Delaware Street, the Quay's main thoroughfare. There was no unity among Quay merchants. Some worried about the number and type of drinking establishments, and others were concerned more with higher rents that pinched small shop owners. The Canizaro ship was on the rocks.

Despite it all, bars continued to pop up. The number of liquor licenses reached 30. The issue was hashed out at City Hall, where Freddy Bonadonna and members of the Market Area Businessmen's Association regularly attended meetings.

To their horror, there were rumblings that the Quay was being considered as the site for a "combat zone" consisting of all the porn shops, X-rated theaters and adult bookstores in Kansas City. Already, they were concerned about the question of adult entertainment in light of the announcement that Ed Herzmark was looking to open an X-rated theater called The Chelsea Quay at 200 W. Fourth St.

Hoping to halt the tide, the Market Area Businessmen's Association took action. For starters, in June 1975 it circulated a petition opposing the introduction into the Quay of X-rated theaters, porn shops and the like. Second, the association pressed the City Development Department to create for the Quay area a comprehensive plan barring such businesses and also limiting the number of liquor licenses. Taking into account that government grinds slowly, the association also called for a moratorium on granting new liquor licenses while the comprehensive plan was hashed out.

The next four to five weeks were intense. Merchants met almost daily with various elements of city government, and Bonadonna played a prominent role. Accompanied by members of the Market Area Businessmen's Association, Bonadonna approached Councilman Hernandez, pushing him to sponsor a liquor-license moratorium. To draft a fair but binding resolution would take several weeks, and while that process was under way City Councilman Joe Serviss won adoption of a resolution declaring a six-month moratorium on accepting license applications for motion-picture theaters. The Serviss moratorium, passed July 10, 1975, did not apply to liquor license applications. The issue of moratoriums would have ramifications Bonadonna could never have imagined.

IRONICALLY, JOE CAMMISANO never got his Fabulous Forties bar on Wyandotte off the ground. He sold out to Anthony Simone, son of Thomas "Hiway" Simone, whose new business, Faces, opened in January 1975.

Nevertheless, Cammisano had not given up on the Quay. He now set out to open a place called Uncle Joe's at 223 W. Third St. On June 9, 1975 — just as word of a proposed moratorium was circulating — he applied for a liquor license.

Cammisano's plan was no secret, so Freddy Bonadonna asked his father to check with Willie Cammisano to make sure that Joe was set with his liquor license before a moratorium kicked in. Word came back that all was well with Joe's application, and Freddy pushed on to make the moratorium happen.

Not long afterward, David Bonadonna called his son and chewed him out. Hadn't he been told, David asked Freddy, to leave Cammisano alone?

Left in the dark, Freddy invited his father down to talk it over. From him, Freddy learned that Joe Cammisano's license had not been approved after all, and that the Liquor Control director's position was that it would be held up by the moratorium. The next day David Bonadonna returned, telling Freddy the situation was to the point where someone was going to get killed. Willie the Rat was furious.

It made no difference that they had made a point to check on the status of Joe's license. It also made no difference that the only moratorium on the books was aimed solely at X-rated theaters, as was the petition circulated in the Quay.

None of it had anything to do with Joe, but the Cammisanos were convinced it was all part of Freddy Bonadonna's plot to keep Joe out of the River Quay. Once the Cammisanos got something in their head, there was no way in the world anyone could reason with them. Once again, all Bonadonna could do was to appear to do Willie Cammisano's bidding by trying to kill the proposed liquor-license moratorium.

At first, Bonadonna stood firm. He was unwilling to betray all those who had come to trust him and who looked to him in difficult times. Reminded that dire consequences followed if one messed with the Cammisanos, he relented. He had one condition: Joe Cammisano must make a commitment that he would not introduce adult entertainment.

At his father's insistence, Freddy Bonadonna paid Joe Cammisano a courtesy call at Uncle Joe's on West Third Street. Joe ignored his greeting and simply grunted, shaking his head as if chiding a misbehaving child. Hardly had their conversation begun when Cammisano exploded. He called Bonadonna a little S.O.B. and asked, Don't you know somebody could get killed jacking around the way you are?

He ticked off a litany of offenses and affronts directed at the Cammisanos, dating back to when Joe first came into the Quay, and warned Bonadonna to get away from politics or someone could get hurt.

Freddy's father jumped into the fray, telling Cammisano that there was no need to talk about killing anyone because the Bonadonnas were trying to help. For the next half-hour the argument raged on until they were able to settle Joe down. They got him to promise he would not operate a "girlie" joint, pointing out that it was critical if Freddy Bonadonna was going to help him.

Back at Poor Freddie's, emotionally drained and stung by Joe's threat, Freddy predicted exactly how things would pan out. He would exert whatever influence he could in Joe's behalf, and the Cammisanos would continue to deny that he had done a damned thing. There was no question Willie Cammisano was capable of murder, but Freddy did not see Joe in the same light.

David Bonadonna simply reminded his son what he had taught him about how Willie handled anyone perceived to abuse any member of his family. The Bonadonnas would commit themselves to help, David reminded his son, and help was what the Bonadonnas had to give. They would see Willie and pledge their assistance, and as proof of Freddy's efforts David would accompany him every step of the way.

Father and son met with Willie, and he assured them that Joe would run a clean business. Not to let the opportunity pass, Willie advised Freddy to quit all the organizations he belonged to, leave politics alone and stick to running his business.

It was a no-win proposition, but on a Monday morning near the end of July 1975, the Bonadonnas set to work. First they made an unsuccessful attempt to see Mayor Charles Wheeler. Then they visited Councilman Hernandez. Freddy couldn't tell Hernandez what was going on with the Cammisanos, so he simply asked Hernandez to do him a favor. He mentioned only a serious problem that forced him to backtrack on what everyone had worked so hard to accomplish. Simply put, it was imperative for Joe Cammisano's liquor license to be approved, and the Bonadonnas needed Hernandez's help. The councilman warned them that, if the Cammisano license was issued, then other licenses, including the one for the X-rated theater, would have to be approved, too. Whatever it took had to be done, Freddy answered. It didn't matter any more.

Freddy was not the only one holding back. Councilman Hernandez had not seen fit to tell him that a problem had surfaced affecting his moratorium. Based on a legal decision, the initial draft moratorium had to be amended to exempt pending liquor license applications that were deemed to have been grandfathered in. Joe Cammisano's liquor license would be approved despite the moratorium.

Freddy called Willie Cammisano, letting him know the matter had been successfully taken care of. Seeing conspiracies everywhere, Willie still was not completely satisfied. Suspicious that the petition against X-rated theaters was only a smokescreen to block his brother, he told Freddy to get him a copy. Apparently, Willie had been led to believe that several Quay businessmen, probably out of fear, denied that they had anything to do with any petition. Now Willie would check the names himself, and God help anyone who had lied to him.

A copy of the petition in hand, David and Freddy Bonadonna took it to the Cammisano brothers at Uncle Joe's in the Quay. Freddy couldn't hold back any longer. He angrily told Joe Cammisano that getting Joe's license freed up had nothing to do with Joe's threats, and that Freddy would not have lifted a finger if his father hadn't asked him to.

"You don't scare me and nobody you know scares me," Freddy added.

Willie downplayed anything his brother might have said, describing it as angry talk. Nobody is going to get killed over anything, Willie said. Forget it, he said, it was just a misunderstanding.

The watered-down moratorium, which would extend for three months, was officially approved July 31, 1975. The River Quay community and Freddy Bonadonna personally had suffered a double whammy. Joe Cammisano's liquor license was issued on August 1, 1975, and soon thereafter work began on the Chelsea Quay X-rated theater. The only ray of sunshine was that Joe Cammisano, as a condition for his license, had to sign an affidavit saying he would not employ go-go girls or other exotic dancers on his premises unless others in the area did so.

Fred believed that the matter was settled and that things could return to normal. Elsewhere, however, events were taking place that would have a profound effect on the Quay.

CHAPTER XI

CIVELLA BATTLES THE GOVERNMENT — AND CANCER

ABOUT TWO AND A HALF YEARS HAD ELAPSED in the government's case against Nick Civella *et al* on charges of interstate gambling when, in May 1974, the defense seized on a new legal twist. The U.S. Supreme Court had invalidated the use of electronic surveillance in certain other cases on grounds that the U.S. attorney general, John Mitchell, or his official designee had not signed off on the wiretap applications, as the law required. Civella's defense lawyers alleged that the same defect applied in the case of the Kansas City Boss and filed appeals.

It seemed a bottomless pit of legal maneuvers. While the appeal worked its way to the high court, the claim of prejudice against Italian-Americans surfaced. In a pretrial hearing, Civella openly accused U.S. District Judge William H. Becker of being prejudiced against him. His outburst was such that Judge Becker threatened to put him in jail for contempt of court.

Civella's disdain for legal restraints resurfaced in August 1974, when he decided to defy restrictions on his travel imposed by his bond. He had important business to attend to, and, by God, he was going to handle it.

The move blew up in his face.

On August 6, FBI agents tailing Charles Moretina, an Outfit enforcer, watched as he parked in the lot of a shopping center in Kansas City, North. Moretina remained in his car. Not long afterward another vehicle pulled up. Out stepped Nick Civella, who quickly entered Moretina's car. The next thing the agents knew, they were heading north on Interstate 29, following Moretina and Civella and finally reaching the airport in Omaha. Feeling safe and secure, Civella, carrying only a small briefcase and flying under the name

J. Sanders, caught a flight to Denver. There he changed planes for Las Vegas, arriving at 8:14 p.m.

As J. Sanders, Civella checked into the Dunes Hotel, which was owned by a longtime associate, St. Louis mob attorney Morris Shenker. Two pieces of luggage were waiting for Civella, as was a lady friend, Marie Guastello. They shared a suite, compliments of the hotel casino's host, Artie Selman. Noted on the registration card of "Mr. Sanders" were the words, "very important person," and an instruction to give the guest anything he wanted compliments of the hotel. The word, "anything," was underlined.

Filling in for the Organized Crime Squad supervisor that day, I was kept abreast of the agents' trip to Omaha, and alerted our Las Vegas office to Civella's travel. Not only had a mob boss sneaked into their city, but also he was one of those excluded persons listed in the Nevada Black Book. Las Vegas FBI agents and gaming authorities went to scoop him up, but they were too late. When Gaming Control officials asked hotel management to produce "J. Sanders," they could not find him. Civella had been tipped off, but his odyssey was far from over.

Marie Guastello checked out on August 8, 1974, with four pieces of luggage. She caught a flight to Denver, arriving at 10:10 p.m. There to watch the flight arrive was Denver FBI agent William Malone. About 55 minutes later, Civella arrived on a flight from Phoenix. He and Guastello then boarded a Frontier flight to Kansas City.

Passengers aboard, doors secured and jetway retracted, the airliner pulled away from the terminal. Malone, who was the Denver FBI's organized crime expert, remained in the terminal, waiting until he saw the jet in the air headed east.

Then, lo and behold, there came the jet heading back to the terminal. The pilot told his passengers that the plane was experiencing a mechanical malfunction and was returning to the terminal to have it inspected. He instructed the passengers to remain in their seats. Alarm bells must have gone off in Civella's head; evidently he believed it was a ruse directed at him. He bullied his way off the plane. Taking it all in, agent Malone followed Civella as he grabbed a cab to a nearby motel, where he registered as Joseph S. Meyer of Kansas City. Malone determined that Civella had a 6:30 a.m. wake-up call, and returned the next morning in plenty of time — only to find that the sly Civella was long gone.

Based on the agents' reports, a motion was filed August 12 to revoke

Civella's bond, requiring yet another hearing. Caught red-handed and embarrassed, Civella had to reveal the details of his trip in open court. Although he apologized to the court for any disrespect, he had to have the last word, and complained that restrictions on his right to travel were unfair.

Years later, the reasons for Civella's trip would become clear.

For the time being, Civella got away with his quick journey. The court declined to revoke his bond. On September 16, 1974, the Nevada Gaming Control Board filed a complaint charging that the Dunes had catered to a subject listed in the Black Book. The board recommended a $50,000 fine. However, in December the Gaming Commission set the fine at a more modest $10,000, which was little more than lunch money for owner Morris Shenker.

Then came yet another windfall for the defense. In December 1974, U.S. District Court Judge John W. Oliver was presiding over a case in which Teamsters kingpin Roy Lee Williams was charged with a labor-law violation. Williams' defense conjured a theory that the federal Strike Force had no authority to operate in the Western District of Missouri. Oliver ordered that certain documents requested by the defense be produced. When the Strike Force failed to produce them — explaining that a decision to do so had not yet been made by the Department of Justice — Oliver dismissed the case against Williams with prejudice, meaning it could not be re-filed. Oliver also ruled that he found no congressional approval for special department attorneys to enter cases. That appeared to fly in the face of history. Since the 1930s the Department of Justice had sent special attorneys to prosecute cases in Kansas City.

Now that the judge had opened the floodgates, defense attorneys swooped in like sharks with blood in the water, claiming the issue as their own. Nick Civella's attorney raised the matter, and Judge Oliver threw out another case in his court in which Ross Agrusa had been charged with a federal firearms violation on the same grounds.

Fortunately, when a defense attorney raised the issue in a case pending before District Court Judge Elmo B. Hunter, he ruled in favor of the Strike Force. Appeals were filed by the Strike Force in the Roy Lee Williams case, and the defense in the case before Judge Hunter. The Eighth Circuit Court of Appeals agreed with Judge Hunter, overturning Oliver's rulings. The door closed for Civella. However, it only further delayed the prosecution.

OLIVER'S RULING SHOWED how a judge's decisions on procedural matters could affect organized crime prosecutions long before a verdict. After a verdict, a judge could have an even greater effect through sentencing.

Early on, tough sentencing was recognized as an essential element in the abatement of organized crime. The 1967 report of President Johnson's Commission on Law Enforcement and Administration of Justice advocated greater punishment when a violation was committed as part of an organized crime business. It urged extended prison terms for offenders who occupied a management position.

A Senate Judiciary Committee report cited a study documenting the low probability that organized crime figures could be rehabilitated. Longer sentences were needed, the report said, to insulate the public from further criminal conduct by organized crime figures for whom Cosa Nostra is a way of life. That purpose is defeated, the report continued, when a prison term suitable for an ordinary offender is imposed on an organized crime leader.

In the wake of the committee report, the Organized Crime Control Act of 1970 included a provision for expanding sentences up to 25 years for those characterized as dangerous offenders. Five years later, an organized crime task force reported that only by long prison terms and heavy economic penalties would organized crime activities be reduced.

With that as background we come to the case of James Duardi, a recognized and active member of the Civella Crime Family.

In the early 1970s Duardi was hard at work attempting to establish a gambling and prostitution enterprise in northeast Oklahoma. His effort was aided by Nate Brancato and Clifford Bishop, two associates of the Kansas City Outfit. Also in league with Duardi was a district attorney based in Miami, Oklahoma, Frank Grayson, and one former and one current investigator in Grayson's office, Jack King and Michael Husong. The district attorney's office was to provide protection for the operation; among other things, the scheme called for bribing local law enforcement. The hub of the operation was to be the Mr. Yuk private club in Grove, Oklahoma.

As events unfolded, the owner of the club, Jess Roberts, got cold feet. When he tried to back out of the deal, he was driven to an Oklahoma back road, shot three times in the stomach and left for dead in a ditch. He survived, however, and agreed to cooperate by testifying to the conspiracy and the brutal attempt on his life.

The six — Duardi, the two other Kansas Citians and the three from the Oklahoma prosecutor's office — were charged with conspiracy to introduce gambling and prostitution in Grove in violation of the interstate transportation in aid of racketeering statute. Judge Oliver would preside.

When time came for the trial, Oliver barred the Strike Force from presenting any evidence of the attempted murder of club owner Roberts, a critical part of the conspiracy, ruling it was "too prejudicial to the defendants."

The trial jury came back with guilty verdicts, and the case had all the earmarks of complying with the special dangerous offenders provision of the 1970 Organized Crime Control Act. A detailed motion was filed supporting expanded sentences for Duardi, the overseer of the crime, for King and Bishop, the shooters, and for Brancato.

Judge Oliver denied the motion. He declined a Strike Force request for a hearing to establish the allegations contained in the motion and ruled that the government had failed to prove that the four defendants were dangerous.

We investigators were stunned. The scheme was a classic example of an organized crime operation, orchestrated by a known mob figure. It had involved gambling, prostitution, bribery of local officials and an attempted murder. One of the accused, Clifford Bishop, was on federal probation at the time of the offense; by the time of sentencing he was in federal prison, his probation having been revoked.

Not only were the sentences for Duardi and the rest not expanded, as appeared warranted, but the modest two-year terms they received did not even meet the maximum called for by the offenses for which they were convicted. The Strike Force attorney tried to make a statement at the time of sentencing, but was cut off. If he had anything to say, Oliver told him, he should put it in a memorandum.

Putting an exclamation point on the matter, Bishop's resume also included a burglary conviction in Jackson County, Missouri. On the patriotic date of July 4, 1972, Bishop had broken into a Macy's store; he was convicted and received a three-year sentence. That sentence for burglary exceeded the sentence meted out by Judge Oliver in the Oklahoma matter, a case in which Bishop attempted to take a man's life.

JAMES DUARDI AND HIS CO-DEFENDANTS Bishop and King were poster boys for the dangerous-offenders sentencing provision, and for the need to lock up organized crime types for long periods, recognizing that chances of their rehabilitation were nil. Yet after serving 15 months of the

Carl Spero

Joseph Spero

Michael Spero

Nick Spero, whose body was found, shot in the head and chest, in the trunk of a car in Clay County in 1973.

John Joseph Calia, a Spero pal

Joe Cammisano at his establishment on the 12th Street Strip, the It Club.

Willie Cammisano's garage — his fortress — in the North End.

Willie "The Rat" Cammisano in 1941, 1950 and 1961.

Stino Circo

Sal Capra sought lower-level seats to the 1980 World Series. The Boss, by then showing signs of his illness, sat in them until a controversy erupted.

Robert Hernandez

James Duardi

Nate Brancato

Clifford Bishop

Frank Grayson

Carl Civella in the mid-1970s

already minimal two-year term imposed by Judge Oliver, Duardi went free, able once again to prey on the community.

Not only did he returned to his old ways and old haunts, but by the late 1970s Duardi's fortunes were reported to be on the rise. According to informants, he held sway in southern parts of Kansas City. For years, Duardi operated out of the Old Fortress bar, later renamed the Austin City Limits, at 1205 E. 85th St. The bar had been the scene of an attempted arson.

As Duardi became increasingly active he expanded his interests. Although normally undisclosed, those interests were suspected to be the J&L Refrigerated Trucking Co. of Lee's Summit; Booths Tow Service; Auto City at 7030 Troost Ave., and the Wild Horse Average Saloon and bingo parlor at 616 E. 135th St., all in Kansas City; and the Red River Saloon at 95th Street and Metcalf Avenue in Overland Park, Kansas.

Tracking Duardi was one of the principal assignments of FBI Special Agent Cullen Scott, who joined the Organized Crime Squad in 1980. Scott recalled that Duardi was, indeed, a tough guy straight from central casting. He carried a fearsome reputation, but at the same time was approachable, even charismatic. Scott found him to be an active racketeer, involved in gambling, labor rackets, politics and arson.

It seemed that any business Duardi frequented was a business from which he made money, whether he was on the payroll or not. Scott's investigations led him to believe that Duardi capitalized on pull he had with several area banks and with the Teamsters union through his association with Sam Ancona, the go-between for Nick Civella and the union.

Duardi used that pull to gain control of businesses.

His relationship with George Lehr is instructive. Lehr was a well-known Kansas City political figure who was widely recognized as a man of integrity. Largely because of that reputation and partly because he knew Roy Lee Williams and Sam Ancona, Lehr in 1981 was appointed to head the troubled Teamsters Pension Fund.

As it happened, in 1980, when Lehr was chairman of Traders Bank, he personally authorized $300,000 in marginal loans to the J&L Refrigerated Trucking Co., in which Duardi had more than a casual interest.

Lehr acknowledged that he had "discussed" the loans to J&L with Duardi, who he understood was "more than an employee" but not the owner. Duardi received authority to write checks on the company, facilitating his takeover. J&L's owner, James Elgin, claimed that Traders Bank had imposed that condition on him. Within a year, Traders' loans to J&L were in default. The matter drew the attention of agents from the FBI and the IRS Criminal Division. Soon agents of Alcohol, Tobacco and Firearms were dogging Duardi's trail, too. Lehr's reputation suffered a blow at the hands of a *Kansas City Star* expose.

In the early 1980s Agent Scott found that Duardi had set up shop at Booths Tow Service. Later events caused speculation that Duardi's foothold at Booths was tied to a loan from Central Bank, the same bank that had financed several racketeers and River Quay figures. In 1981 Central Bank's chairman, Dominic F. Tutera, granted a loan to Booths Tow on condition that Tutera have the option to buy 25.5 percent of the firm. Agent Scott had found a handwritten note to that effect in the subpoenaed records of the bank. The loan from Central was to pay off a loan Booths Tow owed to another bank, and to settle a $162,000 tax lien against the company by the IRS.

Federal law prohibits bank officials from receiving personal gain in exchange for providing banking services. Tutera was charged with that misdemeanor offense and in February 1986 he pleaded guilty.

U.S. Magistrate Calvin K. Hamilton sentenced him to a suspended one-year sentence with three years probation and a $5,000 fine. The sentenced was suspended, Hamilton said, because Tutera had no previous conviction and was in ill health. Nevertheless, the magistrate stated that Tutera had failed to live up to the trust placed in him by the public.

Oklahoma again was on Duardi's radar in August 1982, when he attempted to lay his hands on a quantity of dynamite. As in the Grove affair, he teamed up with Jack King and Clifford Bishop. Bishop was to pick up explosives in Oklahoma and give them to King for delivery to Duardi in Kansas City. Before King could finish the delivery, he was nailed by ATF Agents and earned a 22-year prison term for his efforts.

The explosives eventually made their way to Duardi, delivered by an unnamed individual in May 1983. Six months later a bomb was set to destroy the Wild Horse Average Saloon, which was operated by Duardi associates. It failed to detonate but the saloon and bingo parlor were damaged by a resulting fire.

Stemming from their inquiry into the loans to J&L Refrigerated Trucking, IRS Criminal Division investigators got Duardi indicted in March 1985 for evading taxes from 1978 to 1980 and for filing a false return in 1981. In another instance of Duardi's poisonous effect, his attorney, Michael

Drape, was charged with and convicted of furnishing perjured testimony to the federal grand jury investigating Duardi's taxes. Drape received a five-month sentence.

In May 1985 the axe again fell on Duardi. The ATF's investigation of the explosives delivery in May 1983 led to charges that Duardi and Thomas Hargrove of Tulsa, Oklahoma, conspired to transport plastic high explosives from Oklahoma to Kansas City. In a second count, Duardi was charged with possession of dynamite transported from Oklahoma. Adding to Duardi's woes was an additional charge of extortion leveled against him for his effort to collect $20,000 owed by Fred Marks, a leader in the gypsy community, to a third party.

As part of a plea agreement combining the explosives, tax and extortion charges, Duardi in open court admitted to the offenses charged. In admitting to the extortion charge, he used what might be considered a gross understatement: "Fred Marks could reasonably have construed the language I used as a threat against him to use physical violence or other criminal means to effect the repayment of this debt."

Duardi was sentenced to eight years in prison, well short of the 15-year total that could have been meted to a felon charged with transporting a bomb, tax evasion and extortion.

WHILE DUARDI AND OTHER SOLDIERS OF THE CRIME FAMILY carried on their work, the Boss continued fighting his own legal battles. They provided a candid glimpse at the character and personality of the man.

Nick Civella prided himself on being an avid reader, and nowhere was that more evident than in his own legal research. The Boss' longtime lawyer, James Patrick Quinn, at one point acknowledged in court his client's "unusual nature." From 1971 to 1977 Civella not only participated in hundreds of meetings with other lawyers and legal experts on wiretapping, he also became his own legal research "artist."

He subscribed to books and magazines, supplementing Quinn's own library of wiretap and search-and-seizure law. Wiretap law was in its infancy at the time, and Quinn said that Civella became a student of it, debating various legal issues with his own lawyers. His legal scholarship continued even as his eyesight failed and the Boss took to wearing thick-lensed glasses. Now, he had to be chauffered by his right-hand man, Pete Tamburello.

Armed with his research, Civella showed he was more than willing to contribute to his own defense. In the process, he created courtroom firestorms.

They began with the defense's challenge in 1974 to the FBI's authorization to wiretap the Trap at Fifth Street and Troost Avenue. The wiretap had uncovered the gambling operations taking place at the Office, the mob's gambling hub headquartered there. The defense argument centered on whether U.S. Attorney General John Mitchell had actually initialed the authorizing documents.

Both sides summoned handwriting experts whose findings were diametrically opposed. By early January 1975 an independent, court-appointed expert declared Mitchell's initials were authentic. The defense shot back with a motion contesting the finding on the grounds of the expert's lack of impartiality, along with a motion to disqualify Judge Becker.

Civella accused the judge of discussing the case outside the courtroom, allegedly making statements to the effect that the only way to control a rise in gambling activities was to eliminate Civella. As the story went, the judge would see that Civella was removed from the scene for a very long time, saying, "the Godfather escaped at Apalachin but I'll see to it that he won't make it out of my courtroom." Where did this come from? Civella's sources, he claimed, were persons employed by the federal government who in the past had furnished Civella correct and accurate information, thus leading him to believe the informants were responsible and trustworthy. Civella refused to name the sources, and Judge Becker denied the motion.

By March 1975 Civella was persisting in his assault on Judge Becker's impartiality. The setting was a pretrial hearing.

Civella rose from the defense table to address the court. He asked the judge to disqualify himself, making it clear he was doing so without his attorney's knowledge. Civella complained that the court had discussed the situation with the man who later was chosen as the independent court-appointed handwriting expert. In this conversation, which took place before his selection, the expert made known his previous opinion in a similar documents case favoring the government, leading to the question of his impartiality.

"With concern for the consequences of this next statement, I feel I must make it," Civella said. "I submit that this court's actions in this matter were highly questionable, improper and probably illegal. So once again in the interests of justice I would implore you to withdraw from this case."

With patience and restraint, Judge Becker granted the defense time to find a handwriting expert to make the examination, further delaying the course of justice. Civella again rose to debate the issue at hand. Judge Becker instructed him to confer with his attorney about matters to be raised with the court, to which Civella responded, "We are represented by frightened counsel and you've done a good job of frightening them at this hearing today."

Finally, the trial was scheduled for April 1975, four and one-half years after the first indictment was returned. Then, Judge Becker transferred the case to another judge, creating yet another delay. On May 4, the case would be tried before Judge William Collinson in Springfield, Missouri.

ALL OUT OF LEGAL MANEUVERS, Civella was forced to bow to the weight of wiretap evidence and gave in. Once a trial began, he realized, he couldn't beat the case. That was the beauty of electronic surveillance. On May 5, 1975, Civella, his nephew Tony Civella, gambling chief Frank Tousa and bookmaking subagent Joseph "King" Barletta signed stipulations acknowledging the government's conspiracy charge, and waived a trial by jury.

Judge William Collinson, now presiding, formalized the matter, finding the defendants guilty, ordering a pre-sentence investigation and advising the parties there would be no plea-bargaining. To the benefit of the defendants, Collinson barred the government from their normal practice of recommending a sentence.

So much for the dangerous offenders provision. Apparently, in the judge's eyes the Landie murder was not considered an affront to the criminal justice system. It was another windfall for the Outfit members. Throughout the case, they had whined constantly about selective prosecution and prejudice against Italian-Americans.

The judge's rulings laid waste to those complaints. Two months later, five of the defendants were back in court for sentencing. Nick Civella, Tony Civella, Tousa and Thomas Fontanello all received sentences of 3½ years. The Civellas were fined $5,000, and the other two were fined $2,000. Defendant Philip Saladino had died, and Joseph Barletta received a two-year sentence. Once again, sentences meted out to hard-core organized crime figures fell short of the maximum called for by the law they were convicted of.

WHAT DOES A BOOKMAKER like Frank Tousa do to keep busy

and make a living while free on bond under indictment for gambling? For Tousa it was easy. He simply went back to what he did best, running the Outfit's bookmaking operation.

As surely as night follows the day, the Family's gambling operations continued unabated — despite the 1970 raid on the Office and the charges that came afterward. Just as surely, the FBI kept pace with the changing face of the enterprise, its structure and the identities of the players. Tousa's management role in the continuing operation of the sports book was established and the principal participants identified.

An application for electronic surveillance of the operation was approved by the Department of Justice, and the documents outlining the operation and Tousa's role in it were submitted to a judge in 1973. The judge happened to be William Collinson. In 1973, he was still two years away from receiving the original gambling case, the one that centered on the operation at the Trap in which Tousa had been indicted and was free on bond.

On October 5, 1973, wiretaps were activated on three residence telephones and two telephones at the Necco Tea & Coffee Co. at 3616 Independence Ave. A secret microphone also was placed at Necco. It was the first of two 20-day periods of authorized electronic surveillance.

The gambling book was in full swing and the electronic surveillance proved productive in widening the net for those contributing to the operation. On December 9, 1973, FBI agents fanned out to execute search warrants for Frank Tousa and three other bookmakers, and also to execute a search warrant at the Trap. The agents seized cash and gambling records. The search warrants issued by Judge Collinson and the affidavit accompanying the request for them provided a broad view of the bookmaking network and Tousa's role in it.

By April 1975 Judge Collinson had inherited the Civella *et al* case, and in July that year presided over sentencing. Collinson had the benefit of the extensive evidence of Tousa's continued management of the Outfit book while he was under indictment. Nevertheless, he handed down a sentence that was less than the maximum called for.

Some five months after that sentencing, Tousa and 12 other subjects, including three leading bookmakers, John A. Costanza, Peter J. Simone and John J. Sciortino, were charged with conducting an illegal gambling business in two separate indictments stemming from the 1973 investigation. Despite a slam-dunk government case, Tousa and Costanza chose to put the government to the test and expense of a trial. It took the jury all of two hours to find them guilty.

Tousa once again stood before Judge Collinson to be sentenced. Would Tousa's utter disregard for the justice system, violating conditions of his bond and continuing to foster a vital activity of the Family, have any impact? Apparently not.

Tousa was sentenced to three years to run concurrently with his earlier 3½ -year sentence. Effectively, Tousa received no additional time. Even as a repeat offender and the main cog in the bookmaking operation, he fared better than any of the others.

The sentences in both organized gambling cases presided over by Collinson would deter no one from entering the gambling arena or from becoming involved with mobsters. Nor would they deter the Family itself from continuing its operations.

TWENTY DAYS AFTER BEING SENTENCED and while still free on an appeal bond, Nick Civella on July 30, 1975, entered Menorah Hospital for examination. He remained there five days. The diagnosis was grim: bladder cancer. Four months later, he went under the knife at the University of California Los Angeles Medical Center.

The Nick Civella who returned to Kansas City was described as a shadow of his former self, and there were predictions that his days were numbered. Among other things, Civella's health problems would lead to new legal strategies that further delayed his going to prison.

It stood to reason that his illness and need for medical care along with his court woes would preoccupy Civella for some time to come. Out of necessity, his role in Outfit affairs was restricted and that would have ramifications he could not have foreseen.

AT THE VERY TIME HIS BROTHER'S ILLNESS was discovered, Cork Civella decided to quit his long-running wholesale meat business. Looking back, the reason seems more than coincidental. Clearly, he was taking up for his brother, moving into the mainstream of the Family's business and involving himself in day-to-day operations.

Cork Civella — white-wigged, flamboyant and often volatile – had always been considered a ranking member of and a force in the Kansas City Crime Family. Until now, however he had been overshadowed by Nick

Civella. After the death in 1968 of Thomas Simone, considered the No. 2 man in the Outfit, Nick Civella promoted Carl DeLuna to a position akin to "street boss," overseeing ongoing operations and considered heir apparent. But blood is thicker than water, and when the time came Cork Civella took the reins while DeLuna remained street boss.

Cork became a fixture in the City Market, holding court at the DeFeo Produce Co., and a regular at the Trap. He represented a change in the order of things, bringing a style and philosophy different from that of his brother. Nick Civella favored an approach more reasoned and thoughtful and less volatile than his brother's. There is little question that the new leadership dynamic affected the course of events transpiring in the River Quay and on other fronts.

CHAPTER XII

RIVER QUAY 3

ONE LOOK AS HIS FATHER WALKED IN THE DOOR of Poor Freddie's was enough to signal Freddy Bonadonna that trouble was in the wind. You were right, David Bonadonna told his son: Willie and Joe Cammisano are now saying that you fooled them, that you made an ass out of Willie, and that you haven't done a thing to help Joe get his liquor license.

Initially, the Cammisano brothers had been told that the person responsible for getting Joe's license freed up was Nelson Martin, who was then Liquor Control night supervisor and a Bonadonna nemesis. It was reported that Martin had been ordered by his director to stop associating with people connected to organized crime. Subsequently, David continued, the Cammisanos were told the responsible party was none other than State Representative Alex Fazzino.

Either way, Willie believed that the help had come from someone other than Freddy Bonadonna. That led to a knock-down drag-out argument between David Bonadonna and Willie Cammisano, and a falling out between them.

If that's what they want to think, Freddy said, then screw them.

Of course, it was not as simple as that. Right or wrong, his father warned, an angry Willie Cammisano meant that Freddy was in danger, and the situation could get David killed. Be cautious who comes around you, David told his son, especially any of the North End element. Don't leave your car in the lot out back, the elder Bonadonna continued, and if you have a gun carry it.

As for himself, David was old school; he knew the ways of the Outfit and thought he could take care of himself. Freddy pleaded with his father to quit hanging around Willie at the garage. That plea fell on deaf ears.

Rather than let things sit, Bonadonna father and son agreed to make one more try at peacemaking. As usual, Willie Cammisano was at his garage but he would not talk inside, insisting they go out to a car. David got in the back seat and Freddy in the driver's seat. Cammisano, ever on guard and wary, sat down on the passenger side but left the door open, planting his feet on the sidewalk.

From the beginning, Cammisano went on the attack. He called both Bonadonnas liars, accusing Freddy of trying to make a fool out him. He also said he knew Freddy hadn't done a damned thing to help his brother; he knew who really had gotten Joe the liquor license. Cammisano and David Bonadonna got out of the car and went at each other hot and heavy, the elder Bonadonna telling Cammisano that he was just as tough as he. The rift between the two men was widening rapidly.

A period of quiet followed, which those savvy in the ways of Cosa Nostra know to be a dangerous omen. After the argument, David Bonadonna stayed away from Willie Cammisano until the day before Christmas 1975, when Willie made an overture, inviting Dave to come back into the fold. That, too, represented a dangerous omen. There is an adage that says, Keep your friends close and your enemies closer.

JOE CAMMISANO, PROBABLY FEELING that everything had gone his way, made it crystal clear what was in store for the River Quay when he was quoted September 11, 1975, in *The Kansas City Star*. In his view, limiting the number of liquor licenses in the Quay was a bad idea.

"If a man has got money and wants to invest it," Cammisano said, "I don't think anybody should stop it."

Now he was of the mind to petition the Liquor Control Department to release him from his commitment not to employ go-go girls or exotic dancers.

"Why would they want to stop go-go girls?" he asked. "I don't think they should hold me to it."

And to Quay merchants interested in preserving the historical nature of the area, he had this to say: "The biggest whorehouse that was ever in Kansas City was on Delaware. There were saloons and whores. They ought to ask their fathers and grandfathers about it."

For anyone wondering whether this was simply Joe being Joe, shooting off his mouth, the answer came not long after he opened his bar. There, on the building housing Uncle Joe's, was a huge signboard picturing a scantily clad woman announcing, GIRLS-GIRLS-GIRLS.

ABOUT THE SAME TIME, one of Willie Cammisano's sons started dropping in afternoons at Poor Freddie's. Freddy Bonadonna took the opportunity to express his hope that Willie Cammisano understood he wasn't looking to make anyone angry with him. His greatest desire, he said, was to put an ugly situation to rest. It was suggested to Freddy that he express those sentiments personally to Willie, and it might help if Councilman Hernandez accompanied him. His hopes raised, Freddy asked Hernandez to come down: It was a matter of great urgency.

Hernandez listened as Freddy brought him up to date, explaining how Willie Cammisano believed Freddy had failed to help Joe Cammisano with his license, leading to bad blood between the Bonadonnas and the Cammisanos. Hernandez agreed to accompany Freddy and they headed to Willie's place on Monroe Avenue.

There, Hernandez was introduced to and shook hands with Willie. Bonadonna began by saying they had come to clear the air, to explain exactly what he had done to help Joe Cammisano and to put an end to the feud.

However, there would be no explaining. Willie exploded before Bonadonna could utter another word.

I don't care who got the license, Willie screamed.

Hernandez tried to get a word in edgewise in Freddy's behalf, but Willie ranted on, telling how he would kill every S.O.B. in this town who jacked with his brother. And if his brother wanted to use go-go girls, wanted to run whores, whatever he wanted to do he could, and any S.O.B. who got in the way, including politicians, Willie would kill them and go to jail forever. Unaware of exactly who Willie Cammisano was, and also unaware of his fearsome reputation, Hernandez started arguing, believing he could use his city position as a shield. That only fueled the fire in Cammisano's belly and he ranted on. Willie finally settled down, but seeing the situation as hopeless, Bonadonna and Hernandez left.

Hernandez was angry and shaken, telling Bonadonna it had been like a scene from "The Godfather." Bonadonna tried to downplay the incident, saying that's just how Willie was and he didn't mean anything by it. Freddy let his father know what had happened. Again he was instructed to be cautious and alert to his surroundings, and to stay armed.

IN NOVEMBER 1975, FREDDY had started to wilt under the pressure of intense personal attacks and bitter conflict over the second parking lot, the one on the south. Articles in *The River Quay Journal* labeled him the "parking lot hog."

After operating the controversial south lot for eight or nine months, he decided to walk away. At a meeting of the River Quay Bar and Restaurant Association, Bonadonna announced that the south lot was available, and he made suggestions about how to use it for the benefit of owners and customers. Willis Castle, the City Market manager, also contacted people interested in the lot, confirming that the south lot was available and inviting them to his City Market office to work out a deal.

By April 1976, the lot still sat unrented. Castle was on the phone asking whether Bonadonna wanted to take it back. Understandably reluctant, Freddy first called *The River Quay Journal* and asked that it publicize the lot's availability. From all of Bonadonna's tormentors there was no response. When Castle again offered the lot, Freddy took it.

Incredibly, at a meeting of the Bar and Restaurant Association Bonadonna once again was confronted about the lot and pressured to give it up. That was the last straw. He let loose, defiantly reminding the assembled group that twice its members had had the opportunity to lease the lot, and twice they had done nothing. The lot was his and there was no one in the room, including Joe Cammisano, who was going to make him give it up again.

Joe Cammisano chimed in, claiming he knew a way to make Freddy give up the lot; there were people in town who could handle that. Defiantly, Bonadonna told Cammisano there wasn't anyone he knew who could scare him into giving up the lot.

Not long after the meeting Bonadonna got an urgent call from Castle, who asked him to see him right away. Castle told of receiving two phone calls from Nick Arello, who owned Papa Nick's and who was president of the Bar and Restaurant Association. Arello wanted the lease on the parking lot starting in July; he offered six months' advance rent. He was told he would have to contact Bonadonna.

After Arello's calls, Castle said, he came under pressure from high political figures, and he implored Freddy to give up the lot. Castle was at first reluctant to identify who was exerting the pressure, but Bonadonnna finally got him to acknowledge the name — State Representative Alex Fazzino. The heavy hand of the Cammisanos, Freddy saw, lay behind the move.

What would you do if your boss told you I could keep the lot? Bonadonna asked Castle. I always obey my boss, Castle responded. So, playing his ace card, Bonadonna called Councilman Hernandez, asking whether it was right for him to be forced to give up the south parking lot if it was properly maintained and the rent paid. Soon, word came down to Castle that Freddy could keep the lot, and that Castle was right in directing inquiries to Bonadonna. That must have infuriated the Cammisanos.

Payback came quickly. Parking lots signs were ripped down or splattered with paint and broken glass was strewn around the lot. Bonadonna's son and some high school kids he had working the lot were hassled. Bonadonna's car was sideswiped three times, windows at his business were broken and entertainers on retainer were hired away.

Freddy reported each incident to his father, who continually cautioned him to be extremely careful, to avoid anyone he suspected was remotely connected to the Crime Family. David identified Family members about whom Freddy should be particularly worried. Freddy had grave concerns but he thought he would be all right as long as his father was alive. That was the way of things in the world of the Family. David Bonadonna was part of that world. He was capable — meaning capable in the use of force, even murder. No one would harm Freddy as long as they knew his father would respond in kind.

FREDDY BONADONNA DID NOT HAVE the pleasure of Willie Cammisano's company again until March 1976. The meeting was occasioned by an event on March 13 of that year, when Freddy's teenage son was home alone. Three men broke into the house, put a baseball bat to the boy's head, threw him into the bathroom and cleaned out the house. At first Freddy was inclined to mark it up as a simple robbery, just bad luck for him and his son. Later David Bonadonna would tell Freddy that the robbery was, in fact, a warning.

With that in mind, Freddy Bonadonna paid Willie Cammisano a visit, asking him to be on the lookout for any stolen merchandise being offered around because it might have come from the burglary and theft at the Bonadonna residence. Fat chance that Willie would lift a finger on Freddy's behalf; the approach was a ploy on Freddy's part allowing him the opportunity to describe in detail the security precautions he had since taken for his home. In turn, Willie took the opportunity to warn Bonadonna that he had better get out of politics, leave Hernandez alone and stick to running his place.

At his wits' end, his family put in grave risk, Freddy proposed to his father that he simply surrender, give up the parking lots, quit everything, whatever they wanted. David was emphatic in rejecting the idea, telling Freddy he was to give up nothing. A line had been drawn in the sand and David Bonadonna was finished doing Cammisano's or anyone else's bidding. They had gone too far and now Freddy was to tell anyone who had a beef to go to hell and take it to David Bonadonna.

IT APPEARED THAT THERE WAS NO END IN SIGHT to the conflict buffeting the River Quay and Freddy Bonadonna. Joe Cammisano remained front and center, joining John Amaro and Lonnie Roccaforte in a new venture. In May 1976, Cammisano applied for a liquor license for Il-Pagliacci House of Pasta at 400 Wyandotte St., formerly the site of Mama Angelina's. The place became available when Ross Abbate, the husband of Mama Angelina's former owner of record, got caught up in a deadly soap-opera affair, murdered by the cook over a liaison Abbate had with the cook's wife. The license application for Il-Pagliacci was held up by Councilman Hernandez's moratorium, leading the Cammisano group to exert pressure every place it could. Adding insult to injury, Hernandez told them that, if they wanted a license in the River Quay, they had to go through the Bonadonnas.

The license for Il-Pagliacci was denied in June 1976. The Cammisano group appealed the ruling and a hearing was set for June 23. Just before the hearing date, two of the three members of the Liquor Control appeal board disqualified themselves. Denver Vold and Tom Tierney cited conflicts of interest; they acted as legal counsel to individuals and entities in the River Quay. The license denial stood.

About midnight of the day Tierney announced he was disqualifying himself he got a call from a fuming Joe Cammisano. Cammisano called him names, and warned Tierney that nobody crossed him. Tierney was shaken. Because Alex Fazzino had called him earlier, asking him to help Cammisano if he could, Tierney decided to complain to him. The next day he told Fazzino that he was not getting involved in the matter and to keep Cammisano away from him.

The news of Joe Cammisano's setback put David Bonadonna on extra-high alert. He told Freddy to consider himself at war, meaning it was imperative he take every precaution for himself and his family. They want you out of politics, David said, and they want you to give up the parking lots and the business. However, he continued, I told Willie Cammisano you were not giving up anything.

There was no more pretense. David had come right out with a warning to Willie: if any move was made against his kids they would have to deal with him. More than likely, David Bonadonna had signed his death warrant.

Indeed, David predicted he was going to be killed by Willie Cammisano. Once that happened, he told Freddy, within three months they will come after you. When I'm killed, he said, you will not last, so you'll have to flee the city.

David had accepted back in December 1975 Willie's invitation to come back around, just like old times. The friendly overture, David knew, was meant only to keep him close. He was fully aware that was how the mob operated: Put you at ease and act outwardly cordial and friendly until the right time and place came to safely commit murder.

ON JULY 22, 1976, A THURSDAY, the right time and place arrived. At 2:18 p.m. that day an anonymous caller reported to the Kansas City Police that a dark green Mustang was parked on Wabash Avenue between Eighth and Ninth streets, behind an apartment complex, with a "bunch of blood running out of the trunk."

Police found the car at the rear of the Chip Village Apartments, 2310 E. Ninth St. What appeared to be blood was, indeed, leaking from the right side of the trunk. Forcing open the lid, the officers looked down on the body of 61-year-old David Bonadonna.

The elder Bonadonna had been shot beside the left ear. He was wearing an orange shirt that, ironically, Willie Cammisano had given him as a present. The autopsy revealed Bonadonna had been shot five times, all apparently with a .32-caliber automatic.

The next day homicide detectives Pete Edlund and Clarence Gibson came upon a critical piece of information. Sometime between 10 a.m. and 11 a.m. the day of the murder, an attendant at the Mobile Service Station at 3600 Independence Ave., had seen a black-vinyl-over-green 1965 or 1966 Ford Mustang with wire-spoked hub caps back out of a garage or a driveway by the garage on the West side of Monroe Avenue. The description matched David Bonadonna's car, the one in which he was found dead, and the garage where it was seen was only a half a block from Independence Avenue and the service station.

The attendant, who clearly knew his cars, told detectives his attention was drawn by the driver's difficulty in handling a manual shift, the very kind of transmission in David Bonadonna's Mustang.

Two garage-style buildings, separated by an alley, stood in the area pointed to by the witness. One of them, at 536 Monroe Avenue., belonged to Willie Cammisano. Willie's place, it was learned, was locked up the afternoon Bonadonna's body was found. Willie would tell homicide detectives he had not seen David Bonadonna on July 22, but had seen him the day before. That was when Willie gave his close friend three shirts, one of which he understood David was wearing when his body was found.

Freddy Bonadonna last talked with his father earlier that week. On the evening before his father's body was found, Freddy turned in early, suffering with an ear infection. After a visit to the doctor the next day, he headed down to the Quay about 4:30 or 5 o'clock. Because it was too early for work, Freddy changed his mind and instead went to visit the father of his godchild. It was left to his distraught friend to break the news to Freddy that someone named Bonadonna had been found in the trunk of a Mustang.

Freddy felt as if his heart had been hit with a hammer. He called his brother, hoping it was not their father. Of course, it was. Family members gathered at Poor Freddie's. Meanwhile, a traumatized Freddy Bonadonna had to throw himself into something, so he went to the basement and started to clean it out.

Surely, the final straws were the failed appeal of Joe Cammisano's liquor license denial, which occurred less than a month before the murder, the fact that Freddy still ran all the parking lots, and the fact he was still the man to see in the River Quay.

Consumed with the loss of his father, and fearful for his and his family's well being, Freddy Bonadonna quit his memberships in various Quay organizations, terminated the leases on the parking lots and avoided his political associates. He put out word that he wanted to meet with the Outfit's street boss, Carl DeLuna, but DeLuna had no interest.

ARMED AT ALL TIMES, Freddy Bonadonna no longer worked

nights at Poor Freddie's nor did he go out at all at night unless he was in the company of trusted people he had known for years. His burglar alarm at home was engaged night and day and floodlights remained on all night. He kept a weapon within easy reach, and he even avoided his backyard pool unless with a group. Freddy Bonadonna was in a state of siege.

The burden of working every night was too much for his brother Tony Mike, so Freddy agreed to relieve him on Thursday nights. He no longer greeted his customers, preferring to stay in the background. Friends warned him about parked cars with people inside who watched the place. Afraid that a bomb would be planted in his car, he traded it in for a new one his wife would use. It contained an alarm. For his exclusive use, Bonadonna bought another car, installed an alarm in it, too, along with a Citizens Band radio and had the windows darkly tinted. He was in contact with the police, and the FBI arranged for him to have a bulletproof vest.

One morning he found a message scrawled across the hood of his new car hood: "Hi, Fred. We were here."

At 3 o'clock one morning he was awakened by the blaring of the car alarm. Someone had popped the car trunk, apparently unaware of the alarm. It confirmed his fear that they would try to kill him with a car bomb.

The River Quay was a dead zone. Business at Poor Freddie's fell off badly and that, combined with the pressure from Freddy's enemies, persuaded the brothers to sell. There was no rush of buyers. Only one bargain-basement offer of $18,000 was forthcoming. Had the mob put out the word that no one was even to think about buying the place? Probably.

HIS FATHER MURDERED, himself a marked man, the River Quay finished and his business up for sale, Freddy Bonadonna still had to endure the wrath of the Cammisanos. This time it was caused by a visit to Willie's garage on August 7, 1976, by the FBI and the Kansas City Police, armed with a search warrant. The search-warrant affidavit, filed in U.S. District Court late that afternoon, detailed the whole sordid River Quay story. Joe and Willie Cammisano played starring roles culminating in the murder of David Bonadonna, which was laid at their doorstep. That afternoon *The Kansas City Star* printed the story in an article by J.J. Maloney headlined, "FBI Ties Killing to Showdown over Quay."

Shortly afterward, Freddy's brother DD Bonadonna got in touch with Freddy and told him he had met with the Cammisanos. They were upset with the unfavorable publicity they had received in *The Star* and wanted Fred to speak in their defense.

Are you crazy? Freddy asked his brother. There was no way he would do anything of the sort.

DD grew angry. He berated Freddy and accused him of causing their father's murder.

On the heels of his brother's approach, Freddy found Willie's son Vince Cammisano sitting in Poor Freddie's waiting for him. Vince proclaimed that his father would not have killed David Bonadonna and asked why Freddy remained mute in the face of the bad publicity.

Freddy replied that he was willing to do anything to put an end to his nightmare and to the pressure the Bonadonna family was experiencing. Vince suggested a visit to *The Star* with a statement that Freddy Bonadonna did not believe Willie Cammisano was responsible for his father's murder. That, Vince suggested, would take the pressure off.

The thought of it was sickening, but Freddy believed he had to try. On August 12, 1976, brothers Freddy, Tony Mike and DD Bonadonna, along with Vince and Willie Cammisano Jr., appeared at *The Kansas City Star* building at 18th Street and Grand Avenue to be interviewed by reporter J.J. Maloney. Following the script, Freddy told Maloney that Willie Cammisano had been like a father to his family and could not have been involved in his father's murder.

Maloney, however, had sized up the situation. Instead of writing an article in narrative style and focusing on what Freddy and the others had to say, he set out verbatim excerpts of the interview, complete with Maloney's retorts. The article did not have the effect that the Cammisanos were looking for, and they no doubt placed the blame on Freddy.

The River Quay was in free fall. In December 1976 a headline in *The Kansas City Star* trumpeted, "Exodus of Taverns Strikes Quay," reporting that 11 liquor establishments had closed down along with two other business enterprises and now the Warehouse had closed after a fire the previous week — all in an area that once had been prominently featured in the Prime Time campaign of the Chamber of Commerce.

After the murder of David Bonadonna, the business manager of a closed delicatessen said: "People were afraid to go down there. I've talked to a lot of people who didn't want to be down there after dark."

CHAPTER XIII

BOMBING OF THE TRAP

THE HANGOUT CALLED THE TRAP, now officially renamed the Columbus Park Social Club, resembled a storefront. It was part of a four-story brick building owned by Nick Civella, and stood at 1048 E. Fifth St., just west of Troost Avenue, in Kansas City's North End.

For years, the Trap served as a gathering place for members and associates of the Civella Crime Family. There they socialized, conducted business and engaged in high-stakes card and dice games, a daily menu item. In more favorable times — before it was raided twice by the FBI — the Trap had been the hub for Outfit bookmaking operations.

At 1:20 a.m. on September 29, 1976, only three people were at the Trap when someone threw a pipe bomb at the sheet-metal-lined back door. The explosion blew the door off its hinges. The club suffered damage, but none of the three people inside was injured. The bombing was not an attempt to kill anyone, ATF and local investigators agreed, but rather was meant as a warning.

Such a brazen, overt act directed at a place symbolizing the Civella organization represented a threat to the established criminal order. No doubt, there would be retaliation — whatever steps were necessary to save face and erase any perception that the Outfit had lost control.

Suspicion immediately fell on Freddy Bonadonna. As that reasoning went, the bombing was an act of retribution for the murder of his father and for his being stalked. If those suspicions were correct, the Outfit more than ever would want to put Freddy down. As it turned out, things were more complicated than that.

MOST OFTEN THERE ARE unintended consequences from acts like the bombing of the Trap. It seemed to solidify the Family, and Willie

Cammisano was an example. Until the bombing, from outward appearances, he had not been on intimate terms with the core of the Family. Some viewed Cammisano as acting independently, yet — as a "made" member of the Family — never doing so in a way that would create conflict. Cammisano maintained a low profile, avoided open association with other members at the Trap or various night spots and kept his own circle of associates. That lent credence to reports he was not a Nick Civella favorite and led to speculation about his true position. A clearer picture, however, was emerging.

Coinciding with Cork Civella's entry into the Outfit mainstream, the murder of David Bonadonna and the bombing of the Trap, Cammisano closed ranks with the core members of the Family. Now, FBI agents and police detectives found, Cammisano participated in strategy sessions and associated openly with other crime figures at the Trap. That was critical in presenting a unified front, and the timing could not have been better. The organization would have to confront what was loosely labeled the Carl Spero faction.

AT 2:30 A.M. THREE DAYS AFTER THE BOMBING of the Trap, the telephone rang in the home of Albert Brandmeyer in Leawood, Kansas. The alarm company was on the line, reporting an attempted break-in at Brandmeyer's Mohawk Meat Co., 1615 E. Eighth St. Throwing on his clothes, Brandmeyer hurried to the company. There he discovered that a hole had been made in the building large enough for a man to crawl through, but nothing else was amiss. Nothing further to be accomplished, he returned home.

It was a short night. Before 6 a.m. Brandmeyer returned to the company. Shortly after he arrived, there came a knock at the door. Opening it, he found a man brandishing a revolver.

The robber took $9,000 in cash and $10,000 in checks and forced Brandmeyer to drive him to 30th Street and Tracy Avenue, where the assailant made Brandmeyer climb into the trunk of the car. Before fleeing, the robber pumped five shots through the back seat and into the trunk. Were it not for the protection of the spare tire, Brandmeyer would have been seriously wounded or killed.

Brandmeyer had for many years been a partner with Cork Civella in the B&C Meat Co. at 1119 E. 12th St. In 1960, Brandmeyer had been recruited to provide alibis for Felix Ferina and Tiger Cardarella in the attempted murder of Kenneth Bruce Sheetz. Civella ostensibly sold his interest in B&C around fall 1975, and Brandmeyer moved the business, changing the name to Mohawk Meat Co. Whether or not Civella had actually divested himself of interest in the business was questionable; his longtime paramour Donna Rau had a financial interest in Mohawk, and other circumstances indicated Civella retained a hidden stake.

The robbery and assault of Brandmeyer had all the earmarks of having been orchestrated by someone with inside knowledge of the business. The way the robbery went down piqued investigators' interest. Why did the armed robber have to kidnap Brandmeyer and then shoot up the car, potentially resulting in a homicide? It seemed something else was in play besides a simple robbery. Was someone delivering a message? Within weeks, an answer was forthcoming.

About October 22, 1976, a Kansas City Police detective identified Leonard "Arab" Crego as the culprit. Crego had ties to Carl Spero, John Brocato and John Cuezze. In the past, Cuezze had been a part of B&C Meat Co.

Crego was an imposing, scary character. He had served time in prison and his chances for parole had hinged partly on showing he had a job lined up. Reportedly, Carl Spero arranged for Crego to be hired at the Ozark Meat Co. in Springfield, Missouri, which was operated by Spero's pal Cuezze. Ozark Meat was one of several bait-and-switch meat outlets that had cropped up in various parts of the country, masterminded by Kansas City lawyer Patrick R. Faltico.

Law enforcement uncovered information that Crego, Carl Spero and John Brocato had teamed on various "scores." Spero had also carried Crego as an employee of the Feron Basement Co. in Blue Springs, Missouri, a company begun by Jimmy Feron and later taken over by Spero. Symbolic of what seems to befall people in the clutches of organized crime, on November 2, 1980, Jimmy Feron's body was found in a ditch beside Cement City Road, an isolated part of Sugar Creek. Missouri. Feron had been shot five times in the head at close range. Police later found his pickup truck parked in the lot of the Morgan Steak House on Blue Ridge in Independence, Missouri. The murder was never solved.

As for B&C-Mohawk and Brandmeyer, the pieces lined up. Cuezze, a Spero pal, had worked there and Crego was Spero's boy. Spero was doing all he could to embarrass the outfit, and B&C-Mohawk was an Outfit-connected operation. Everything pointed directly to Carl Spero's having set up the Mohawk Meat Co. caper.

Cork Civella's longtime connection to the company made it a symbol of the Family; an attack on the company was an attack on the Civellas. After the Mohawk Meat assault, Spero moved to the top of the Outfit's list of suspects in the bombing of the Trap. Such acts of defiance meant someone would have to pay — someone like John Brocato.

CHAPTER XIV

JOHN BROCATO, THE CREDIT UNION OF AMERICA AND MURDER

IN THE MACHIAVELLIAN WORLD OF COSA NOSTRA, relationships are often contradictory and convoluted. Even members of the family, let alone outsiders, never really know who is friend or foe, or when friend becomes foe and vice versa. According to Freddy Bonadonna, after his father's murder John Brocato started spending time at Poor Freddie's. Already on edge and leery of strangers, Freddy was puzzled by and suspicious about this turn of events. Had the outfit sent this person to set him up?

He discussed his fears with brother Tony Mike, and was told that he need not worry. Brocato had a history with the Cammisanos and had no use for them. In fact, Brocato and Carl Spero were extremely close.

However, if Freddy was initially puzzled he would have been downright confounded if he had known that Brocato also was close with John Amaro. Amaro had strong ties to the Outfit, which soon would be looking to kill Spero. Amaro also had ties to the Cammisanos, and was helping them in their pilgrimage to infiltrate the Quay and destroy Freddy Bonadonna.

Brocato was under investigation in connection with an arson fire at the Central Envelope Co. at 541 Central Ave. in Kansas City, Kansas, on December 7, 1975. The fire resulted in $25,000 in damage. A witness observed five-gallon plastic containers being transferred into the company from a pickup truck that was traced to Brocato.

Adding to his legal woes, Brocato become entangled in a Federal Housing Administration loan-fraud scheme along with a number of River Quay and organized crime figures, uncovered by police detectives in Kansas.

OVERLAND PARK INTELLIGENCE UNIT detectives Don Palmer and Dave Lequire, both savvy investigators, were an integral part of a brotherhood of local and federal officers dedicated to organized crime matters. On a routine work day in March 1976, they received a tip from a Prairie Village Police detective that well-known criminal figures Joe Boothman and Benny Avery were visiting with a manager at the Credit Union of America office at 9760 Metcalf Ave. in Overland Park. According to evidence developed later, John Brocato had gone to the credit union with the two.

Palmer and Lequire, their interest piqued, dropped what they were doing and drove to the credit union office, where they saw a car with Missouri license plates. They followed Boothman and Avery — evidently Brocato already had left — from the credit union to the Valley View Bank on 95th Street and watched as the two men entered the bank. Now extremely intrigued, the detectives followed them back to Missouri, and then returned to the bank to inquire. They learned that Boothman and Avery had cashed $7,500 checks written on the Credit Union of America.

Convinced there was something nefarious about what they had uncovered, Palmer called me at the FBI office, and within the hour Flosi and I met with him and Lequire. Despite a full plate of investigations at the time, we recognized that the alert detectives had uncovered something that needed to be addressed.

The ensuing investigation uncovered a sizable Federal Housing Administration loan fraud with links to the River Quay. Plagued by a myriad of interruptions, the case would be three years in the making.

As it turned out, the manager of the Credit Union of America, Larry Bellmeyer, had colluded with James Giordano, owner of Atlas Builders & Remodeling Experts in Kansas City, Missouri. They had devised a fairly simple plot involving FHA home-improvement loans. Giordano recruited individuals, who in turn recruited others, to apply for the loans. Bellmeyer approved the loans knowing the applications were falsified and the loans would not be repaid. Most active in recruiting loan prospects, among them Boothman and Avery, was John Brocato, who accompanied six individuals when it was time for Bellemeyer to approve their loans.

Twenty loans of $7,500 each had been approved by Bellmeyer and a share of the loan money was kicked back to him. When we executed a search warrant at the Credit Union of America, we found a drawer full of loan applications that were part of the scheme but not yet approved.

Boothman, Avery, Bellmeyer and Giordano were indicted and charged with fraud against the government. Giordano pleaded guilty and received five years in prison. Bellmeyer cooperated fully with the FBI, agreeing to wear a wire, and in return received a one-year sentence, all but 60 days suspended, and two years probation. Avery and Boothman chose to stand trial.

During their trial, Strike Force attorneys introduced 17 pending loan applications as part of the scheme. Among others, the loans went to River Quay figures Joe Cammisano, Louis Ribaste, Lonnie Roccaforte and Angelo Vitale. Outfit member Peter Simone, car dealer Joe Sivigliano and jewel thieves Frank Robertson and Jimmy Joe Sollome also were identified as having received loan money.

Because the jury was unable to reach a verdict, Boothman and Avery at first went free. Then they were retried and both were found guilty and sentenced to five years in prison. In 1981 Louis Ribaste, the former River Quay bar owner, pleaded guilty to charges stemming from the investigation, receiving a 60-day sentence followed by a two-year probation. He was the other loan recipient charged.

THE LEGAL ENTANGLEMENTS BROCATO faced were substantial. His association with Carl Spero, however, was a cross Brocato would have to bear.

In mid-afternoon on the first day of November 1976, John Brocato was believed to have stopped at a North Kansas City gasoline station to fill his tank. He was never seen again.

Fifteen days passed before one of his brothers filed a missing-person report. Magically, the very next day another Brocato brother — claiming he was "acting on a hunch" — made a run to Kansas City International Airport. In the short-term parking lot, he found John Brocato's car and called two of his siblings to join him. The three Brocato boys opened the trunk and there, stuffed inside, was the body of their brother, 32-year-old John Brocato.

Airport records revealed that Brocato's 1975 Chevrolet Caprice had entered the short-term lot on November 8 and been logged there each day afterward. The coroner ruled that Brocato died from strangulation three to five days before the body was placed in the trunk. That implied that he had been murdered nearly two weeks before he was found. Parts of his body were frozen; overnight temperatures had fallen below freezing in those two weeks,

Blood trickled from the trunk of David Bonadonna's automobile in July 1976. His body, clad in a shirt given to him by Willie Cammisano, was stuffed in the trunk.

The Columbus Park Social Club, informally "the Trap," was the Outfit's headquarters. A bomb placed there in 1976 clearly was meant as a warning to the inner circle.

John Brocato, suspected in various criminal enterprises, wound up dead in the trunk of his car at Kansas City International Airport in November 1976.

From *The Kansas City Star*

and daytime temperatures had not been much warmer.

Brocato's family was reluctant to cooperate in the murder investigation, police were quoted as saying. The same was true of Brocato's associates, who feared retribution.

When reporters asked about the brother's impulse to search the parking lot at KCI, lead detective George Henthorn said: "There is no way in the world I'll believe he had a hunch to go up there. I believe there is more to it than that."

If, indeed, Brocato was last seen alive November 1, that would place his disappearance just nine days after a Kansas City Police detective identified Leonard Crego as having robbed, abducted, and attempted to murder Al Brandmeyer, a crime laid at the doorstep of Carl Spero.

How did these dots connect?

A plausible scenario would have Brocato lured in, swept off the streets, held captive and tortured to squeeze information out of him — information of vital interest to the Family. Who was behind the bombing of the Trap? Was he or Spero involved? Was Spero behind the Mohawk Meat caper? What is Spero plotting? Would Brocato cooperate and "deliver up" Carl Spero and Freddy Bonadonna to the Outfit?

Then Brocato was strangled and stuffed in his car trunk.

CHAPTER XV

RIVER QUAY 4

FREDDY BONADONNA'S WORLD was in turmoil. His father had been murdered, he was stalked by mob assassins and the River Quay and his business lay in ruins. John Brocato had appeared mysteriously at Poor Freddie's and then been murdered. Now, further complicating Freddy's life, two more unknowns appeared.

One was Harold "Sonny" Bowen, who had been one of the jewel thieves associated with Carl and Nick Spero. The other was Bowen's pal Gary T. Parker, known on the streets as "Parker T." Bowen was a friend of Tony Mike Bonadonna, but at first that was not enough to put Freddy Bonadonna at ease. He would soon discover there was a lot more to know about Bowen.

On January 19, 1976, Bowen was released from the California prison where he had served time for the robbery of a jewelry salesman in 1971 in Palo Alto. Bowen returned to Kansas City, but once a thief always a thief.

On March 7, 1976, he was arrested along with his old jewel-thieving running mate Johnny Joe Calia, who was still an ally of the Speros. Bowen and Calia were caught rifling the trunks of cars parked in the garage at Kansas City's Municipal Auditorium. The loot included several shotguns, and because both men were ex-felons they were indicted on April 2 for violating the Federal Firearms Act. The next day, Bowen pleaded guilty and received a one-year sentence followed by five years probation.

A month later Calia also pleaded guilty, but he received a stiffer sentence of three years followed by two years probation. The discrepancy in sentences was puzzling at first and then turned downright suspicious when Bowen was sent to nearby Leavenworth Penitentiary and Calia ended up almost 500 miles away at the federal prison in Texarkana, Texas. Although Calia later was transferred to Leavenworth, that did nothing to mitigate his ill feelings. He put out the word that Bowen had cooperated with the feds to save himself and could not be trusted. In support of his good buddy and jewel-robbery accomplice, Carl Spero lent his voice to Calia's, labeling Bowen as untrustworthy.

Bowen was under a dark cloud in late 1976 when he was released from prison to a halfway house and began frequenting Poor Freddie's. At first Freddy Bonadonna was leery of Bowen's intentions, wondering whether he was an Outfit plant seeking to set him up. Bonadonna changed his opinion when he found that, like himself, Bowen was a marked man and the two developed a friendship. That only cemented the Outfit's commitment to kill them both.

In mid-November 1976, about the same time that John Brocato's body was discovered at the airport, Freddy Bonadonna was awakened by an early-morning phone call. On the line was a shaken Sonny Bowen. After getting off work, Bowen said, he had gone to his car and found blood all over the back seat. Come over right now, he asked.

His mind racing, Bonadonna feared the call might be a ruse. He put Bowen off, agreeing to meet him later that morning. At 8:30 a.m. he arrived at his business just as Bowen pulled up.

Sure enough, the back seat of Bowen's car was stained with big splotches of blood. The seat fabric contained numerous small perforations. Under the floor carpet, the two found what appeared to be a small piece of a blasting cap. It didn't take a crime-scene expert to tell them that someone had tried to plant a bomb but had bumbled the job and been wounded when the cap detonated, pieces of it peppering the back seat. Bowen refused to call the police. Although assigned to a halfway house, technically he was still in custody and he feared being sent back to the penitentiary.

When Bowen took his car to have an alarm installed, it was discovered that the insulation of a tail light wire had been stripped — exactly what one does when wiring a car bomb.

Foolishly, Bowen let it be known that he planned to retaliate and that he had important members of the Outfit in his sights. Inevitably, word got back to them. It only encouraged the Family to re-double its efforts to murder Bowen.

Rumors began circulating that Freddy Bonadonna was recruiting people to join him and Bowen in challenging the Family. The rumors were false. Bonadonna was trying only to stay alive, and the only people helping him were in the same boat.

News that the mob was out to get Bowen reached Kansas City Police and the FBI's Organized Crime Squad. When law enforcement authorities find out that lives are threatened, they must warn the potential victim — even if the person is mobbed up and even if he has committed murder for the mob.

Agent Lee Flosi had spent long hours tracking mob-connected jewel thieves; on December 2, 1976, he looked up Sonny Bowen, told him he was the subject of an intense effort by the mob to kill him and offered protection. Bowen didn't argue, but he declined the offer of protection and rejected Flosi's recommendation that he leave the city. I'll be sure, he told Flosi, to alter my routine.

How reliable was Flosi's information? It had come from an informant who had personal access to Bowen and who had his trust. The informant had been ordered to make the hit and according to his instructions yesterday wasn't soon enough.

Complicating matters, Flosi and his informant were up against a Cosa Nostra tradition: anyone failing to carry out a murder assignment would be murdered. With Bowen standing fast despite imminent danger, and the informant in a precarious position, something had to be done.

A temporary solution lay in Bowen's custody status. He had not completed the prison sentence stemming from the federal firearms conviction, and parole authorities agreed that the seriousness of the matter warranted action. On December 7, 1976, Bowen was ordered back into custody and off he went to the Johnson County Jail. However, only 21 days remained on his sentence. Then he would be on a three-year probation and things would be back to Square One.

Flosi, along with Strike Force Chief David Helfrey and Bowen's attorney, Kenneth Simon, paid Bowen a visit. Again he declined any assistance and declined to cooperate. He also refused to consider a suggestion that he serve his probation anywhere but Kansas City.

Bowen walked out of jail on December 28, 1976, picking up where he left off, haunting Poor Freddie's with his pal Parker T. and his future very much in doubt.

MEANWHILE, WORD FROM THE STREET was that the Outfit was planning yet another murder. The intended victim was renegade Carl Spero. On December 9, 1976, Flosi and I found Spero on a jobsite and told him what we and the police were hearing. We impressed on him that he should accept as gospel what we were saying and assured him that we were not jacking him around, as many in organized crime believed when feds approached. Spero listened without much reaction or comment. It seemed he accepted that we were serious, but he refused our request for his cooperation, our offer of protection and our advice that he leave town.

BY NOW FREDDY BONADONNA WAS CONVINCED that Sonny Bowen posed no threat. Indeed, he saw Bowen as a lifeline because of his familiarity with many in the Family, so he enlisted Bowen and Parker T. to watch his back. Bonadonna wanted them to be around any night he was at work and to serve as his eyes and ears. After work, Bowen accompanied Bonadonna to his car and then tracked him until it was clear no one was stalking him. There were nights when Bowen recognized cars belonging to mob figures, requiring evasive action.

Joining the mix of characters frequenting Poor Freddie's was a rough-and-tumble character named Mike Ruffalo. Bonadonna in his early years had encountered Ruffalo, who was older, around the old North End neighborhood but he did not know him well. He recalled that Ruffalo lived on the wild side, had become an armed robber and associated with Outfit types in the North End.

As the story went, Ruffalo once committed so many robberies that he was forced to flee to California to escape the heat his crime spree had generated. A Kansas City Police official who had a channel to Outfit members confronted Cork Civella, threatening that all the Outfit's gambling operations would be shut down unless he made Ruffalo return to Kansas City and confess. Civella reached Ruffalo and ordered him back home, promising that if Ruffalo agreed to confess he would walk away with nothing more than a probationary term. Once back in Kansas City, Ruffalo discovered he had been had. No deal existed, and he was going to the slammer for up to five years.

Knowing that Ruffalo had been deceived by Cork Civella, Freddy Bonadonna could only hope that he posed no danger. Besides, Ruffalo was courting David Bonadonna's widow, his second wife and Freddy's stepmother, who worked at Poor Freddie's.

Unfortunately for Bonadonna, Mike Ruffalo was a man who wore many hats, and some would not be to his liking.

THE CLOCK WAS TICKING DOWN and Sonny Bowen knew it. He was preoccupied and obsessed with his own predicament, and with that of his new pal, Freddy Bonadonna. Both of their lives hung in the balance, but life had to go on.

In mid-February 1977 Bowen and his girlfriend went apartment hunting.

Of all places they could have chosen, the two settled on Apartment 303 in the Vivian Oaks Apartments at 5000 North Oak St. In the same complex lived Nelson Martin, the Liquor Control agent who had it in for Freddy Bonadonna. Manager of the apartments was Martin's wife, who was identified in a news account as having worked for Joe and Doris Cammisano. She handled the rental agreement for Bowen and his girlfriend. The move-in date was Friday, February 18.

Mrs. Martin would later tell agents she knew and liked Joe and Doris Cammisano as well as John Amaro and was acquainted with Willie Cammisano and Tony Civella. As for Freddy Bonadonna, she had "seen him and heard a lot about him and did not like him."

That night of February 18, Bowen and his girlfriend had dinner at their new apartment. About 11 p.m. he left and headed for the Quay to look after Freddy Bonadonna when closing time arrived. By the time his girlfriend was ready for bed, Bowen had not returned to the apartment. Some time in the early morning hours she was awakened when Bowen and Parker T. entered the apartment. Later, after Parker T. left, Bowen told her they had arrived at 4 a.m.

On the same Friday evening, John Amaro had followed a nightly routine. First he stopped at Uncle Joe's bar in the Quay to visit with his close friend, Joe Cammisano. After closing each night, the two were in the habit of heading up to Sambo's Restaurant on Burlington Street in North Kansas City. The place had become a gathering point for River Quay bar owners after closing hours.

On this evening, however, Cammisano had taken ill and left Uncle Joe's early. Amaro stayed till closing time, having drinks with Cammisano's son Charles, and then headed up to Sambo's, arriving about 2 a.m. It was now Saturday, February 19.

Amaro went to a table where Pat O'Brien and his date were seated and had a cup of coffee with them. A half-hour later, he left.

At 2:42 a.m., someone called 911 to report shots fired in a

neighborhood north of the river. A policeman was dispatched to 1508 N.E. 50th Terr. He was flagged down by John Amaro's wife, Bena Amaro, and directed to their residence. In the garage the officer found the body of John Amaro slumped in his car. He had been shotgunned and showed no sign of life.

Homicide detectives at the crime scene deduced that two men had ambushed Amaro as he pulled into the garage. The brunt of the wounds were on Amaro's left side. Death resulted from a single pellet that caused a massive wound at the top of his left shoulder, severing an artery and veins leading to the left aorta, and injuring his upper left lung.

On the ground outside the garage authorities found a blue suede leather athletic shoe. Across from the residence, on Flora Street, detectives noted that grass had been pressed down along a track apparently made by a car. At one end of the track they recovered a blue nylon windbreaker with a Falstaff beer design on the left breast. Nearby they found a white glove.

With daylight, the search expanded. It turned up the murder weapons, two shotguns recovered from a ditch on the north side of Vivion Road just west of Highland. The butt, stock and barrel of each were sawed off.

The ramifications of the murder were seismic. The Amaros lived just up the street from the residences of Nick Civella, his brother Cork Civella and his nephew Tony Civella. All were in Filumena Acres, a residential development that was also home to other Outfit associates. Committing a murder in Filumena Acres was the ultimate sign of disrespect and defiance toward the Family. Someone had tried to send a message that no one associated with the Outfit was safe anywhere.

This severe breech of mob protocol led to the conclusion that Amaro was slain by individuals outside the Family. That was supported by detectives' belief that the murder lacked the earmarks of a professional gangland execution.

Mob protocol nevertheless quashed any thought of cooperating with authorities. Relatives who gathered at the Amaro residence acted hostile toward investigators and refused to submit to interviews. What happened to the Family or within the Family would be handled by the Family.

Before the day was out, the Outfit was on to the responsible parties. Flosi's informant, the same one who had been ordered to murder Bowen, filled Flosi in on what took place. The informant, who enjoyed a personal relationship with Bowen, had been summoned to Bowen's apartment that morning, before news of the murder hit the airwaves. Bowen confided that he had murdered Amaro in the belief that the bold action would attract the informant to his cause. No matter what Bowen may have believed, however, the informant was under the thumb of the Family. He was obligated to report to them immediately what he had learned, and that is exactly what he did.

Machinery was put in motion to accomplish what in the eyes of the Outfit had been dragging on too long — Bowen's murder. The Outfit had been tracking him and it knew about his activities. Before Bowen even moved in to his new apartment, the Outfit knew its location, and already had tried but failed to trap him there. His trackers knew the times he could be found at Poor Freddie's and his favorite watering holes. Armed with that intelligence, it was only a matter of finding Bowen at one of those places. Outrage over the slaying of Amaro meant that the caution normally exercised in such an undertaking would be thrown to the wind.

ON MONDAY, FEBRUARY 21, 1977, SONNY BOWEN and his girlfriend each got home about 5 p.m. There were still mundane tasks that accompanied settling into a new apartment. For one, Bowen had a batch of phonograph records but no record player. He rang up a woman who apparently had a record player for sale, obtained a description so he would recognize her and arranged to meet her at Poor Freddie's. He left the apartment about 7 p.m.

At Poor Freddie's Bowen hung around till just before 9 p.m., when he told Tony Mike Bonadonna to keep an eye out for a redheaded woman asking for him; he would be back in five minutes. Sure enough, the redhead appeared, looking for him. When he didn't come back after an hour, she left.

For reasons that will never be known, Bowen had headed to Mr. O'Brien's Cocktail Lounge on Broadway north of Armour Boulevard. It was one of his regular haunts and was owned by Tom Ribaudo, whom Bowen considered a friend. Arriving about 9 p.m., Bowen exercised little caution. He parked on Broadway right in front of the place.

He grabbed a seat at the bar, chatted up one of the bar girls, made a few calls and socialized with some of the other regulars. Then Bowen moved to the third booth from the front door, where he sat by himself. At some point Ribaudo joined him and the two talked, leaning across the table toward each other with their heads close in what appeared to be a private conversation. At 10:20 p.m. Bowen called his apartment, said he was still waiting for the woman with the record player and if she didn't show in a half hour he would head home.

While Bowen was socializing, John Amaro's family and friends gathered for his wake. The event took place at the long-established Sebetto Funeral Home in a modest building at Fifth and Campbell streets in the heart of the old North End. Several Outfit members were in attendance, paying their respects. Probably the somber occasion only reinforced the urgency of their mission. Bowen had proved himself a difficult target, one who would not be lured in or easily cornered, so when word reached the right ears at the wake that Bowen was at Mr. O'Brien's, a plan was quickly formulated. The matter would be taken care of that very night, even if it meant doing so in a public place filled with patrons and employees.

Around midnight at Mr. O'Brien's, Ribaudo left Bowen's booth, apparently headed for the restroom. As a female patron carrying a cup of coffee approached Sonny's booth, four men wearing ski masks entered the bar from a rear door. They shouted for everyone to get down.

The place was dimly lit and the juke box played loudly — ideal conditions for the assassins' task. Two of the intruders, armed with shotguns, moved directly to Bowen's booth. He was seated so that he looked right at them as they fired at point-blank range. The four escaped the way they had entered, by the rear door. It was 10 minutes past midnight, February 22, 1977.

Bowen suffered gunshot wounds to his left forehead, the midline of his neck and the right side of the base of his neck. The shots grazed his left forearm, chin and jaw. Two of the four spent shotgun shell casings lay on the seat of the booth across from him.

That morning a citizen's call led police to a high bank near the tennis courts in Hyde Park on Gillham Road between 37th and 38th streets. There the police found the two shotguns used to kill Bowen.

When the police forensic team inspected Bowen's car, they found evidence of fragments from an exploded blasting cap and stains on the rear floor that appeared to be blood. What had been known only to Bowen and Freddy Bonadonna now saw the light of day.

Not only had Freddy Bonadonna lost his most important ally, but he also faced the realization the Outfit had pegged him as Bowen's accomplice in the Amaro murder. Now that he was isolated, they would move quickly to eliminate him.

For Freddy it was the final straw. On receiving word of Bowen's murder, he fled the city.

CHAPTER XVI

THE OUTFIT'S PURGE

THE CIVELLA GAMBLING PROSECUTION had reached the six-year mark in April 1976 when the Eighth U.S. Circuit Court of Appeals in St. Louis upheld the convictions of Nick Civella, his nephew Tony Civella and Frank Tousa.

Tousa surrendered to start his jail term in October 1976. On a technicality the convictions of Thomas Fontanello and Joseph Barletta were overturned and then reinstated by a higher court. They were ordered to report to prison in December 1977.

Nick and Tony Civella remained free on appeal bond pending a U.S. Supreme Court ruling on whether the government's electronic surveillance was properly authorized. In February 1977 the high court turned down the Civellas' petition.

Nick Civella was left with one final legal maneuver to avoid jail — his health. He petitioned the court for probation or for a reduced sentence to be served at his home. Tony Civella asked for a reduction in his sentence.

The Strike Force opposed the defense moves, labeling Nick Civella a "hardened professional criminal who is incorrigible and thoroughly unrepentant." However, Judge Collinson granted a stay, allowing Civella time to produce evidence that he could not survive a prison term.

March 29, 1977, was a thoroughly unpleasant day for Nick Civella. He had to endure a court hearing that produced detailed testimony about his operation, about the colostomy bag he had to wear, about the procedure to change the bag and other intimate matters. As for his life expectancy, estimates ranged from two years to five years to "couldn't say." In the never-ending process, the court ruled Civella had to undergo a 90-day study of his health beginning April 11 at the U.S. Medical Center for Federal Prisoners in Springfield, Missouri.

On April 15, 1977, Judge Collinson ruled on Tony Civella's request for a reduction in sentence, and in open court proclaimed, "The court states positively that all statements in the pre-sentence report indicating that the defendant was reputedly a member of an organized crime group in Kansas City were totally disregarded." It was yet another windfall for the Civellas. The judge cut his sentence by six months to three years. Tony Civella was ordered to report to the federal prison in Texarkana, Texas.

For the agents and prosecutors who dogged Tony Civella, the disregard by the judge was hard to comprehend. Much had been exposed about organized crime in the 20 years since the Apalachin conclave, and numerous cases in the Western District of Missouri had established the existence of the Crime Family, the millions of untaxed dollars siphoned out of the city, and the leading role played by Tony Civella.

When the 90-day health study of Nick Civella was completed, Judge Collinson granted Civella a six-month reduction in his sentence to three years. On August 1, 1977, the prison doors finally closed behind the Boss, seven and one-half years after Super Bowl IV.

WHILE CIVELLA'S LEGAL BATTLE WAS GRINDING ON, detectives assigned to the multi-jurisdiction Metro Squad aggressively pursued leads in the slayings of David Bonadonna and Sonny Bowen. In the process, police and FBI agents got reports that Gary T. Parker — Parker T., who had been Bowen's running mate — would be next. The Metro Squad set out to impress on him the danger he faced.

A Kansas City homicide detective, Clarence Gibson, and Sergeant Sam Scott of the Liberty, Missouri, Police found Parker the evening of February 22, 1977. At first reluctant, he eventually agreed to accompany the officers to a midtown Kansas City hotel for safekeeping and for a heart-to-heart talk. On the chance he hadn't figured it out, the detectives explained to him that, as a known running mate of Sonny Bowen, the mob considered him a likely accomplice in the murder of John Amaro. Parker was in grave danger.

However, the detectives' concern for his welfare was lost on him. Parker seemingly had no clue about the precariousness of his position. He believed he could simply go about his life as if nothing had happened.

Police nevertheless remained concerned, so they monitored his comings and goings. Two days later, they saw him leave a bar at 18th Street and Grand Avenue, exposed to any harm that might come his way. Officers picked him up, relieved him of a .38-caliber Colt pistol and took him to police headquarters for further questioning.

Parker not only refused any form of protective custody, but also made it clear he wanted everyone to back off. The efforts by police and the FBI, he said, were creating "heat on him." He denied any involvement in the murder of John Amaro but refused to submit to a polygraph exam or to consider the possibility of immunity for testifying about the killing.

As the Metro Squad toiled on with its investigation of the Bonadonna and Bowen slayings, at the FBI office it was clear the time had come for an intensified effort focusing on the string of interrelated events beginning with the murder of David Bonadonna. As the River Quay case agent, I was assigned to lead a team composed of Organized Crime Squad agents supplemented by agents from other squads in our office to pursue the investigation.

The Kansas City Police Department had done its best in behalf of Gary T. Parker, so it was agreed that the FBI would have a go at him. On March 9, 1977, Parker was invited to the FBI office. His attitude had changed because he had heard from his own sources that he was being stalked. Hanging over the interview was Parker's suspected participation in the Amaro homicide. When he was advised of his rights and questioned about the murder, Parker bristled. Confronted with holes in his stated alibi — his girlfriend failed to corroborate his claim of having been with Sonny Bowen at her residence in the hours before the murder — he walked out in a huff.

The simplest course would have been to abandon him and wait for the call reporting that his body had been found. However, if Parker could be persuaded to cooperate, not only would the odds of preventing his murder increase, but also evidence might be gained against those bent on killing him. With that in mind, I arranged to meet with his attorney, Kenneth Simon, hoping he could persuade Parker to work with the FBI. The plan proposed to Simon called for Parker, with his cooperation, to be discreetly observed. With luck, agents could identify and neutralize whoever might try to set him up.

Simon succeeded. He persuaded Parker that it was in his best interest to work with the FBI. Details were worked out with Parker by Agent Tom Lavin, who had developed a rapport with Parker and his girlfriend, and Agent Carl Nau. Each day Parker was to provide an itinerary that allowed the agents to keep track of him.

When the plan was set in motion on March 21, 1977, we believed it was workable.

However, a flaky Parker viewed it as some sort of game. On purpose, he created various difficulties for the agents trying to track him. His folly almost cost him his life.

On the night of April 1, 1977, he received a telephone call from Vince Picone, who was under indictment for his role in an Outfit bookmaking ring. Picone offered to pay Parker $150 he owed him. Without alerting the agents, Parker agreed to meet Picone at the Auditorium Bar and Grill at 14th and Wyandotte streets.

A warning buzzer should have gone off immediately in Parker's head, but instead he had his girlfriend drive them to the bar. There they found Picone sitting in his car in the parking lot, obviously nervous. He came to their car, handed over $100 and asked Parker to meet him in 30 minutes at Louie's tavern, believed to be a bar run by Tony Mike Bonadonna on Truman Road, where he would pay the remaining $50. In his precarious position, Parker should have smelled a rat and fled for safety. Instead, off they went to the bar.

Fortunately for Parker, his brain had not gone completely dead. The couple parked across the street from the bar to survey the landscape. Soon they saw Picone drive slowly by. Now, he was accompanied by a man with graying, receding hair. Picone and his passenger appeared to scan the bar's parking lot, probably looking for Parker's car.

Then a second car cruised by on the side of the street where Parker and his girlfriend were. The car, driven by a 35-year-old man with dark hair and a dark mustache, stopped alongside. The driver stared intently at Parker and his girlfriend.

Having seen enough, the two beat it out of the area.

Parker waited four days to tell FBI agents about the incident. The agents laid out photos to help him identify the people he had seen, and he pointed to a photo of Willie Cammisano as the man who rode with Picone. Parker, highlighting his own foolishness, acknowledged that he knew Picone was heavily indebted to Outfit loan sharks. He also knew that Freddy Bonadonna once had refused to give Picone a ride to his car, afraid Picone was setting him up as a means of settling his debts. From the outset, Parker should have known that never in a million years would Picone repay anyone who was known to be only steps away from the grave.

Unfortunately, Parker learned nothing from his close call. Eventually his antics endangered the agents who were trying to follow him, putting an end to the effort to protect him. That left Parker on his own.

Meanwhile, conflict between Carl Spero and the Civella Family continued to escalate. In reality, it amounted to a vendetta rather than to a power struggle because the Speros never would have been strong enough to replace the established order. The grim reality of such conflict provided a multitude of opportunities for investigators — opportunities that could lead to inroads against the Family.

IN JANUARY 1977, A FRESH FACE APPEARED in the North End, tooling around in a flashy yellow Cadillac. In his pocket he carried the lease to the vacant restaurant space next door to the Trap at Fifth Street and Troost Avenue.

Gary Ward planned to open a new restaurant, primarily a sandwich shop, named Ward's. As owners of the building, Nick Civella and his wife signed the lease but in negotiating the lease a crucial bit of information was omitted. Gary Ward was a fictitious name and so was the name of his partner, Bob Newton. In addition, both were undercover FBI agents.

The Crime Family is close-knit. Its members and associates inherently suspect anyone new, anyone with whom they do not have a history. "Ward" and "Newton" had instructions to remain friendly but aloof, displaying no interest in what was going on next door at the Outfit's social club. Like experienced fisherman, they would throw out the bait, sit patiently and let the Outfit come to them. The bait would be an innovative gambling business not seen before in Kansas City. Ward's Restaurant would be promoted as an offsite betting courier service. For a fee, it would run customer's horse-race bets to the Ak-Sar-Ben racetrack in Omaha, Nebraska.

Counting on the fact that all forms of gambling fell within the domain of the Family, it would be only a matter of time before the sharks appeared, first to investigate and then probably to move in. In addition, because of the strategic placement of Ward's Restaurant, the agents could document the comings and goings of all Family members, associates and fellow travelers.

To our frustration, the concept of FBI agents' running horse wagers to Omaha made government lawyers squeamish. Authority to proceed with that part of the plan was denied. Despite that setback, the operation still held enormous potential based on the strategic location of the restaurant and the potential that it would become a hangout. With enough time, curiosity alone would attract attention to the business and another form of bait could be devised.

Predictably, several mob heavyweights stopped in periodically at Ward's, where they engaged in guarded, serious conversations. For the most part the undercover agents, playing their role as uninterested restaurateurs, could not pick up anything from those conversations.

Then one afternoon an extraordinary event took place. Two men entered and settled in a booth. Possibly because of the import of their conversation and the absence of other customers, the two let their guard down. They paid little attention to the presence of "Gary Ward," who was able to overhear snippets.

The fact that the two were talking at all seemed like a chapter out of Machiavelli. One was Carl Spero, subject of a murder plot against him. The other was Cork Civella, who was leading the effort to kill Spero. The date was February 26, 1977.

CIVELLA: You're not in any trouble with my outfit. There's nothing to worry about…. I can say this with authority.

Civella went on to say that he did not know who killed Spero's brother Nick Spero, but indicated he did know who murdered John Amaro, and "someone can use a shotgun besides them." The name Freddy was mentioned, obviously referring to Freddy Bonadonna, and Civella continued.

CIVELLA: I don't care how long it takes ….. they should have gotten him a long time ago. It doesn't matter if it takes six months or years, we'll get him. That'll be my legacy after I'm gone. Someone will get him.

Spero spoke of somebody being in hiding, somebody who had fled the city earlier in the month. That would have been Bonadonna. Civella answered that he wanted to get one of his people next to him to find out where he was. Spero was then offered the job to find and kill Bonadonna. If it was a good, clean job, Civella said, Spero could do it. If it could not be done cleanly, he said, he would not jeopardize Spero.

CORK CIVELLA WASN'T THE ONLY ONE who had Freddy Bonadonna on his mind. On May 19, 1977, Kansas City Police Detective

Robert Warren stopped at Uncle Joe's in the River Quay and visited with owner Joe Cammisano, whom Warren had known for years. After chatting about this and that, Cammisano took Warren to the back of the bar where the two could talk in private. He wanted to talk about Freddy Bonadonna. Bonadonna had screwed things up badly in the Quay, Cammisano said, and he surely would like to know where he was. Cammisano wouldn't do anything himself, he told Warren, but he would get the word to the right people.

"I'll keep my eyes open," Warren responded. He immediately reported the incident to his commander, Major Sid Harlow. Later Warren recounted the incident in testimony in federal court.

Incrementally the undercover operation was progressing, as evidenced by the Civella-Spero meeting. With time, the potential of Ward's would have been realized. However, the rug was pulled out from under the plan after only six months when Bill Williams, special agent in charge of the Kansas City FBI Office, ordered the operation shut down. To this day I do not understand why that happened. It was a bitter pill to swallow, especially in light of future developments.

THE OUTFIT HAD TO FACE THE FACT that murdering two of its primary targets in a traditional, safe and secure, up-close assassination was not likely. Spero knew what was afoot and would not be lured into a trap, nor was he fooled by Cork's friendly chat at Ward's Restaurant. Also, Parker's recent experience should have taught him the same lesson. The enforcers would have to take chances, as they had with Sonny Bowen. That meant risking a mistake, or injuring bystanders, or facing an unexpected event that jeopardized the operation. To succeed, they must have everything in place: getaway cars, weapons and clothing. They had to be ready for a quick strike when the opportunity presented itself. And the opportunity would come only by continuing to stalk their prey.

Unexpectedly, the pursuit was interrupted by Nick Civella's legal situation. In December 1976, when Civella still was waiting on a decision by the U.S. Supreme Court, word on the street was that all planned executions were to be put on the back burner to avoid any negative publicity for the Boss. Civella's appeal to the high court was unsuccessful, but the murder moratorium was extended when Civella's sentence was delayed by the question of his health.

Apparently, however, the moratorium was not all-encompassing.

At 2:11 a.m. on March 27, 1977, the serenity of the early morning hours in the deserted River Quay was broken by a thunderous explosion heard across Kansas City. It leveled the massive building housing Judge Roy Bean's and Pat O'Brien's bars, a building owned by Freddy and Tony Mike Bonadonna. Debris was blown three blocks north and one block south, and windows were broken in buildings in a four-block radius. No one was hurt in the blast, which authorities determined was caused by explosives

"They used 10 times as much of the stuff as they needed to blow these places up," said an agent for the federal bureau of Alcohol, Tobacco and Firearms. "This was definitely meant to be a message to someone."

The hearing on Nick Civella's health — the one in which his condition was laid out in intimate detail — lay two days away. Was the bombing carried out anyway in an attempt to throw suspicion on Freddy Bonadonna, implying that he had bombed his own building to collect insurance? Or, having failed to murder Freddy Bonadonna, had the Outfit simply decided to "murder" his building?

At any rate, the bombing was far from an isolated instance. About 5:45 a.m. one day four months later, a two-alarm fire was reported at Joe Cammisano's Uncle Joe's tavern. Damaged was listed as $75,000 to the building and its contents. Cracks in the foundation, a blown-out wall and a strong odor of natural gas suggested to fire inspectors some sort of explosion. As it turned out, a section of the building's gas line had been removed.

A month after that, again in the early hours, a fire broke out at The Godfather Lounge. A sprinkler system had activated, minimizing damage and preventing a possible explosion. It was determined that the gas line had been broken to feed three small fires set in a first-floor storage area. The rear door was found unlocked and there was no sign of forced entry.

As for the moratorium on murder, it continued while Nick Civella underwent his 90-day examination at the Federal Medical Center in Springfield. With that finished, Civella was formally sentenced to three years and entered prison on August 1, 1977. The moratorium was over, and the crime family struck immediately.

SEEMINGLY OBLIVIOUS TO EVERYTHING and to everyone, Gary T. Parker went about his life with a business-as-usual attitude. He planned a trip with his girlfriend and needed to borrow his parents' trailer. So on August 5, 1977, a Friday, Parker ventured out to an unincorporated section of Jackson County near Blue Springs, Missouri, where his parents lived. They found him in good spirits and looking forward to the trip.

That afternoon, between 2:30 and 3 o'clock, Parker stopped by Fimco, a kitchen and bath equipment supplier at 1300-1400 Jackson Ave. where he had been employed for several months selling cabinets to contractors. It was a brief stop to chew the fat with the sales manager, and after 15 minutes he left.

Next, Parker drove to Louie's Tavern at 4127 Truman Rd. He parked his 1964 Ford Falcon station wagon in the lot on the west side of the bar facing the building. Louie's was owned by Tony Mike Bonadonna, Freddy Bonadonna's brother, and a partner. According to the owners, the bartender and some of the regulars, Parker visited the bar periodically, sometimes cashing his paycheck there. In the two hours he spent at Louie's, Parker played a couple of games of pool, chatted up one of the regulars and drank three beers. To all he seemed relaxed and carefree.

About a quarter to 5, Parker ordered a can of beer to go and left the bar. He placed the beer on the roof of the car and proceeded to open the car door.

An enormous explosion literally blew him apart. What remained of Gary T. Parker was scattered over Truman Road. Torn parts of his torso landed atop a two-story building north across the street from Louie's. Beneath the twisted remains of Parker's vehicle was a crater, evidence that the bomb had been placed beneath his vehicle. Most likely it had been detonated by a remote-control or pressure device.

Whether he was sincere or simply playing a role, Parker's view of his lot in life had played out there in the parking lot of Louie's. Six months earlier, in February, when Parker was brought in by police detectives for questioning, he proclaimed:

"I don't give a f--- if I'm gonna get killed or not .... I don't give a f--- if they smack me when I walk out of here 'cause I've said I've lived my life. And I've always said I'll never live till I'm 35 and I may be right."

Gary T. Parker was blown apart five months short of his 35th birthday.

BY MID-APRIL 1978 WORD WENT OUT that Nick Civella's poor health put him in line for early parole. Our eyes and ears on the street reported that there was to be a concerted effort to handle unfinished business before the Boss was released from prison, which was scheduled for June 14. After that, there would be no further acts of violence, creating an aura of Civella as peacemaker, bringing stability to a chaotic time.

Supporting these reports, surveillance and spot checks by the Kansas City Police Intelligence Unit and FBI agents indicated an obvious escalation of activity on the part of the enforcement arm of the Family. The frequency of meetings, secretive and furtive in nature, had increased dramatically at the Trap and at the restaurant next door, now known as Wimpy's. "Walk-and-talk" conversations were observed among mobsters, aimed at avoiding electronic surveillance by chatting while strolling the sidewalks. Frequent forays in cars had all the markings of reconnaissance missions. Cork Civella would later be overheard complaining to his brother about the efforts to stalk Carl Spero: "Our guys got exposed: Raguse (Joe Ragusa), Vince (Vince Abbott). Every time they seem to go some place the f----n' coppers, they see them behind 'em." You could feel the sense of urgency in the air.

The loss of the FBI's undercover operation at the restaurant next door to the Trap was sorely felt by investigators. The challenge was to come up with something in its place that capitalized on the wealth of intelligence at our disposal.

On the third floor of the U.S. Courthouse at Eighth Street and Grand Avenue, Gary Hart, who had taken over as Organized Crime Squad Supervisor in September 1977, called me in to discuss the lay of the land and a fresh report by an informant that the Outfit hit team was zeroed in on a specific target. Hart's view, supported by Strike Force chief David Helfrey, was that there were sufficient grounds to bug the cars used by Outfit enforcers to stalk the target. I was to get to work on an affidavit supporting a request for court-authorized electronic surveillance. Together with Helfrey, we worked on the affidavit till 1 a.m. the next day, and then we worked steadily on the project for three days. The completed paperwork was submitted to the Department of Justice and to FBI headquarters.

We were preempted, however. The Outfit made a move that threw a monkey wrench into our plans. In quick succession, it cleaned up two pieces of business that were not on our radar.

At 3 a.m. May 2, 1978, a police patrol car spotted a white-over-green 1969 Chevy Camaro parked in a lot behind an empty frame house at Independence and Prospect avenues. The Camaro's doors were locked, its headlights were on and its windows were up. Peering into the vehicle, a patrolman saw the body of a man sprawled in the front seat. Myron Mancuso, 37, had been shot twice in the head and once in the hand.

Two days later, the body of 30-year-old Michael Massey was found in a stolen car parked in the 4900 block of Wyandotte Street. Massey had been shot four times in the head.

If either Mancuso or Massey was the unknown murder target spelled out in our affidavit, there was no longer a basis for a federal judge to authorize electronic surveillance; the deed had been done. A mad scramble ensued to reach the informant. It took a day or so, but we learned that neither Mancuso nor Massey was the principle target referred to by the informant.

On May 5, 1978, with the affidavit and application amended to reflect the latest events, the court authorized the planting of microphones in vehicles owned by Charles Moretina, Vince Abbott and Joe Ragusa, identified as members of the Family's enforcement arm. A host of agents did brilliant work, enduring long hours and overcoming severe obstacles and tense times to install microphones in several of cars. Unfortunately, the microphones were plagued by technical difficulties and did not function properly. Before the problem could be fixed, events made the justification for the court order null and void.

WHEN YOU ENVISION AN OLD-FASHIONED neighborhood tavern, the Virginian fits the bill. Anthony Todaro, born in Italy, arrived in Kansas City in 1917, and for a time operated an ice cream delivery service. In 1948 he converted his delivery service to an ice cream parlor at 1315 Admiral Blvd. Four years later he converted the business again, this time to a tavern selling beer, whiskey and sandwiches. Todaro died in 1961, and his son Frank Todaro took over running the tavern. Anthony's wife and Frank's mother, Millie Todaro, took care of the lunch trade.

Frank Todaro was a lifelong friend of the Spero family, especially brothers Michael and Carl Spero. The Speros' father and mother had worked at the tavern when it opened, making it a place Carl and Michael favored. Carl was in the habit of visiting the Virginian each Saturday, normally in the afternoon, and the Saturday falling on the 16th of May 1978 was no exception.

That day was particularly busy for Spero. He spent time at a basement repair job, then looked over a new piece of equipment and in the process was cited twice for traffic infractions. Spero had scheduled a meeting at the Virginian with attorney Daniel Matula, and was running late. Arriving home, he cleaned up and hurried to the tavern.

To his surprise — and purely by happenstance — brother Michael

Spero, a Teamsters business agent, was at the tavern when Carl arrived. Michael arrived about 7:30 p.m. Later, brother Joe Spero joined them.

A phone call came in for Carl, and on the line was John Caresio. Caresio and another man had been arrested by the Kansas City Police on July 13, 1977, for robbing a jewelry salesman — the kind of crime with which Spero was quite familiar. Free on bond, Caresio needed to show a place of employment. Carl Spero told him he was putting together a basement company and would be willing to vouch for Caresio as his employee. Caresio stayed in touch, occasionally visiting Spero on a job site.

Caresio's call to Spero at the Virginian was made to see whether the deal was still on. He also asked whether Spero planned to be at the tavern a while; Caresio needed to talk with him. Assured that Spero would be there for a while, Caresio asked him to wait.

Spero then called Johnny Joe Calia, one of the cadre of jewel thieves Spero had run with years before. Calia had been released from prison a month earlier, having finished his sentence for looting shotguns and other items from car trunks at Municipal Auditorium. His accomplice in those robberies was Sonny Bowen. Because Bowen got a lighter sentence than Calia, Carl Spero suspected he had made a deal with investigators. He had put out the word that Bowen could not be trusted.

On this night, Carl Spero was told by Calia's wife that he wasn't home. Spero asked her to have Calia call him at the Virginian.

Now there were two people who knew exactly where Carl Spero was and where he would remain for a while.

At the Virginian, Carl kept his appointment with attorney Dan Matula. The two talked at the bar. Michael and Joe Spero were seated at a table near a back wall, directly across from the front door. Around a corner from where the two brothers were seated was the back door to the tavern.

John Caresio had yet to show up for his promised meeting with Carl Spero.

That night, two veteran detectives from the Kansas City Police intelligence unit, Harold Nichols and Tommy Walker, were surfing mob hangouts to document the movements of key Outfit figures. Coming to the Virginian tavern, they slowed down upon seeing Carl Spero just outside the front door. He was talking on the telephone, the line from the receiver stretching out the door. It was about 10 p.m. when Nichols and Walker drove past and proceeded west on Admiral Boulevard.

At that very minute, unseen by the two detectives, three or four masked men burst through the back door of the Virginian tavern. One had a shotgun, the others handguns, and they marked their arrival by firing shots into the air. Before anyone had a chance to react, Joe and Michael Spero were shot. Carl, still on the telephone but no longer outside the tavern, instantly realized what was afoot. He fled through the front door onto Admiral Boulevard.

The intruder with the shotgun chased after him, firing several times. Carl made it to Virginia Avenue just north of Admiral Boulevard, and then collapsed. The assailant raced back into the tavern and escaped out the back door with his accomplices. Climbing into a car parked on Virginia Avenue, the murderers drove south to Eighth Street, turned east and drove to Highland Avenue, where they headed north to the 700 block.

Detectives Nichols and Walker had made it to Admiral and Oak streets when their police radio came alive. Shots had been fired at the Virginian Tavern. Speeding back east to the Virginian, they found Carl Spero lying in the street, conscious and lucid but unable to move.

"Do you know who did this, Carl?" they asked.

"Yeah" he replied.

"Are you going to tell us who?"

The answer, predictably, was no.

Inside the Virginian, Michael Spero lay dead on the floor, shot once in the top of his head and once in his left leg above the knee. Joe Spero, shot once in the right arm, was taken to a hospital in fair condition. Carl Spero, with a shotgun wound in the back, was rushed into surgery. Several days later he was reported as paralyzed from the neck down.

The two detectives estimated that two minutes had elapsed from the time they saw Spero in the tavern doorway to the report that shots had been fired. Nichols figured that the murderers probably were entering the back door as they drove by. It was a vivid illustration of what might have gone wrong for the gangland executioners when they had to "cowboy" a murder.

The getaway car, a white 1976 Ford LTD, was found by police parked in the 700 block of Highland. The engine was still running, and a shotgun lay outside the car, its brand name and serial number obliterated. The car had been stolen from 46th and Summit streets more than two months earlier and obviously had been stashed away in anticipation of the day it would be needed.

The next morning a passerby came upon two .38-caliber revolvers near

Seventh and Woodland streets. The weapons had been part of the loot taken 11 years before from the Gateway Sporting Goods Co. Of 2,000 weapons stolen in that burglary about 300 had surfaced, some in Kansas City, others as far away as Alaska.

The paralyzed Carl Spero was moved to Colorado to a private rehabilitation facility. He returned to Kansas City months later. His broken body confined him to a wheelchair, yet his will was undamaged and his mind set on retribution.

ON JUNE 14, 1978, HAVING SERVED NINE MONTHS in prison, Nick Civella received an early parole because of poor health. In January of that year, prison authorities had transported Civella to the UCLA Medical Center in Los Angles for a examination. His cancer had recurred, requiring another operation, and in March he went under the knife.

Now he was going home, but instead of returning to a clean slate and a period of tranquillity, Civella faced the first real threat to the safety of his clan since taking over as boss in the early 1950s.

Not long after the shooting at the Virginian Tavern, the two surviving Spero brothers, Carl and Joe, began plotting revenge. They aimed to cut into the Outfit's criminal endeavors and otherwise wreak havoc. Joining them were their close friend Mike Cuezze and Conrad Metz, a tough character. The Speros also recruited a fringe player, Lyle Neal, a 37-year-old ex-convict.

The immediate task: find some dynamite.

CHAPTER XVII

RIVER QUAY PROSECUTION

BOUNCING FROM CRISIS TO CRISIS and investigation to investigation was akin to the antics of a circus juggler. Time and again, agents and attorneys of the Strike Force set aside the work required to bring charges in the River Quay case and diverted their attention to murders, bombings, the conflict between the Speros and the Civellas and other endeavors of the Family.

Despite all the detours, agent Lee Flosi and I met regularly with Strike Force chief David Helfrey and his staff about the River Quay. As early as August 1976 subpoenas were issued to call witnesses before the federal grand jury.

One went to Missouri State Representative Alex Fazzino. The subpoena, it might seem, would have given Fazzino a chance to tell his side of the story and to answer allegations that he had exerted political influence in behalf of Outfit-connected individuals. However, when he appeared on August 24, 1976, he refused to answer questions, citing his right under the Fifth Amendment to the Constitution not to incriminate himself.

Fazzino would not say whether he knew Willie or Joe Cammisano, John Amaro, David Bonadonna, Nelson Martin or Willis Castle, or knew of the business known as Poor Freddie's. He refused to answer whether he had any knowledge of the murder of David Bonadonna, or of efforts to alter the character of the River Quay by illegal means, or of threats and violence directed at River Quay business owners. As for parking lots in the Quay, he would not talk about whether he had discussions with Willie Cammisano or with Willis Castle or had intervened in the matter.

Almost six months later, on February 22, 1977, Fazzino appeared before U.S. District Judge Elmo B. Hunter. In open court, Fazzino said he would again take the Fifth if asked the same questions. The judge then granted Fazzino immunity from prosecution arising from those questions. If

Fazzino persisted in refusing to answer questions, he would be sent to jail for contempt.

Fazzino complied and testified. Afterward, a *Kansas City Star* reporter asked him to explain why he had invoked the Fifth Amendment.

"I thought it would be the safest thing to do," Fazzino replied. "I didn't know what they were going to ask me about."

Besides, he continued: "My lawyer told me to. If they had just called me and asked me to come down I would have been glad to. I have nothing to hide."

To investigators that raised the question, Why had he taken the Fifth in the first place?

DD Bonadonna, Freddy's brother, was the only other witness who took the Fifth and to whom immunity from prosecution was granted. Nevertheless, he continued to refuse to talk and was sent to jail for contempt. He only spent a day there, however, because an indictment was returned immediately afterward, which ended the justification for holding him. DD Bonadonna never had to testify.

The push for a River Quay prosecution received added emphasis from the special investigative team that was formed after the Bowen murder and that I headed. It focused on the chaos in the Quay and all related events leading up to that murder. In an intensive month of pounding the bricks, the team accumulated a wealth of information adding to and supplementing evidence obtained through grand jury sessions.

The final pieces of the puzzle fell into place when Freddy Bonadonna surfaced and talked to investigators.

Although Bonadonna had fled the city and gone into hiding after Sonny Bowen's murder, he had stayed in touch with Flosi. The two discussed his future and his limited options. For Bonadonna the decision was gut-wrenching, but he agreed to come in from the cold. He would testify as a cooperating federal witness and then face the unthinkable, to disappear with his family.

Secretly he returned to Kansas City on March 14, 1977. He testified before a federal grand jury and then was whisked away from his hometown, his extended family and his friends, and formally admitted into the witness protection program.

The long and tortuous journey to prosecution in the River Quay case culminated with a one-count federal indictment returned June 16, 1977. It charged Willie Cammisano and Joe Cammisano with extortion.

In legal terms, the accusation outlined a conspiracy on the Cammisanos' part to obtain from Fred Harvey Bonadonna the good will, parking lot leases, customer patronage and other valuable rights and interests in the business known as Poor Freddie's by the wrongful use of actual and threatened force, violence and fear.

If convicted, the Cammisanos faced a maximum sentence of 20 years.

THREE MONTHS LATER, another crisis arrived at the hands of the Cammisanos. Early in September 1977, agent Flosi got word from one of his most productive informants that the Cammisanos had put the informant in the trick bag, a place from which it would be difficult to escape. The informant had been ordered by the Outfit to provide a false affidavit to the Cammisanos' lawyers discrediting Freddy Bonadonna and providing other falsified information that would aid the Cammisanos' defense.

In short order, Flosi and I met with the informant to flush out the facts and determine how precarious the informant's situation was. The informant had a bad feeling: Gene Shepard, an Outfit associate tied closely to Cork Civella, was becoming suspicious of him. Once, he had warned the informant that he would dump his son into a well if the informant ever did anything wrong — a veiled reference to our informant's talking to the authorities.

The informant already was in disfavor for having failed to murder Sonny Bowen when he was ordered to do so. He had dodged the bullet on that one, but if he failed to provide the affidavit to the Cammisanos' lawyers he would surely be killed for defying the Outfit. Flosi's informant was treading water, trying to figure out how to extricate himself.

We went to Strike Force chief David Helfrey and filled him in on the dilemma. As we feared, Helfrey confirmed that we were in a no-win situation. FBI agents and federal prosecutors could not knowingly allow someone to offer perjured testimony. If the informant was called as a witness by the Cammisanos and perjured himself, Helfrey, representing the government, would be obligated to reveal to the court and the defense his status as an informant, and to say that his testimony was known to be false.

We met again with the informant and the news was not good. He had been unable to find a way out of his predicament. We in turn told him of the legal bind we were in and what he could expect if he offered perjured testimony. Bluntly, there were only three options, none attractive.

First, he could defy the mob and risk being killed. Second, he could comply and offer perjured testimony and be outed as an FBI informant, which would definitely get him killed. Third, he could cooperate as a witness and enter the witness protection program.

Adding to the complexity was that our informant had a 10-year-old son whom he was raising on his own and who was the light of his life. The boy's mother had left the family and had had little to do with the boy since. We knew her to be untrustworthy. Her male companions were Outfit-connected and she worked in Outfit-connected businesses. If the informant went into witness protection without the boy, there was no doubt that the Outfit would use his son to force the informant back to Kansas City.

Finally, a decision was made. He chose Option Three, to cooperate and go into witness protection. Soon the Crime Family would learn the informant's name: Mike Ruffalo.

Ruffalo was an especially valuable asset. He provided timely inside information about Outfit operations and strategies. He was the informant who had warned us of plans to murder Sonny Bowen, Carl Spero and Gary T. Parker. On the other hand, he had also been a valuable asset for the Family. Having befriended the Bonadonnas, Bowen and Parker, he provided the Family valuable intelligence about them. He walked the tightrope, as did Freddy, and both ended up in witness protection.

The loss of Ruffalo as an informant for the future was a blow to the Organized Crime Squad, but the lives of Ruffalo and his son would be changed for the better. Helfrey and the U.S. Marshals Service made arrangements for both to evaporate into the witness protection program.

In the early-morning darkness of November 10, 1978, Flosi and I checked out the FBI's camper vehicle and drove to Ruffalo's residence. Having packed what they could carry, Mike and his son got into the camper with us to face the unknowns of a new life and a new identity.

WHEN GENE SHEPARD COULDN'T FIND his running mate Mike Ruffalo or Ruffalo's young son, red flags went up. Shepard's concern was well founded.

Together, Shepard and Ruffalo had carried out many an assignment for the Family. Before long, Shepard found himself charged in one of those assignments, a bombing at a lounge in Kansas City, Kansas. His partner in that crime, Ruffalo, now filled in the details in the role of a cooperating government witness.

The bombing had taken place at the Red Apple Lounge, a private club owned by Clarence Wade "Jack" Anderson. It occurred in late May 1978 as part of the violent business that needed to be wrapped up before Nick Civella was released from prison.

Although Anderson was the owner of the Red Apple, the liquor license was in the name of Antoinette "Toni" LanFranca, an employee at the lounge. Symbolic of the tangled world of underworld relationships, LanFranca was going out with Cork Civella and Carl Spero at the same time. Also she was the daughter of Amy Irene Gilliland, who was living with Gene Shepard.

In April 1978 LanFranca and Anderson got into an argument over an incident that occurred during a Red Apple employees' jaunt to Las Vegas, a trip sponsored by Anderson. LanFranca told the story to Cork Civella, including her mistaken belief that Anderson had fired her. Her story evidently sparked in Civella's mind a scheme to take over the Red Apple.

Civella went to Shepard and Ruffalo. He ordered them to devise a plan to intimidate Anderson in such a way that he would not know where the threat came from and would run to Cork Civella for protection. In turn, Civella would send his people purportedly to look out for Anderson but in fact to muscle him out of the business. The move, Civella believed, would impress LanFranca. Civella pushed them to hurry.

Shepard and Ruffalo decided to put a bomb under Anderson's car, and Civella agreed to the plan.

On May 22, 1978, a bomb was assembled at Shepard's residence and the two drove to the Red Apple Lounge. Ruffalo set the bomb under Anderson's empty 1977 Lincoln Mark V and used Shepard's cigar to light the fuse. As they drove out of the parking lot the bomb exploded, destroying Anderson's car. The two headed back to reported their success to Cork Civella.

The success was short-lived. Anderson never came to the Outfit for help, and Toni LanFranca married Carl Spero. In 1981 both Shepard and Civella were charged with conspiracy and with transporting an explosive device across state lines. In separate trials in April 1982, Civella was acquitted. Shepard was convicted and sentenced to five years.

Civella's plot had failed.

HAVING TIES TO THE CRIME FAMILY, however, could still bring benefits.

Ambushed as he drove into the garage of his Northland home, John Amaro was shot to death by two men in mid-February 1977. The slaying occurred in the neighborhood favored by Crime Family leaders, and probably was meant to send them a message.

Sonny Bowen became an ally of Freddy Bonadonna. The Outfit suspected that Bowen was a killer of John Amaro.

Only three days after John Amaro's death in 1977, four men wearing ski masks and carrying shotguns entered Mr. O'Brien's on Broadway, where Harold "Sonny" Bowen was sitting in a booth. They shouted at patrons to duck and aimed at Bowen killing him and leaving spatters of blood on the seat and walls.

The FBI operated under cover in 1977 at Fifth Street and Troost Avenue, next door to the Trap.

Before entering prison for his gambling conviction in 1977, Nick Civella's appeals for leniency centered on his declining health.

Death knell for the River Quay came with an explosion in March 1977, when an entire building housing several bars was obliterated. Four months later, Uncle Joe's tavern, run by Joe Cammisano, burned. Before the 1970s ended, Willie Cammisano, below, pleaded guilty and Joe Cammisano, bottom, was found guilty of River Quay-related crimes.

From *The Kansas City Times*, June 27, 1978.

The Crime Family suspected Gary T. Parker of aiding in John Amaro's murder, and authorities warned him his life was in danger. Parker reacted nonchalantly at first. Eventually he was done in by a bomb placed in his car outside a tavern on Truman Road. The date was August 5, 1977.

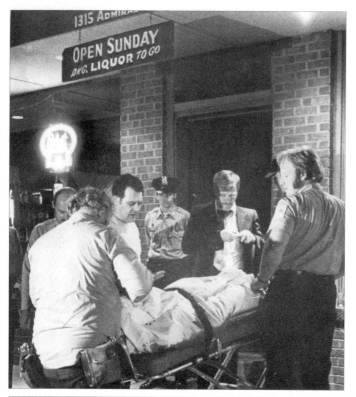

In May 1978 gunmen burst in on the Virginian Tavern and shot Michael, Joe and Carl Spero. Michael died, Joe was wounded and Carl was paralyzed. The surviving Spero brothers plotted revenge.

Civella associate Gene Shepard warned his partner in crime, Mike Ruffalo, against cooperating with authorities. Ruffalo rejected the advice, entering witness protection with his son.

Donna Ruffalo. Mike Ruffalo's wife, had plenty of mob connections, and her pleas for the return of her son from Mike's custody were viewed with suspicion.

Associated Press/Charles Harrity

April 1980: Freddy Bonadonna, shielded by a screen, prepared to testify before the U.S. Senate Permanent Investigations Subcommittee in Washington. Senator Sam Nunn of Georgia headed the committee.

Ruffalo told agent Flosi how, with Civella's influence, he had been handed a job as a "security aide" with the Columbus Park Safety and Energy Project. The project was part of the federally funded Comprehensive Employment and Training Act, called CETA, administered by the Kansas City Department of Urban Affairs.

CETA was enacted to provide jobs for the poor and hard-core unemployed. The task of the Columbus Park project was to install smoke alarms, safety locks and other items in the city's depressed areas. Another CETA project, the Northeast Student Services Project, was responsible for counseling students at Northeast High School. All told, various CETA projects had received $360,000 since their inception.

Both projects were headquartered at 3239 Independence Ave., the business address of Gene Shepard. For 19 months beginning in January 1978, Shepard was listed as project director and security aide for the Columbus Park project, and his live-in girlfriend, Amy Irene Gilliland, was carried as a "student service counselor" for the Northeast project at a salary of $764. Besides Ruffalo and Shepard, other "security aides" on the payroll included Outfit associates John Cuezze and Frank Costanza, a close Shepard associate, along with Toni LanFranca and Donna Rau. Both women had been companions of Cork Civella. Hired as a "project aide" was Carl Vincent Civella, son of Tony Civella and grandson of Cork. Carl Vincent Civella's female companion Shelly Mitchell also was on the Northeast project's payroll.

The FBI launched an investigation, which led to an expose by *The Kansas City Times* in April 1980. As for the effect of the CETA effort, the newspaper quoted the vice principal at Northeast High School as saying, after checking with school counselors, "I can't find anyone who knows about such an operation."

THREE MONTHS AFTER RUFFALO entered witness protection, signs bubbled to the surface that the Family was going to try to find him and force him back to Kansas City. The first sign came from Ruffalo's ex-wife, Donna Ruffalo, when she petitioned the Jackson County Circuit Court for custody of their son, Michael "Mikey" Ruffalo Jr.

Before entering witness protection, Mike Ruffalo had legal custody, under which Donna got weekend and some holiday visitation rights. Now Mike was in no position to return to Kansas City and contest the case, and on July 24, 1979, Donna Ruffalo won full custody of the child. For the time being, Mikey remained in hiding with his father.

In July 1980 Donna, working with the American Civil Liberties Union, sued Mike Ruffalo, the U.S. attorney general and the U.S. Marshals Service, seeking the return of her son. She claimed her rights to due process had been violated and asked $3 million in damages.

All along, Donna Ruffalo portrayed herself as a doting, aggrieved mother struggling to raise two children, and her alleged plight received national publicity. The tide of sympathy for her would turn, however, as the case wound its way through the justice system and a far different picture of Donna Ruffalo came to light.

U.S. District Court Judge Howard Sachs initially ruled that the government did not have to produce the boy. The ruling was appealed to the Eighth Circuit of Appeals, which decided that Donna Ruffalo's rights had been violated. The appeals court, however, stopped short of ordering the boy's return. It left that decision to the presiding judge in Kansas City after a full hearing into the safety of the boy and his father.

In a series of intense federal court hearings in May 1983, Donna Ruffalo's image as the aggrieved mother was bloodied. It was revealed that she had willingly given up custody of Mikey in 1975. In 1976 she had done the same with an illegitimate daughter, Angela, who was born that year. Meanwhile, she fraudulently drew Aid to Dependent Children benefits for both.

Rather than the doting mother who was claiming to have visited her son daily, Mike Ruffalo's affidavit — supported by testimony from his son — said she visited the boy only once every three or four months.

Donna Ruffalo also was described as a pawn for the mob in their attempt to force Mike Ruffalo back to Kansas City. That allegation was at the crux of the matter, and the government offered other witnesses to support it.

Agent Flosi had known Ruffalo since about 1971. After years of frequent personal contacts, Flosi could attest to the absence of Donna in Mikey's life. Ruffalo's dedication to raising the boy meant that his meetings with Flosi had to be arranged around parental commitments, and often meetings were cut short or cancelled entirely. Flosi told his story in court as did I, along with another informant who had been placed in witness protection, Donna's daughter, Angela, and Mike Ruffalo. It was a story of an uncaring mother with mob boyfriends playing her part in an Outfit-directed plot.

Most important, Mikey, now 13 years old, testified about his mother's lack of interest in him and his half-sister, and of his desire to stay with his father. He also said he feared what would happen to him if forced to return, and also what would happen to his father — who surely would come to Kansas City to retrieve him.

A week after Angela testified about being unwanted and abandoned, Donna Ruffalo, drunk and angry that Angela had testified, went to the home where Angela lived with a woman she described as her "foster grandmother" — an acquaintance who had taken her in and raised her. Donna called police and demanded that the girl be turned over to juvenile authorities.

That didn't fly, so she took Angela by cab to the juvenile facilities, where Donna alleged that Angela was using drugs, lied that Angela's caretaker didn't want her and demanded that juvenile authorities take custody of her. The government described these as acts of retaliation.

At the conclusion of the hearings, Judge Sachs ruled that the government was not required to produce the boy. He labeled Donna Ruffalo's suit a "vehicle of intended homicide."

Although she had "unclean hands in filing the suit," the judge continued, "even a wicked mother has some rights that should be respected." As a result, Donna was allowed one visit with her son every three months at a secure neutral site.

On her first scheduled visit to Mikey, Donna made a big mistake. She disobeyed a U.S. Marshal's instruction not to use the telephone and called her current boyfriend, criminal figure Jake Wilhelm, from the airport. The trip was aborted, and her visits were reduced to three a year.

As for her suit asking millions of dollars from the government, a trial was held in June 1984. The judge awarded her $17,000, and reduced her permitted visits to two a year. As a footnote to the matter, in November 1980 Donna Ruffalo, whose resume was not exactly sterling, was hired by the ACLU.

In the end, the Cammisanos had done Mike Ruffalo Sr. and Jr. a huge favor. Once in the witness protection program, Mike Ruffalo successfully made the transition out of a life in the underworld with only a dim future for himself and his son. His life stabilized, he earned a legitimate living and he raised his son to be a solid citizen. Mike Ruffalo died April 16, 2009, having stayed on the straight and narrow from the time his new life began.

ONCE IN WITNESS PROTECTION, Mike Ruffalo was not available to provide a perjured affidavit in behalf of the Cammisanos or to do their bidding to otherwise discredit Freddy Bonadonna.

In a surprise move, Joe and Willie Cammisano entered guilty pleas to charges of conspiracy on October 23, 1979, the day their trial in the River Quay case was to begin. Under terms of a plea deal, the government recommended a sentence of no more than five years for Willie Cammisano and 18 months for Joe Cammisano. The government's willingness to deal on the sentences stemmed partly from its desire to save Freddy Bonadonna from having to testify, which he was averse to doing anyway.

Equally surprising as his guilty plea, less than a month later Joe Cammisano petitioned the court to withdraw the plea. According to Joe, he had agreed to the deal only to help his brother get a lighter sentence. Two days before the trial date, Joe claimed, Willie told him that if he turned down the deal down it would hurt Willie. That left Joe with an overpowering sense of duty that clouded his judgment.

His request was denied and Joe appealed the ruling.

At the time of sentencing defendants are allowed to make a statement.

Willie made his statement simple, telling the judge, "You could give me a little less time if you'd like to."

Simple was not Joe's style, and he let it all hang out. Defiantly, he proclaimed his innocence, accused his attorney of selling him down the river and lashed out at everyone associated with the case — specifically Strike Force chief David Helfrey, Mayor Charles B. Wheeler, Councilman Robert Hernandez, *Kansas City Star* reporter J.J. Maloney and, of course, Freddy Bonadonna.

As it happened, an appellate court ruled that Joe Cammisano could be allowed to withdraw his plea. He would have a trial after all. It began August 6, 1979.

Freddy Bonadonna was the star witness. He provided the jury a story of five years of conflict in the River Quay. Five days into the trial, after deliberating only 29 minutes, the jury found Joe Cammisano guilty of extortion.

To this, he was quoted as saying, "I believe the jury lied."

While the case was on appeal Joe Cammisano died and by law the conviction was vacated by the appeals court.

His brother Willie, meanwhile, was in for more grief.

IN NOVEMBER 1979 WORD CIRCULATED that the U.S. Senate Permanent Investigations Subcommittee, dormant since the 1950s when it was chaired by John McClellan, was being rejuvenated. Under the leadership of Senator Sam Nunn of Georgia, the subcommittee would take an updated, comprehensive look at organized crime. By April 1980 a subcommittee spokesman announced that mob violence would be the top item on the agenda, and Kansas City's River Quay case would be first up.

Invited to testify before the subcommittee were Michael DeFeo, now supervisor of western U.S. strike forces and based in Kansas City; Police Chief Norman Caron of Kansas City, and myself as supervisor of the Kansas City FBI Organized Crime Squad. Our testimony on April 30 set the stage for a dramatic appearance by Freddy Bonadonna. Surrounded by U.S. marshals and testifying behind a screen, he held the subcommittee members' rapt attention.

One other Kansas City figure was called before the subcommittee, but he did not come willingly. Willie Cammisano was brought from prison to appear on May 1, 1980. As expected, he invoked the Fifth Amendment to all question posed to him — even after a grant of immunity from prosecution. The subcommittee then chose to invoke for the first time provisions of a 1978 law that made it easier to force witnesses to testify, providing as it did the possibility of jail for civil contempt.

The process began in October 1980, when a federal judge in Washington ordered Cammisano to testify. Willie defied the judge's order. That led to his being held in civil contempt, and on December 29, 1980, the five-year sentence he was serving for extortion was extended until the 97th Congress adjourned on January 3, 1983, or until he agreed to submit to committee questioning. He never did so.

Without the subcommittee's action, Cammisano would have been released in March 1982. With the civil contempt citation added on, he was not released until August 10, 1983.

On the street, speculation swirled as to what role he would play in the Crime Family. His attorney, former federal prosecutor Bruce Houdek, told *The Star* that Cammisano was now retired. If Houdek meant retired from the Family, that was pure fiction.

CHAPTER XVIII

UNFINISHED BUSINESS

T HE BOTCHED ATTEMPT ON Carl Spero's life served only to aggravate an explosive situation. From the mob's standpoint, Spero still represented unfinished business. From Spero's standpoint, he had every intention to strike back. From law enforcement's standpoint, more violence was in the wind.

It was back to the drawing board for Supervisor Gary Hart, senior members of the Organized Crime Squad and Strike Force attorneys. Clearly, electronic surveillance offered the only real chance of developing evidence. What was the best location? That called for analyzing a mass of intelligence, brainstorming with members of the Police Intelligence Unit and canvassing sources on the street. All roads seemingly led in one direction: the Villa Capri Restaurant at 2609 Independence Ave., run by an Outfit associate and active bookmaker, Ross Strada. The restaurant was a favorite congregating point, and a back table was set aside for the exclusive use of Outfit members. Besides being a safe place to conduct business, the Villa Capri also was the center of a bookmaking and loansharking operation.

While files were reviewed, informants contacted and affidavits drafted, other agents and Intelligence Unit detectives maintained watch on the Villa Capri. After nine intensive days of work on the Virginian Tavern assault, approval was received to petition a U.S. district judge for authority to place a secret microphone at that back table in the Villa Capri and in four automobiles that had been the subjects of an earlier court order for surveillance.

Running an electronic surveillance operation is labor-intensive. It ties up agents and prosecutors for extended periods. Such operations also anticipate extraordinary results, and this came to pass the night of June 6, 1978. The restaurant was deserted except for two heavy hitters in the Crime Family, Cork Civella and Carl DeLuna, and the FBI's microphone.

We were looking for evidence of murder and mayhem in Kansas City. However, their conversation, laced with obvious code names, instead concerned "Chicago," the Teamsters and ill winds affecting Family interests — not in Kansas City but in Las Vegas, Nevada.

This unexpected development, rather than providing a solution to the Spero-Civella conflict, set wheels in motion in an entirely different direction. What direction? The conversation left questions that begged for answers. What was the Kansas City Outfit's involvement in Las Vegas? Who were the people referred to by code names? Where did investigative jurisdiction lie? In any case, what could we do about it?

The answers lay in three segments of the conversation. First was DeLuna's opening statement: "I told that guy you and I are going to call him." Second was another DeLuna statement: "Carl, we're going to have to give this guy an answer right now. Tonight." Third, DeLuna's concluding comment: "I don't think we ought to call from here. I think we ought to get a phone." At that point, Civella and DeLuna left the restaurant. There seemed little doubt the telephone they were seeking would be used to call an ally in Las Vegas. Our task was clear: Identify what phone or phones DeLuna was using and tap them.

The pot was boiling over. Nick Civella was released June 14. Two days later, the River Quay case indictments came down. All the while, the Spero situation simmered and the Las Vegas matter waited in the wings, put on hold by reason of internal strife over which FBI office — Kansas City, Las Vegas or Chicago — would take the lead in the investigation. Eventually, the questions over direction and strategy were resolved and Kansas City was assigned the lead role.

DeLuna, the savvy street boss of the Outfit, clearly would be difficult to follow discreetly day in and day out. The job fell to the Kansas City FBI office's surveillance team. The wary veteran mobster took all manner of evasive actions in attempts to "clean" himself.

It was no contest. Our surveillance team was more than up to the task.

On five occasions from June 16 to July 6, the team tailed DeLuna to what was then the Breckenridge Inn at 1601 N. Universal Ave. in Kansas City's East Bottoms. With the agents looking on, DeLuna loitered by a bank of pay telephones, waiting for one to ring. The phone in question had been found.

Years later, Hart recalled in a magazine interview how the FBI

key to the kingdom: legal electronic surveillance.

And so on that night in June 1978 — when agents monitoring Carl DeLuna and Cork Civella at the Villa Capri Restaurant overheard the two hashing out problems in Las Vegas — the door was opened. The results of the electronic surveillance gave rise to a massive investigation that would doom the Kansas City Crime Family.

The Villa Capri meeting led to the uncovering of DeLuna's use of pay phones at the Breckenridge Hotel, which led to wiretaps on those phones. Those wiretaps in turn paved the way for expanded electronic coverage in Kansas City and elsewhere. The result was a tidal wave of information. Combined, the electronic surveillance plus supporting investigation plus statements from critical witnesses painted as vivid a picture of Cosa Nostra at work as one could find.

JOSEPH AGOSTO, CODE-NAMED "CAESAR," claimed to have been born in a Cleveland brothel and sent to Sicily, where he grew up. Immigration officials disagreed, alleging he was Sicilian by birth, had assumed the name Agosto and was in the United States illegally. They tried to deport Agosto for a dozen years before Agosto prevailed in 1978.

He had connections in Kansas City, having spent time here in the 1940s before moving to the West Coast. He met Nick Civella in 1973 when he was invited to Kansas City to join John Amaro in promoting a mob scheme. The plan was to promote a legal services benefit for Teamsters members with money kicked back to figures in the Family. Nick Civella's influence with the Teamsters was critical to the scheme, so Agosto met with him, paying him $75,000 for his help. The scheme, however, failed and Agosto moved on.

In summer 1974 Agosto had an opportunity to build a hotel and casino in Las Vegas. His first move was to head for Kansas City, where he met with Nick and Cork Civella and Carl DeLuna, attempting to arrange a loan from the Teamsters Fund. As those plans progressed, he was instructed to keep in regular contact with DeLuna.

These events, revealed through the Strawman investigation, may well have been the reason Nick Civella in August 1974 had defied the travel restrictions on the bond in his gambling case and flown secretly to Las Vegas.

In late 1974 Agosto's initial plans were sidelined by a tip that the Tropicana Hotel and Casino was in financial difficulty. He recognized a ready-made opportunity. Agosto met with the owner, only to learn that two

Las Vegas figures were negotiating a joint venture with the owner and had applied for a $50 million loan from the Teamsters Fund to seal the deal. If the loan was approved, Agosto would be out in the cold. He headed back to Kansas City to make a new pitch to Nick Civella.

If the loan to the two Las Vegas figures was killed, Agosto would get the chance to gain a foothold — and Civella would secretly gain control of the Tropicana. Civella agreed to the idea.

Now, the top priority was for Civella to block the loan. Then Agosto would negotiate a new deal with the Tropicana's owner. They would then apply for a new Teamsters Fund loan in the name of the owner and of Nick Tano, who was Agosto's partner. As an ex-felon, Agosto could not become a licensed owner.

It was a sweetheart deal, dumped in Civella's lap and not unusual when it came to Cosa Nostra bosses who had union clout.

ABOUT FIVE MONTHS BEFORE Joe Agosto offered himself as Civella's man at the Tropicana, a 30-something wonder boy from San Diego, California, burst on the Vegas scene in a big way.

Allen Glick got his feet wet in Nevada gaming by acquiring an interest in the Hacienda Hotel and Casino. Next, Glick secured a lease for the casino at the Marina Hotel. Then, in a risky and bold financial move, he added ownership of the Stardust and Freemont hotels and casinos by obtaining a $62 million-plus loan from the Teamsters Fund. The loan was approved with the say-so of Nick Civella and of crime family bosses in Chicago, Milwaukee and Cleveland. Glick gathered all four hotels under the umbrella of his Argent Corp. The Stardust was the flagship property.

Without realizing it, Glick had walked into a hornet's nest.

For years, the Stardust had been known as the Chicago mob's hotel. The mob's man in charge of stealing money there was Frank "Lefty" Rosenthal. He was a notorious character in his own right and a gambling wizard, code-named "Craze."

He wore loud clothes, talked loud, boasted and strutted and even had his own television talk show in Las Vegas. Too often, Rosenthal acted as if he were the boss of it all.

Glick, pinned with the code name "Genius" or "Baldy," held himself out as a legitimate businessman. He had no idea, he maintained, that by obtaining the Teamsters loan he would become a mob puppet. A puppet was what Rosenthal made him.

Rosenthal was an ex-felon, having been convicted when he was 32 of conspiracy to fix a North Carolina basketball game. As a result, he was not eligible to hold a gaming license as a "key employee" and so was barred from officially exerting any management control. Nevertheless, Rosenthal openly acted as the de facto boss of the Stardust.

Making matters worse, Glick was told by Milwaukee boss Frank Balestrieri that if he wanted consideration for future Teamsters Fund loans he would have to appoint Rosenthal as his assistant. With little choice, Glick named Rosenthal director of Nevada operations, a strictly advisory position but one that carried a salary of $250,000.

Rosenthal continued to undermine Glick at every turn, and their relationship turned toxic. Eventually, Glick decided to fire him.

In fall 1974 the two sat down in a coffee shop at the Stardust. Glick tried to lay down the law. Instead, Rosenthal laid out the facts: He was placed in his position to help others and not Glick. Glick was not his boss.

"If you interfere with any of the casino operations or try to undermine anything I want to do," Rosenthal told him, "I represent that you will never leave this corporation alive."

Glick left the meeting shaken, describing himself as feeling "like someone who had just arrived from an alien planet." What followed was beyond anything Glick could have anticipated.

Late one evening in March 1975, Glick was having dinner when Rosenthal called him from Kansas City. He ordered Glick to fly there immediately, even if it meant arriving in the early-morning hours. At Kansas City International Airport, Carl DeLuna and Rosenthal picked up Glick and took him to a hotel. On the way, Rosenthal told Glick he was about to meet a very important person. He was escorted into a darkened suite and seated in a chair with a light shining in his face.

Across from Glick sat Nick Civella, whom Glick had never met. The Boss wasted no time. In a cold, calculating manner Civella told Glick that he was not the kind of person he wanted anything to do with.

"Cling to every word I say," Civella told him. "You don't know me, but it would be my choice you would never leave this room alive..... Because of circumstances, if you listen, you may....

"If you don't accept that I was responsible for the loan (from the Teamsters Fund) then either you would not leave the room or somewhere in the short period of time you will get the message by bullet."

And that wasn't all Civella had to say. Glick was informed he had a commitment to "us" and he owed $1.2 million that Civella wanted paid.

"We own part of your corporation and you are to do nothing to interfere," Civella said. "I want that paid..... We will let Mr. Rosenthal continue with the casinos, and you are not to interfere."

Then Civella told a bewildered and intimidated Glick to get out.

Of all the mob bosses who had a piece of the action in Argent, it was Civella who gave Glick his marching orders. That spoke to the stature of the Kansas City Boss in such affairs.

From 1976 through the first two months of 1979, the Civella Crime Family would receive $1,310,000 as its share of money skimmed from the Argent Corp. Chicago, Cleveland and Milwaukee crime families, having participated in arranging the Glick loan, also got a cut, ballooning the total skim stolen from Las Vegas. The skim money came through Chicago, which had deep roots in Las Vegas, and anyone getting in the way of the money stream skated on thin ice. Even after the Strawman investigation surfaced, the Chicago family would continue to receive skimmed money from Las Vegas, part of which was distributed to Kansas City.

WHILE THE ARGENT SITUATION SIMMERED in spring 1975, Nick Civella, still under indictment in the gambling case, met with Agosto in Las Vegas to hash out affairs at the Tropicana. By then Agosto had a tentative financial arrangement established and had obtained the rights to the lavish Folies Bergere show. Civella instructed Agosto to hire Carl Thomas, the skimming expert, as casino manager.

The proposed $50 million Teamsters Fund loan to Agosto's competitors was still months away from being rejected, which would open the way to Agosto. In the interim, his plans for control of the hotel hit a wall.

Mitzi Briggs, a wealthy heiress, infused $6.2 million in the Tropicana, taking over ownership and ending Agosto's influence. Nevertheless, he maintained a foothold at the hotel because of his interest in the Folies Bergere show and so bided his time.

It turned out that Briggs' management style was a disaster. By 1977 she was looking to Agosto for advice. He gained her trust, and she turned over management responsibilities to Agosto, allowing him to hire a crew recommended by Carl Thomas to handle the skimming. The unstable financial situation, however, hampered the anticipated skimming operation.

Also in 1977 the Department of Labor filed suit to remove Roy Lee Williams and other trustees for mismanagement of the Teamsters Pension Fund. That was a severe setback for Civella's plans and for the influence of Midwest crime families.

Equitable Life Insurance Co. of New York City got authority and control over the assets and investments of the Fund. Responsibility for management of Fund real estate investments was assigned to the Victor Palmieri Co., also of New York City. Both firms were outside the control of mob families.

The result was a hiatus in mob-sponsored loans from the Fund. Now the Kansas City Family was out in the cold, unable any longer to influence a loan to gain ownership of the Tropicana.

With Nick Civella on his way to jail in August 1977, Agosto — who still maintained management control of the Tropicana — now reported to Cork Civella through Carl DeLuna. With DeLuna, Civella paid Agosto a visit to discuss the management situation at the Tropicana. Six months later Agosto was called to meet secretly with Nick Civella in Los Angeles, where Civella had been transported by the Bureau of Prisons to undergo a cancer operation. Nick Civella was pleased that Agosto was in a position of authority at the hotel, but expressed his displeasure at not seeing any skim money.

Using Sicilian, the Boss told Agosto he had received *mancu un petu*, which translated to "not even a fart."

"What do you think those people are there for?" Civella asked, referring to the "skim crew." He instructed Agosto to get things going.

That led to a meeting in Las Vegas with DeLuna and Carl Thomas. There, Agosto learned that Thomas had also visited with Civella in Los Angeles about the skim. It was agreed they would begin the operation, but take no more than $50,000 a month. Ten percent of that would be paid to the crew responsible for getting it done.

The first hit from the slots amounted to $11,500. The money was handed over to DeLuna in April 1978 while he was in Vegas. The plan was for future deliveries to be handled by a courier, Carl Caruso, code-named "Singer." Caruso ran regular gambling junkets to Vegas and in years past had worked in Outfit gambling establishments. Two months later, $40,000, referred to as a "sandwich," was delivered to Caruso for transport to Kansas

City. The transfers continued until February 1979.

Later, evidence revealed that for 11 months from 1978 to 1979 the amount stolen from the Tropicana, limited by its shaky financial situation, was $401,000. Because control of the Tropicana was not accomplished by means of a Teamsters Fund loan, the Kansas City Outfit was not obligated to share the proceeds with crime families in other cities. Civella cut the Chicago family in, anyway, forking over $135,000 of the Tropicana skim.

AT THE STARDUST, Glick and Rosenthal were still at crossed swords, and Rosenthal's high-profile antics also led to conflict with gaming authorities, who called him in for a licensing hearing. Rosenthal went into attack mode, creating a publicity nightmare for mob interests. Now, Rosenthal had become a thorn in the side of the mob, rather than the asset he had once been.

Glick also remained in disfavor with the mob. His fate was sealed on April 19, 1978, at a meeting in Chicago among Carl DeLuna, Cork Civella, Chicago Boss Joe Aiuppa, Aiuppa's underboss Jack Cerone, his top aide "Turk" Torello and Frank Rosenthal. Glick was to get his walking papers and Carl DeLuna was to serve them.

A week later DeLuna traveled to Las Vegas. Accompanied by Rosenthal, he met Glick in the law office of mob attorney Oscar Goodman, who made it available for the mobsters to conduct business.

Glick was told he was finished. He should step aside, sell his hotels, and in DeLuna's words, "Do what you gotta do, boy, make your public announcement that you are getting out of this for whatever f-----g reason you want to pick and get out."

To insure that Glick was clear about the message, DeLuna took out a piece of paper and read off the names of Glick's two sons and their ages, chilling him to the bone.

The effects that Glick experienced — from the theatrical meeting in a dark Kansas City hotel room with Civella while a light semi-blinded Glick to the more recent reading of Glick's children's names and ages — were reminiscent of the way Roy Lee Williams had been intimidated in the 1950s. All were vintage Nick Civella.

WITH GLICK'S HEAVE-HO there followed a scramble of competing factions, including the Kansas City Family, to gain ownership of

Argent. Because the Chicago Family had long had the upper hand in control of the Stardust, Argent's flagship, Chicago had the ultimate say. As it turned out, the quest for ownership was the topic of the intercepted conversation between Carl DeLuna and Cork Civella at the Villa Capri Restaurant in June 1978, the conversation that triggered the Strawman case.

As the Strawman investigation gained momentum and the Spero murder investigation continued in Kansas City, agents expanded electronic surveillance. Taps were placed on the home phones of DeLuna, Pete Tamburello and Charles Moretina; at the Quinn & Peebles law firm, and on pay phones at the Muehlebach Hotel. Bugs were placed at the Columbus Park Social Club and the adjacent Wimpy's Restaurant in the North End, and at places where meetings were planned. Among those was the residence at 1512 N.E. 50th St., the Marriott Airport Hotel, the residence of Jack Trombino, the offices of Carl Caruso and the residence of Phil Simone at 1505 N.E. 50th St. Tied to the Strawman investigation, court-approved electronic surveillance also was under way in Las Vegas, Chicago, Milwaukee and San Diego.

New Argent ownership "packages" came and went, entailing sensitive, complex and devious negotiations. Tension developed between outfits in Kansas City and Chicago, requiring the sending of messages and many meetings. The process was complicated by the periods when Nick Civella was in prison.

In fall 1978, Nick Civella was overheard talking with his nephew, Anthony "Stompy" Chiavola, a Chicago Police sergeant and courier of skim money between Chicago and Kansas City. The two were planning a meeting that Civella and DeLuna were to attend. It would take place at the Chiavola residence with the Chicago boss, Aiuppa, his underboss, Jack Cerone, and ranking member, Angelo LaPietra. The planning was detailed, down to the type of wine Civella wanted served. Arrangements were made for Chiavola and his son Anthony Chiavola Jr., also a Chicago policeman, to provide security for the meeting. They were to sweep the area, looking for FBI or other law enforcement.

The Chicago FBI took on the task of covering the meeting. The meeting was to take place in an upstairs apartment of Chiavola's residence, which ordinarily was occupied by a relative. Getting a microphone installed in the lion's den was a formidable endeavor, but accomplished nonetheless. It would be a rare opportunity to be the fly on the wall when two Cosa Nostra bosses sat down to conduct business.

The date was October 22, 1978, and the participants were all accounted for. Then fate interceded. Aiuppa, who suffered from a heart problem, could not negotiate the stairs to the second floor. Instead, the meeting was held in Chiavola's first-floor space.

There is little doubt that it had to do with the Argent Corp.'s new ownership and that Civella argued a Kansas City "package" should prevail. If he had succeeded, Civella would have gained control of skimming from the Argent hotel and casinos. He still would have been obligated to share with the other crime families, but it would have been his call as to who got what.

As it turned out, however, the Argent Corp. holdings were sold to two individuals controlled by the Chicago Family.

RETURNING HOME, CIVELLA turned his attention to sorting out affairs at the Tropicana. He ordered Joe Agosto and Carl Thomas in from Las Vegas for a meeting on November 26 at a neighboring residence in Filumena Acres. That was the meeting in which Nick and Cork Civella were overheard discussing beforehand what it would take to murder Carl Spero.

Once Thomas, Agosto and Carl DeLuna arrived the group hashed through a variety of topics. One concerned the antics of Frank Rosenthal.

Other topics included the Stardust and other hotels and various Las Vegas personalities, but the main item on the agenda was stealing money from the Tropicana. Nick Civella worried that casino people were stealing for themselves, and he had ordered a moratorium on skimming from the Tropicana through November and December 1978. In that time, Carl Thomas was to audit the operation to see whether the unauthorized thefts were occurring.

Thomas assured him there was no stealing, and the time came to lift the moratorium. The group looked to Thomas to explain how that could best be done. In outlining the possibilities, Thomas delivered a textbook dissertation on the various methods of stealing money from hotel casinos, sports books and stage shows.

Civella, speaking of controls that would be required, said, "I'm for, I'm for control of Shepard (a casino manager)....To tell you the truth, a, I'm for control of everybody.... I'd like it to be either me or him (DeLuna) or my brother (Cork Civella) the ultimate control."

Summing up his position, Nick Civella told his guests, "I'm glad you're all here together to touch on various things we have to touch, that there is a compatibility between you two guys, and that, which I'm damned sure I told you sometime back, we'll get you here together.

"You'll get confirmation for whatever you need. Joe'll get confirmation for whatever he needs. We'll be the responsible ones for you and for him."

Time was running out for Civella's grand plans and anticipated good fortune.

THE KANSAS CITY FBI AND LAS VEGAS FBI had never really been in sync in the investigation, and interoffice tensions and conflicts over timing and direction of the case created unnecessary problems that had to be dealt with. In early December 1978 Organized Crime Supervisor Gary Hart and Agent Shea Airey traveled to Las Vegas for a meeting to sort things out.

As a result of that meeting, it was decided that the time had come to "surface" the investigation — to take overt action. In early January 1979 plans were mapped out in conjunction with the Strike Force to serve search warrants in Kansas City and other cities at the moment Carl Caruso made his next delivery of skimmed money. Timing was important; once the investigation came to light in one place, the mob grapevine would deliver the news to other cities, where people involved in the distribution would pull in their horns.

Agosto and DeLuna were overheard discussing delivery of a skim package on January 17, 1979, and a search warrant was rushed into print to seize it. That effort, however, went for naught. Caruso was not on the plane, and it was found that he had arrived earlier than scheduled but without any skim money.

The authorized period of electronic surveillance was due to expire February 1, and when a second expected skim delivery on January 27 did not materialize, an extension had to be applied for. The request was approved in Washington and the court order signed on February 2. Five days later, DeLuna and Caruso firmed up a date of February 14 for a skim delivery consisting of two "sandwiches."

Valentine's Day 1979 saw the weather turn ugly. Fog closed Kansas City International Airport for a time. The lengthy search-warrant application was in the hands of Magistrate Calvin K. Hamilton and while under his review the assembled search teams were briefed. They were instructed not to take any action until Caruso was intercepted at the airport and searched.

That task was to be handled by agents Noel Vetter, Parnell Miles, Bruce Wick and myself, along with Intelligence Unit Supervisor Larry Weishar. By 5:40 p.m. word from Las Vegas indicated that Caruso was on the plane headed to Kansas City. At that time, the judge still had not signed the search warrants.

Caruso was due about 7:40 p.m. at KCI. Finally, just after 6 p.m. the warrants were signed. They still had to be distributed to the various teams and plans had to be firmed up. About 6:30 p.m. we were ready to go.

Next came a white-knuckle trip from the FBI office to KCI airport, speeding north on Interstate 29 in bad weather with low visibility. Our team arrived later than expected, and not long afterward Caruso's flight arrived.

We spread out near the baggage carousel and watched as Caruso, wearing an ascot and blazer over loud, blue-plaid slacks, made his way there carrying an attache case. Apparently sensing our presence, he handed the attache case to his son, who had come to the airport to meet him. The young man headed for the doors. As agents intercepted his son and seized the attache case, I approached Caruso, identifying myself and telling him why we were there to meet him. We escorted Caruso to an airport security room, where his son was allowed to join him. Caruso received his copy of the search warrant and was told to start emptying his pockets.

There has always been a mystique about how skim money was transported: Was it hidden in clothing, in the false bottoms of baggage or in other exotic places? Not so.

Caruso reached into one inside pocket of his blazer and removed a packet of bills held by a rubber band. He did the same with the other pocket. The two "sandwiches" totaled $80,000. To my knowledge, that was the first time a delivery of skim money had been seized by law enforcement. Among other items of evidence seized were $80,000 in gambling markers, representing money owed to a casino.

Then we sent word to the poised teams of FBI agents and police detectives. They moved in on Nick Civella, Cork Civella, Carl DeLuna, Pete Tamburello, Joe Ragusa, Vince Abbott, Charles Moretina and William Cammisano Jr., searching them, their homes and several of their vehicles. A warrant was executed at the North End residence of DeLuna's mother, where three flak jackets and walkie-talkies were recovered.

From Nick Civella the team recovered $110,000 in cash, 40 loose diamonds, financial records and a sheaf of Las Vegas newspaper articles. Cork

Civella was relieved of $25,000 in cash, $45,000 in certificates of deposit and records including a note with coded names and percentages tied to the amount of skim shared with Kansas City Outfit members.

The mother lode was uncovered at DeLuna's home. There the search team found that DeLuna kept voluminous records documenting crime family affairs in Kansas City and elsewhere, and the agents spent the night collecting them. These detailed coded records, kept over a period of years, documented dates, places and content of high-level meetings in various cities and the mob figures involved.

DeLuna also recorded the amounts of skimmed Las Vegas gambling proceeds coming to Kansas City, portions of which were shared with other crime families, and the percentage of the skim money received by various local Outfit members and associates. The search team also toted away $60,000 in cash, which had been stashed in various parts of the house, an instruction booklet on silencers and four loaded handguns.

At Pete Tamburello's home, a key to a safe-deposit box led to $10,000 in certificates of deposit, walkie-talkies, binoculars, two blackjacks, $12,000 in cash, a notebook with financial recordings and five handguns, four of them loaded. Other searches turned up various weapons, a police scanner, ski masks, handcuffs, a beeper tracking device and Citizens Band radios. In all, about $300,000 in cash was seized.

The search of DeLuna's mother's residence, which was just down the street from the Trap, turned up a roster of employees of the U.S. Drug Enforcement Administration, other official government documents and a bulletproof vest similar to those issued to federal agents. The equipment was identified as having come from four or five break-ins of DEA and ATF cars in 1978.

ONE MONTH AFTER THE VALENTINE'S DAY RAID, the investigation took yet another turn. Squad Supervisor Gary Hart was scheduled to be away for two weeks starting March 19, 1979, and as principal relief supervisor I filled in for him.

It was a hectic time, what with the surfacing of the Strawman investigation and the need to handle last-minute details for the long-delayed trial of the Credit Union of America-FHA fraud prosecution. That trial was scheduled to begin the next Monday.

Snow was falling on Friday, March 23, 1979, when about 5 p.m. the

Chicago FBI office called to say that wiretaps had picked up plans for a one-day visit to Kansas City by several individuals connected to Allen Dorfman's insurance agency. Their destination and purpose were not known. The meeting was planned for Sunday, March 25.

The names didn't set off any alarms and, in view of the scarcity of information, I considered whether it was worth paying heed to their arrival. Then I considered that we were better safe than sorry, so I started lining up agents to spend yet another weekend on the job.

At 9:30 a.m. Sunday, March 25, a Chicago agent called with news that changed everything. These weren't nobodies coming to Kansas City, after all. Allen Dorfman himself, a bigshot in Teamster-mob affairs, along with Sol Schwartz, his right-hand man, were going to make the trip. A ranking Chicago outfit member later identified as Joe "The Clown" Lombardo, also was on the way. Their flight arrived at 11 a.m. and their taxi ride was tailed to the Crown Center Hotel, where they registered and were assigned room 1539. While the visitors lunched at the hotel, I made arrangements to secure a room where traffic in and out of room 1539 could be observed.

Our assigned room, 1540, turned out to connect to 1539. Anyone entering or leaving 1539 could be seen through a security peephole. Better still, by placing an ear to the metal framework of the connecting door, we could clearly overhear the conversation next door. That unexpected happenstance was heightened by what came next.

At 1:54 p.m. Nick Civella and Pete Tamburello were seen walking down the hall from the elevators to Room 1539. After some small talk, everyone except Nick Civella and Lombardo left the room.

Lombardo started off by saying that the "Old Man" — a reference to the Chicago boss, Aiuppa — wanted him to see Civella to talk over issues plaguing the Teamsters Pension Fund. For one thing, the Fund administrators were not in their camp. The Labor Department had given direction of Fund assets to Equitable Life Insurance and Victor Palmieri Co., New York firms that were not on the Cosa Nostra team.

The problems had to be resolved to get things running smoothly. Lombardo went on to say that Roy Lee Williams was the one who could get the job done, and that Civella was the only one who could get Williams to listen and act. Civella agreed that Williams was his to handle without interference, just as Lombardo would not want Civella to interfere with Chicago's "people." Civella mentioned that the "Old Man" had already sent word about the situation. He had checked with Williams, he said. Williams agreed changes had to be made, but he disagreed about the methods proposed.

The discussion turned to the issue of a candidate to take over leadership of the Pension Fund. Civella indicated that he had no one in mind nor was he trying to put anyone in, but he did voice objection to Allen Dorfman. If Dorfman was known to be running things, Civella argued, the government would swoop down, and besides Dorfman had an ego problem. Civella mentioned that he and Williams agreed it would be desirable to have Williams appointed president of the International Brotherhood of Teamsters so that he would be the incumbent at the time of the next election. As president of the international union, Williams could name his successor as central conference president, and could count on him to control the Fund trustees. That would ensure continuance of mob influence in Teamster affairs.

About 15 minutes later, Dorfman joined Civella and Lombardo in the room, and there followed a wide-ranging discussion of the various problems they faced. Lombardo summed up this way: We have a lot of work to do to get the Fund back, a lot of moves to make and scheming to accomplish.

Civella raised the issue of talk that Roy Lee Williams was getting money, saying the "Old Man" had mentioned it. Civella said that he considered Williams a good friend and took care of whatever he needed. People were always trying to influence Williams, he continued, by using money to win Williams' loyalty from Civella. In fact, the Boss went on, "We give him money."

Civella said he agreed with all that had to be done to regain control of the Fund, and would see to it a plan was formulated at a meeting to be set up in Kansas City and attended by Williams, Dorfman, and Nick and Cork Civella. He told of other meetings with Williams at the residence of Phil Simone, who managed a trucking terminal. At Simone's Williams felt comfortable and had good reason to visit. Civella instructed Dorfman to travel "legit" using his own name, and union business as a cover.

Taking turns with ears pasted to the door frame, three other agents and I were able to overhear the conversations, awkwardly making notes on hotel note paper. We had never expected to encounter such a situation, so none of us had brought writing materials. The meeting broke up at 4:15 p.m. Lombardo and Dorfman left first and Civella five minutes later. Back at the office while the conversations were still fresh, I roughed out what we had overheard.

The meeting was another windfall, similar to the June 1978 monitoring at the Villa Capri Restaurant. The upcoming meeting in Kansas City had to be capitalized on, and electronic surveillance in Chicago provided what was needed.

The meeting with Dorfman to plan strategies for the Pension Fund was scheduled for April 23, 1979, at Phil Simone's residence, 1504 N.E. 50th St. in Filumena Acres, a few doors away from the house where Civella met with Joe Agosto and Carl Thomas in November 1978. By then the mechanics involved in obtaining authority for electronic surveillance were well honed, and on April 5 a judge signed an order allowing for the planting of a microphone. Once again the daunting task of installing the bug in Civella's own neighborhood was taken on and executed brilliantly by a team of agents.

While agents watched, Sam Ancona picked up Dorfman at the airport about 1:30 p.m. and drove him to a Kansas City shopping center. There Phil Simone was waiting in his silver Cadillac with Roy Lee Williams. Ancona and Dorfman got in Simone's car for the trip to Simone's house, where Nick Civella was waiting.

Our hopes were dashed when the group met in a bedroom that was not covered by the secret microphone. Bedrooms are off limits to court-authorized electronic surveillance. The meeting broke up about 5:49 p.m. Civella walked to his home nearby and Simone drove Williams, Dorfman and Ancona to the shopping center. He left Ancona and Dorfman at Ancona's car, and drove Williams to the Teamsters Hall at 4500 Van Brunt Blvd.

Fortunately, the Chicago bureau picked up on a meeting between Dorfman and Chicago mobster Tony Spilotro on May 1. In it, Dorfman talked about the meeting in Kansas City. Dorfman reported that "Roy agreed with everything." Dorfman was to provide a list of procedures for Williams to follow to resolve the problems with Equitable and Palmieri and with trustees who needed to be ousted.

Dorfman was to be the conduit between Williams and the Fund trustees. He described how, at the meeting in Kansas City, Nick Civella confronted Williams, saying: "How much longer are we supposed to go along with this kind of s--t? We're getting f----d around and nothing is taking place."

The issue of manipulating Williams into a position for the presidency of the international was hashed over. Civella claimed he had a commitment from that "f----n' fussbelly Irishman right in my office." He referred to the current international president, Frank Fitzsimmons, who was known to be suffering from cancer. Fitzsimmons reportedly told Civella he would step down before his term expired so Williams would succeed to the presidency.

Those two high-level meetings formed the impetus for a new investigation in Kansas City of Roy Lee Williams and Sam Ancona. That complemented the investigations in Chicago and other offices directed at mob influence in Teamsters affairs.

AT THE TIME OF THE VALENTINE'S DAY SEARCHES, Nick Civella was on parole. When the "Strawman" case surfaced, the accumulated evidence proved sufficient to once again revoke his parole and send him to Leavenworth. He entered the prison June 11, 1979. Four days later, more than 1,000 pages of documents filed in support of the applications for electronic surveillance were unsealed. They provided the public the whole sordid story.

It would take more than two years to pull the Strawman case together, and in this time the responsibility for managing the case and the Organized Crime Squad became mine. Gary Hart was transferred and on July 30, 1981, I was appointed to his spot. Now the day-to-day legwork would be left to others, notably agents Eugene Thomeczek and Ed Humphrey.

With a host of agents and support personnel and the Strike Force, we worked diligently to build a case from the mountain of electronic intercepts, seized evidence, witness interviews, grand jury material, surveillance reports and more — and to prosecute the bribery case against Civella, Tamburello and Tortora.

On November 5, 1981, the first multi-count indictment was returned in what was labeled the Tropicana phase of Strawman. The indictment addressed the skimming of money from the Tropicana. Named in it were Nick and Cork Civella, DeLuna, Moretina, Tamburello, Caruso and Agosto. Also charged were Billy Caldwell and Don Shepard, who were officials of the Tropicana casino, Carl Thomas and Civella's nephew Anthony Chiavola, the Chicago policeman who also carried skim money between Kansas City and Chicago.

The Strawman prosecution was significantly affected when Allen Dorfman was accosted in a Chicago restaurant parking lot and shot seven times in January 1983. At the time, Dorfman was awaiting sentencing, having been convicted in Chicago along with Roy Lee Williams and Joe Lombardo of conspiracy to bribe a U.S. senator from Nevada, Howard Cannon. One publicized theory attributed Dorfman's murder to the mob's fear that, facing a long jail term, he would cooperate with authorities.

That same month Joe Agosto was convicted in St. Paul, Minnesota, on fraud charges unrelated to the Las Vegas matter and jailed pending his sentencing. With pressure mounting from all sides, Agosto caved in and cut a deal with the government to cooperate in the Strawman case. In a public statement, Agosto said he did not want to become "another statistic like Allen Dorfman."

To Agosto, the idea that the mob was now eliminating people simply on the chance they might turn on them was not acceptable. Adding to his anxiety, only four months before the Dorfman killing, the flamboyant Frank Rosenthal had been targeted for murder. A bomb was placed under his car in Las Vegas. It exploded and blew Rosenthal from the car, but the vehicle was a sturdily built Cadillac and miraculously Rosenthal survived.

AGOSTO WAS THE STAR WITNESS in the Tropicana trial that began May 30, 1983, in the U.S. District Court in Kansas City. After a month's trial, eight defendants were found guilty.

This time, sentences were stiff. Cork Civella and Carl DeLuna each got 30 years in prison, Moretina 20 years and Carl Thomas 15 years. Lesser sentences went to the remaining defendants, down to three years probation for Carl Caruso. Agosto pleaded guilty before the trial. He died before he could be sentenced. Tamburello was acquitted.

In the second or Argent phase of the prosecution, indictments were handed down on October 11, 1983. They encompassed eight counts of conspiracy to control and skim funds from the Argent Corp.'s four Las Vegas hotel and casinos. Named defendants were Cork Civella, DeLuna and Tamburello from Kansas City; Joe Aiuppa, Jack Cerrone, Angelo LaPietra and Joe Lombardo from Chicago; Anthony Chiavola Sr. and Jr.; Milton Rockman, a Cleveland mob figure; Frank Balistrieri, Milwaukee crime family boss and his two sons Joe and John, both attorneys; Tony Spilotro, a Chicago crime family member headquartered in Las Vegas, and Carl Thomas.

With several guilty pleas, Spilotro's severance and Thomas' agreement to testify, the seven remaining defendants went to trial in September 1985. The trial lasted four months and was a hotly contested and star-studded affair. Taking the stand for the government were Cosa Nostra turncoats Angelo Lonardo of Cleveland, West Coast-based James Fratianno and Ken Eto of Chicago. Eto had survived a mob execution attempt, although he was shot three times. Allen Glick and Roy Lee Williams provided dramatic testimony. Williams told the story of how years before he had been "compromised" by Civella and had to follow his lead.

The jury came back on January 21, 1986, with guilty verdicts against five of the remaining defendants. When sentencing time came for those five Aiuppa got 28½ years, Cerone 24 years, LaPietra and Lombardo 14 years each, and Rockman 21 years. Joe and John Balistrieri were found not guilty by the judge, who upheld their motion for a directed verdict.

As for those who had pleaded guilty, Frank Balistrieri received 10 years. Cork Civella and Carl DeLuna were sentenced to 10 and 16 years respectively to run concurrently with their 30-year sentences in the Tropicana case. Pete Tamburello was sentenced to five years, and Anthony Chiavola Sr. and Jr. got five years apiece. Spilotro, who had been severed, was murdered before he could be tried separately.

The last piece of business was resolved in February 1984 with the return of an indictment invoking the provisions of the federal Racketeer Influenced and Corrupt Organizations law, or RICO. The indictment aimed to prosecute the Kansas City Crime Family as a criminal entity. Cork Civella, then 74 years old, Tony Civella, 53, Carl DeLuna, 56, and Charles Moretina, 55, were charged with running a criminal enterprise since 1969, along with Boss Nick Civella. Each pleaded guilty to the charges.

The charge encompassed five "acts of racketeering" engaged in by the criminal enterprise known as the Civella Crime Family:

- From January 1, 1976 to February 14, 1979, the defendants invested in a bingo operation in Kansas City, Kansas, purportedly operated by a veterans organization and skimmed $111,128 of the proceeds.
- From January 1978 to January 9, 1984, Carl and Tony Civella and Carl DeLuna conspired to murder Carl Spero, who was eventually killed in a bombing on January 9, 1984.
- From August 9, 1978, to February 14, 1979, the defendants, except for Tony Civella, attempted to maintain illegal hidden control of the Tropicana Hotel and Casino and skimmed $280,000, which was distributed among defendants and crime family figures in Chicago.

- In the late 1970s, Cork Civella and Carl DeLuna conspired with others to control the Argent Corporation in Las Vegas, skimming $2 million from the Stardust and Freemont Hotels.
- From 1969 to 1982 the enterprise engaged in sports bookmaking using interstate communications to facilitate the operation.

CHAPTER XXII
A FINAL ACCOUNTING

IN NOVEMBER 1982 WORD CIRCULATED that Nick Civella's health had seriously deteriorated. He was diagnosed as suffering from lung cancer. His lawyers moved for an early release from prison, but their effort was rejected by the U.S. Parole Commission.

In late December 1982, a petition containing some 800 names was sent to Washington, asking for an early parole. The petition drive was organized by Phil Simone, President of the American Sons of Columbus organization. Simone, the brother of dead mob figure Thomas "Hiway" Simone, had been a liaison man for Civella in Teamsters affairs and, among other services had made available his Filumena Acres residence for Civella to meet secretly with Roy Lee Williams and Alan Dorfman of Chicago.

Among the petition signees was State Representative Alex Fazzino, who stated: "I think he has been punished enough when he was convicted for a crime he probably didn't commit. I signed it (the petition) and I recommended other people sign it."

A letter from a Catholic priest described Civella as a "very charitable man."

On March 1, 1983, the U.S. Parole Commission ordered Civella paroled immediately because of further deterioration of his health. He returned to Kansas City, where he was taken to Menorah Medical Center.

Eleven days later, at 4 p.m. on March 12, Nick Civella died. He was only days short of his 71st birthday — outlived by his early sponsor, Joe Filardo, who did not die until two years later. Nick Civella's death brought down the curtain on his 30-year reign as boss of the Kansas City Cosa Nostra Crime Family.

About 2,000 people paid their respects at a wake at the Sebetto Funeral Home, Fifth and Campbell streets in the North End neighborhood of

Civella's birth. He was afforded traditional Catholic rites, including the recitation of the rosary. The next morning, March 14, 1983, funeral services were held at Holy Rosary Church. He was buried in St. Mary's Cemetery.

Civella's death mercifully allowed him to forgo the trials and tribulations of the Strawman and RICO prosecutions. They most certainly would have resulted in a long prison sentence and the fate that befell his brother Cork, who died in prison in 1994.

FREDDY BONADONNA DID NOT HAVE AN EASY TIME in the witness protection program. Birth certificates, driver's licenses and other documents he and his family desperately needed to start a new life and to open a business were slow in coming or in some cases never provided. His repeated requests for assistance to the U.S. Marshals Service, which was responsible for the witness protection program, went unaddressed and marked him as a troublemaker.

He left the program in the middle 1980s, but nonetheless had to keep his location secret. He took to visiting his mother in California.

When she died in 2001 an ugly family dispute erupted over his handling of the estate. A civil suit was filed accusing Bonadonna of lying about his witness protection status as a ploy to isolate his mother from other family members. The judge sided against Freddy.

"The judge didn't do his homework," former organized crime squad supervisor Gary Hart told *The Star*. "Just because you're out of the program doesn't mean you're out of danger."

Added to the pressure of years of living in secret, the judgment left him feeling despondent. Two days after the judge's ruling, on April 11, 2002, Freddy told his wife, "I've put you through so much, I can't do it any more."

Then, 63-year-old Fred Harvey Bonadonna left his home and took his own life.

The Bonadonna family already had undergone more strain. After Freddy entered witness protection his brother Tony Mike Bonadonna was hounded to reveal Freddy's location, and also to refrain from testifying against the mob. The fact that Tony Mike owned the bar where Parker T. was murdered by a bomb was seen by Freddy and others as no coincidence, but as a message to both Bonadonna brothers. On one occasion when Freddy came to Kansas City to testify, Tony Mike was allowed to visit him. Freddy was shocked at his brother's appearance. He had aged beyond his years.

Eventually, Tony Mike drank himself to death.

FOR MANY YEARS AFTER APALACHIN, the Kansas City Outfit under the leadership of Nick Civella was not highly regarded compared with brethren in other American cities. That stemmed from an early lack of understanding of the true nature and workings of Cosa Nostra crime families, from failed memories of the city's sordid history and from protection by local politicians who played down the Outfit's influence. In addition, there was the astute leadership of Nick Civella, who proved that the underrating was a gross miscalculation. In addition to presiding efficiently over the Kansas City Family, he was highly regarded in Cosa Nostra circles and wielded great influence in them.

However, no matter how skilled, cunning and intuitive Nick Civella was, the Kansas City Family was no match for what proved to be one of the FBI's most successful bureauwide endeavors — the organized crime program, and in Kansas City the landmark Strawman investigation and prosecution. The dismantling of the Civella Crime Family was a team effort made possible by the dedicated, resourceful and relentless efforts of the Kansas City Strike Force, U.S. attorney's offices, other prosecutors, a variety of federal agencies and local and state law enforcement entities.

Beginning in the Prohibition era, the Crime Family had been an integral part of life in Kansas City. From its people the Outfit sucked untold millions of dollars. It corrupted politicians, officeholders, the criminal justice system, businessmen, professionals and everyday citizens who availed themselves of services the mob provided.

The mob influenced elections, fostered vice activities and other forms of criminal activity and committed murder. Along the way, the Family enjoyed the support of apologists, protectors and fellow travelers who denied the existence of any such organization. As early as 1950, Senator Estes Kefauver recognized the problem.

"A nationwide crime syndicate does exist in the United States of America," Kefauver said, "despite the protestations of a strangely assorted company of criminals, self-serving politicians, plain blind fools, and others who may be honestly misguided that there is no such combine."

It can be safely said that the specter of a criminal syndicate with such a negative impact on life in Kansas City ended with the Civella era. There are those who sought to perpetuate the organization but they found the climate and conditions no longer favorable. The Civella power bases — political influence, union influence, monopoly of gambling operations and others that made the Outfit what it was — are gone.

The Boss' final journey: In March 1983, an air ambulance carried a dying Nick Civella from prison in Springfield, Missouri, to Kansas City. As doctors attended, he was moved to Menorah Medical Center. There, on March 12, he died.

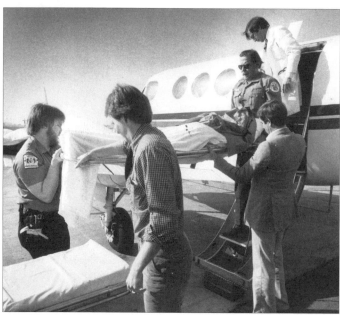

Fred Harvey Bonadonna

5/14/1938—4/11/2002

*Beloved Husband,
Father, Grandfather,
Son, Brother to
Victoria, Relative,
and Friend.*

The funeral program for Fred Harvey
Bonadonna, who committed suicide in 2002.

An ailing Roy Lee Williams was brought to
court to testify in the Argent trial in 1985.
Among other things, he told how he had
been "compromised" by the Civella Crime
Family. Williams died in 1989.

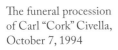

The funeral procession
of Carl "Cork" Civella,
October 7, 1994

Sources

Kansas City *Times* and *Star* newspapers

Kansas City Crime Commission, historical files

Kansas City Crime Commission Publications: Spotlight-1 On Organized
Crime, April 1970 - Kansas City Area Report of U.S. Strike Force
Prosecutions 1971-1979

Freedom of Information Documents Release, Federal Bureau of
Investigation: Case file captioned John Frank Amaro *et al*, RICO,
Kansas City FBI Field Division.

Testimony of Fred Harvey Bonadonna:
Permanent Subcommittee on Investigations of the Committee on
Governmental Affairs, U.S. Senate, May 1, 1980
Trial testimony in U.S. vs. Joseph Cammisano, U.S. District Court, Western
District of Missouri - August, 1979, Case No. 78-00114-CR-W-2

Panel Interview of Fred Harvey Bonadonna, WDAF Radio, Kansas City,
aired August 12, 1979

National Records Administration Center:
U.S. District Court, Western District of Missouri Case Files:
U.S. vs. DeLuna *et al*, Case No. 81-00107-CR-W-8
U.S. vs. DeLuna *et al*, Case No. 83-00124-01/15-CR-W-8

Federal Bureau of Investigation, Kansas City Field Office, by Court Order,
Electronic Surveillance:
Overhears Entered as Exhibits in U.S. vs. Carl Angelo DeLuna *et al*,
U.S. District Court, Western District of Missouri - Case No. 83-00124-
01/15-CR-W-8

Nineteen Affidavits Filed in Support of Applications for Electronic
Surveillance Authority, U.S. District Courts, Western District of
Missouri and District of Kansas, May 5, 1978 to February 2, 1980.

National Archives, Kansas City, Missouri, review of Case Files
U.S. Vs. Dominic Tutera, Case No. CR 86-00026

U.S. vs. Jasper Brancato, Case No. CR 74-00399

U.S. vs. William Cammisano, Joseph Cammisano, Case No. 78-00114-CR-W-2

U.S. vs. James Giordano *et al*, Case No. 79 CR 20009

U.S. vs. Edward Kratty, Anthony Begulia, Case No. CR 79-00040

U.S. vs. Nick Civella *et al*, Case No. CR 80 000023-01/02-CR-10-5

U.S. vs. Carl Civella, Gene Shepard, Case No. 81-CR-20104

Mollenhoff, Clark R. *Strike Force: Organized Crime and the Government.* Prentice Hall.

Index